P9-BZD-105

FIFTY-TWO YEARS A NEWSMAN

For
Alex Blomerth,
a good family friend
and neighbor.

William J Hooten

El Paso
Nov 25, 1986

This book is dedicated to the wonderful men and women with whom I was associated during my fifty-two years as a newsman. My heart warms when I think of the exciting times we had putting out a newspaper.

Fifty-Two Years a Newsman

by

WILLIAM J. HOOTEN

TEXAS WESTERN PRESS
THE UNIVERSITY OF TEXAS AT EL PASO
1974

•

EDITED BY
JOSEPH M. RAY

•

Library of Congress Catalog Card Number 73-91959
ISBN 0-87404-047-7

•

Dustjacket Photograph courtesy El Paso Natural Gas Co.

CONTENTS

CONTENTS *(Continued)*

CONTENTS *(Continued)*

CONTENTS *(Continued)*

Foreword

This book is a record. It is a story of events, tied in with human reactions, human frailties, successes and failures. Its contents may not please everyone. A number of readers might consider some of the chapters as being trivial, even in poor taste. It was written to report what happened, not what the author wanted. Some of the characters may be put in a poor light, some of which they may not have deserved, while other characters may appear in a better light than they deserved. That is the way it was seen through the human eyes of the writer.

In reading this account, it must be taken into consideration that many of the events occurred a long time ago, and some of the persons written about are dead. It is a record of human events, most of which is taken from the columns of El Paso's newspapers. There is some editorial comment which was written by the author. At times, the writer may appear to win, while at other times he goes down to dismal defeat.

It is not intended as the history of one man, but rather as a record of what happened during the almost 52 years he was in the newspaper business. I hope you will find it interesting.

March 15, 1974 W. J. H.

AUSTIN, TEXAS

Dear Bill:

Your letter of reminiscenses brought back many pleasant memories to me, too. I enjoyed reading it, just as I have enjoyed our friendship through the years.

Now that you are free to dictate your own schedule, I hope you are using some of your time to record some of your experiences and some of your thoughts on things that have been or things that you hope will be. Because of the full life that you have led, I know that this could be an interesting volume.

Mrs. Johnson joins me in sending our warm personal regards.

Sincerely,

Mr. W. J. Hooten
3611 Clifton Avenue
El Paso, Texas 79903

May 9, 1972

Fifty-Two Years A Newsman

Downtown El Paso in October, 1926 with crowd gathered near the old HERALD *building to follow the World Series as the game came over the Associated Press telegraph for the last time. I was the telegrapher.*

CHAPTER ·1·

Fifty-Two Years

MUCH CAN BE LEARNED in 52 years if one looks and listens. It was my privilege from August 12, 1918, to March 31, 1970, to occupy a ringside seat and watch the events of the world, nation, state, city and county unfold. On the former date, I went to work for the Associated Press and was assigned to the Douglas (Arizona) *Dispatch.* On the latter date, I retired as editor of the El Paso *Times,* El Paso's largest newspaper, after serving nearly 30 years in that capacity. I was the last Associated Press telegrapher to serve the El Paso *Herald* and the El Paso *Times,* and I was editor of the *Times* longer than any other person. During those 52 years, I saw two world wars come and go. The atomic bomb shook the earth. Radio and television appeared and are having a tremendous impact on our daily lives. The elite passenger trains rose to great heights and importance, then practically disappeared from the scene.

Our country has changed almost beyond recognition since November 11, 1918, when World War I ended, or even since that eventful day in 1945 when World War II was over. I have seen El Paso grow from a city of 70,000 to more than 325,000. Albuquerque has grown from 18,000 to more than 250,000. Tucson was 20,000 in 1920, and now it is pushing 300,000. Phoenix has grown from about 35,000 to more than half a million. Our neighboring city of Juarez has expanded from about 60,000 to more than half a million. The population of Mexico has risen from an estimated 18 million in 1920 to 53 million today.

During my years as an active newspaperman I met many famous people, including Harry Truman, John F. Kennedy, Dwight D. Eisenhower, Earl Warren, Lyndon Johnson, Richard Nixon, Sam Rayburn, Josephus Daniels and others on the home front, and such world figures as Gamal Abdel Nasser, David Ben-Gurion, King Hussein, King Paul, Premier Guy Mollet, and Pope Pius.

During the nine years I was with the Associated Press, I was assigned to the Douglas *Dispatch,* the Douglas *International,* the El Paso *Herald,* the El Paso *Times,* the Albuquerque *Journal,* the Albuquerque *Herald,* the Bisbee *Review,* the *Arizona Daily Star* in Tucson, and the Tucson *Citizen.*

During those years I saw President Woodrow Wilson rise to great heights. The world hung on every word he spoke. Upon his return from the Paris Peace Conference, his heart was broken when the Senate refused to approve the League of Nations.

I took the flash from the Associated Press wire revealing that the armistice had been signed. That was at 1:00 a.m., November 11, 1918; soon every whistle in Douglas was blowing. A sleeping city was awakened and began to celebrate. The soldiers at Camp Harry J. Jones, under quarantine for influenza, broke camp and came storming into town. Bedlam broke loose. It was that way all over the United States, and much of the rest of the world. In those days, the people received their information by word of mouth and from newspapers. Today, radio and television break the news first, but the newspapers report in depth.

I recall copying the fight between Jess Willard and Jack Dempsey, the Dempsey-Carpentier battle, which ushered in the million dollar gates, the Dempsey-Firpo fight, and others. It was a great thrill to sit behind the score boards of the old El Paso *Herald* and the *Times* and copy the World Series. Great crowds assembled in the streets in front of both newspapers, since in the days before television and radio that was the only way they had to follow the game.

I thought my business life was set, and that I would retire from the Associated Press after 30 years, but the automatic machines came along to replace telegraphers; for me that happened on September 5, 1927. Captain H. D. Slater, then publisher of the *Herald* and the *Times,* offered me a job as a reporter. I snapped it up, and soon I was plunged into the daily events of El Paso and saw a half-century of the history of this community made.

CHAPTER ·II·

Telegrapher's Perspective

Early Years

AS A PART of this narrative I should like to tell a little about myself and my early years. I was born in Chocowinity, North Carolina, September 5, 1900. I was forced to leave school in the middle of the ninth grade at Christmas, 1915, because of a death in my family which ended my home. I had gone to Albuquerque, arriving February 7, 1918, from Norfolk, Virginia. Two of my brothers, Archie and Leland, were ill with tuberculosis in Albuquerque. My oldest brother Leland died the night I arrived.

My brother Archie and I got jobs telegraphing for the Western Union in Albuquerque. The Associated Press telegrapher for the *Journal,* Guy Gaines, convinced Archie and me that we should join the Commercial Telegraphers Union of America. A week later I went to the Western Union to have lunch with Archie and he told me both of us were fired. The Western Union in those days did not tolerate labor union membership among its employes. Archie and I were automatically blackballed from Canada to Mexico in the Western Union and Postal. We pooled what money we had and took a train for El Paso on April 27, 1918.

The two of us called on W. A. Roberts, chief dispatcher for the old GH&SA Railroad. I shall always owe a debt of gratitude to Dr. E. W. Rheinheimer: when I went for my examination, he asked me how old I was. I told him 21, when I was only 17. He passed me without batting an eye. Archie and I went to work in the Fabens depot where A. Boone was station agent. I had the second trick and Archie the third. We boarded with the Pat O'Donnells in the Island Inn.

Two weeks later, Archie received a telegram from the Associated Press offering him an assignment with the El Paso *Times.* He left immediately for El Paso. The railroad sent a lad, apparently right off the ranch, to take his place in Fabens. This young man began showing attention to the young Mexican-American girls. Early one morning he came to the Island Inn and woke me up, with his hands and arms dripping blood. He had been attacked and knifed at the depot. I decided I did not like the atmosphere in Fabens and two weeks after my brother left I did likewise. I came to El Paso, rented a typewriter, and proceeded to try to learn to be a press telegrapher, sitting in with my brother.

A week later, the Postal in El Paso offered me a job. The local manager told me that the Postal had waived objections to the union for the duration of World War I. I went to work in the Postal office, which was just across the street from Hotel Paso del Norte on West San Antonio Street. Roy Martin, one of El Paso's political figures at that time, had the Exchange Club, a few doors from the Postal, and operated a bookie joint. I handled the entries and results from the racetracks for him.

My brother Archie in the meantime had returned to Albuquerque and was on *The Journal.* The last week in July, 1918, Archie met the Western Union chief operator O'Neill on the street in Albuquerque. He told Archie that I belonged with him and to tell me to come back to work for the Western Union in Albuquerque. I quit my job in El Paso and returned to Albuquerque.

I began to handle the Denver wire, the fastest in the office. O'Neill told me at the end of my third day's work that I would have to write a letter of withdrawal to the Commercial Telegraphers Union of America and give the Western Union a copy. My card had expired and I had not renewed it, but that was not sufficient for the Western Union.

I did not show up for work the next morning. I arrived at the office about 10 o'clock. O'Neill was having a fit, trying to man the Denver wire with an old man and an old woman, and the two of them could not handle it. I told O'Neill that I did not want to be fired twice by the Western Union, so I had quit, and I wanted my pay for the days I had worked. I was still only 17. I checked with a friend in the Western Union a few years ago and the fact I had quit on short notice was still on my record.

For the next week, I underwent some intensive training and coaching from my brother and Charles O'Halloran, who was the AP telegrapher on the Albuquerque *Herald.* The Associated Press offered me my pick of assignments in several states — telegraphers were scarce during the war. I chose Douglas, Arizona, and went to work on the *Dispatch* August 12, 1918. Thus I began my newspaper career, a little less than a month short of my eighteenth birthday.

Three Die In Road Race

Upon returning to El Paso in September, 1919, I was assigned to the El Paso *Herald* by the Associated Press with the rank of traffic department representative. Soon a story broke about which I sent out details over the

AP wire. On November 3, 1919, a road race was held between El Paso and Phoenix. It was a big event mainly because there was practically no paving between El Paso and the capital of Arizona. In some instances, drivers had to choose a route from a series of ruts or even to make their own road across the mesa. Three men died as a result of that race.

John T. Hutchings of Alamogordo, driving Buick Car Number 10, was shot in the back and killed near Lanark Station. A warrant charging murder was issued by Justice of the Peace Cruz Garcia of Las Cruces on information sworn to by Oliver Lee, noted New Mexico cattleman and mechanician in the Hutchings car, against Major F. M. Scanland, a patient at the base hospital at Fort Bliss. Major Scanland said they were target shooting and it was only an accident. The *Times* said on its front page of November 5 that Major Scanland was held pending action of the grand jury on a murder complaint. Complaints against seven other members of Scanland's party were withdrawn.

The El Paso *Herald* reported on November 3, 1919, that S. O. Bottorff of El Paso and his mechanician, Lloyd Brown, were killed near Vail while trying to negotiate a curve; news dispatches said their heads were severed in the accident.

The race between El Paso and Phoenix was won by Hugh B. Miller of Phoenix, who averaged 41.9 miles per hour.

Major Scanland was tried in Las Cruces for the shooting death of Hutchings before Judge Raymond E. Ryan. Judge A. B. Henehan of Santa Fe was special prosecutor, and Major W. H. H. Llewellyn was chief defense counsel. On March 13, 1920, the jury returned a verdict of involuntary manslaughter and Scanland was given a sentence of one to ten years in prison.

Execution of a General

In the days of Pancho Villa, easily one of the outstanding Mexican military men was General Felipe Angeles. In some quarters, Angeles was considered to be the brains of the Villa forces. He attended the French Military Academy and was credited with perfecting the French 75, that great artillery piece of World War I.

Dr. Cleofas Calleros of El Paso, a well known historian, told me that Angeles was captured by forces of President Venustiano Carranza on November 15, 1919. The first report of Angeles' capture appeared in the El Paso *Herald* November 20, 1919. A Washington Associated Press dispatch of November 21, 1919, said many officials and private citizens in Washington and other cities had sent telegrams to friends in Mexico urging them to persuade President Carranza to spare Angeles' life. On

November 24, 1919, the *Herald* said Angeles would be tried in Chihuahua City. It also stated that Angeles was calm and showed signs of recent illness, and that he tearfully received a telegram from his wife in New York.

The *Herald* headline of November 26, 1919, said, "Angeles Is Fearless At Execution." The *Herald* report said General Angeles was "sentenced to death last night and shot this morning," following his conviction by four Carranza generals on charges of rebellion.

Thereby hangs a story, because the Associated Press had no Chihuahua City correspondent. With the help of my friend, Napoleon Lucero, a telegrapher and also a Juarez businessman, I helped arrange for a railroad dispatcher in Chihuahua City to write the story and send it out over the railroad wire. He wrote it in Spanish and it was translated by Gilbert Cosulich, the Associated Press correspondent in El Paso and Juarez, who was bilingual in Spanish. I sent that dispatch all over the United States by Associated Press wire.

Here it is, as it appeared in the El Paso *Herald* of November 26, 1919:

Chihuahua City — Gen. Felipe Angeles, revolutionist, was executed at 6:35 a.m. today inside the barracks of the 21st Regiment of cavalry by a firing squad. Many spectators were present. Gen. Angeles died without visible emotion or fear.

Gen. Angeles himself chose the north wall to stand against to be killed and arranged details of his execution with the Carranza officers and men detailed to the task. He was remarkably cool.

Opposite the revolutionary stood five soldiers with rifles ready. They fired one volley into the breast of Angeles. Angeles fell forward. He then was lying on the floor of the barracks. The left side of his face was on the floor.

An officer stepped up to the already dead man and delivered the "coup de grace." This was a shot from the pistol of the Carranza officer. It entered behind the right ear of Angeles.

A military surgeon arrived and performed the legal autopsy. Later the body was taken to the home of a woman friend and buried from there.

Gen. Angeles spent the few hours between being sentenced and the time of execution with friends and a priest. During most of the night they discussed philosophy, mathematics, politics and religion. He quizzed the priest and friends on different questions and appeared to have little concern in the fate awaiting him.

He slept the hour and a half, between 3:00 and 4:30 o'clock. Arising, he dictated letters to Mrs. Angeles and his son Albert and Manuel Calero. He wrote, personally, letters and autographs for friends to be delivered after his death which he carried with him to his stand for execution. He recommended farewells be sent a long list of friends.

During his trial, Angeles gained sympathy and on all sides it was freely expressed his life should have been spared. His address of three hours to the court Monday, in which he upheld America and Americans, was widely discussed.

Thus ended the life of a gallant and intellectual Mexican general. I shall never forget the part I played, with the assistance and cooperation of "Nap" Lucero, in getting that vivid account of General Angeles' execution as written by the railroad dispatcher in Chihuahua City.

Trial in Tombstone

In the spring of 1920, a trial occurred in Tombstone, Arizona, which attracted nationwide attention. It all began on July 12, 1917, when citizens in Bisbee, Arizona, rounded up striking copper miners, who allegedly were members of the I.W.W. (Industrial Workers of the World), their friends and sympathizers and deported them by rail to Columbus, New Mexico. As a result of that deportation, a Bisbee hardware dealer named Harry E. Wootton was indicted and his trial set for Tombstone, then the seat of Cochise County. The Phelps Dodge Corporation retained W. H. Burges, a highly successful El Paso attorney, to defend Wootton.

Phelps Dodge set up a news bureau in Tombstone to cover the trial. I recommended that the Associated Press set up its own bureau in Tombstone. They did so and assigned Reed Hays, AP correspondent in El Paso, to cover the trial. I was asked to find a telegrapher to send to Tombstone; I recommended Bill Ammons, who was employed.

Attorney Burges set up a defense for Wootton based on the law of necessity and self-defense. The *Herald* said March 15, 1920, A. A. Worsley, special prosecutor, made his statement to the court, insisting that, because the 1,186 striking copper miners and sympathizers were already at the mercy of the men who later shipped them out of the State, the law of necessity and self-defense could not be invoked to justify the Bisbee deportation. The defense claimed that the deportation was justified on the ground of self-defense, since the men deported were about to help overthrow the government and destroy the community of Bisbee. Special Prosecutor Worsley said there were a U. S. marshal and deputies, a governor and the sheriff who might summon and call to their aid every male citizen to preserve law and order.

During that trial, I left the El Paso *Herald* and returned to the Douglas *International.* I went to Tombstone several times during the trial. Gilbert Cosulich of the El Paso Associated Press bureau had replaced Reed Hays in Tombstone. The trial lasted more than a month, with the jury returning a verdict of not guilty for Wootton. El Pasoan W. H. Burges made legal history in his conduct of the defense for Wootton.

Murder on a Newspaper

On March 14, 1922, Fred McClure, circulation manager of the *Times,* was arrested for the murder of Miss Louise Frentzel, his secretary, who was described also as his sweetheart. McClure told the police that Miss Frentzel had shot herself the night before in a fit of jealousy while in his car on the new Alamogordo Road near William Beaumont Hospital. He was reported in the *Herald* of March 20, 1920, as saying that her body was dumped out at Alabama Street and Altura Boulevard.

Will Pelphrey, El Paso County Attorney, called on L. M. (Bud) Rutherford, the *Herald* news editor, and me because he learned that we had been riding in my new Ford on the Alamogordo Road on the night of the shooting. Pelphrey, Rutherford, and I went to the vicinity and conducted a search for the pistol used in the death of Miss Frentzel, but we found nothing.

Later during the investigation, Miss Frentzel's body was exhumed at Evergreen Cemetery. Police said it was impossible for her to have shot herself in the manner described by McClure. McClure told detectives that he had received mail under the assumed name of "John Gaffney" to conceal his criminal record for automobile theft in Ohio. At McClure's examining trial before Justice of the Peace R. B. Rawlins, the state's case was presented by County Attorney Pelphrey and Assistant District Attorney C. L. Vowell. Defense attorneys were J. M. Harris and Victor Moore.

McClure was tried three times in El Paso on a charge of first degree murder. Tom Lea was his attorney. His first two trials resulted in conviction and sentence of life imprisonment, but he was granted a new trial each time. On December 5, 1925, he was found guilty and sentenced to 25 years. Mrs. McClure was in tears as the verdict was returned; the defendant was unmoved. The *Times* said, "The loyalty of Mrs. McClure to her husband during this and the other trials of her husband was a highlight of the case." She had fought for his freedom for more than three years, working in downtown stores to earn money for his defense. The *Times* reported his sentencing on December 6, 1925.

The *Times* in May, 1928, quoted Mrs. McClure as saying she was leaving El Paso for Dallas to join her husband who, she said, had been pardoned. The pardon was not confirmed in Austin dispatches. The McClures dropped from sight. Then on March 24, 1934, the *Times* on its front page quoted an Associated Press dispatch as saying a bandit slain during an attempted bank holdup at Alto, Texas, had been identified as Fred M.

McClure, formerly of El Paso. A follow-up Associated Press dispatch from Cleveland quoted police of that city as saying they believed it was the same McClure who formerly worked in the circulation of a Cleveland newspaper and engaged on the side in automobile theft.

Days of The Klan

Early in the 1920s El Paso underwent a unique experience: the Ku Klux Klan made its appearance. The El Paso *Times*, under the leadership of Editor James S. (Jim) Black, conducted a vigorous fight against it. On September 15, 1921, he wrote of the dangers of the Ku Klux Klan: "Apparently the Ku Klux Klan with its ghostly trappings has not considered El Paso a safe place for night riding with masked face, but the general opinion elsewhere seems to be that it essays to set up a sort of super-government."

The Klan was mentioned in the School Board election in April, 1922. Those running for office were Charles S. Ward, composing room foreman of the *Herald,* Dr. J. Hal Gambrell and Attorney S. J. Isaacks on one ticket; and Attorney W. H. Burges, Dr. J. B. Brady and U. S. Stewart, president of the City National Bank, on the other. There was talk that the Ward-Gambrell-Isaacks ticket was backed by the Klan. The *Times* supported the Burges-Brady-Stewart ticket. The *Herald* was not enthusiastic, but it endorsed the Ward-Gambrell-Isaacks ticket. Captain H. D. Slater, *Herald* publisher, wrote that he had been informed those men were not members of the Klan. I remember riding to the home of Charley Ward on Tularosa Street early on that April morning with Bud Rutherford, *Herald* news editor, to tell Ward that he and other members of his ticket had been elected.

Even prior to the School Board election, the *Times* became aware that it was in for a fight. It was soon apparent that the Klan was not composed of fly-by-night people, but that some of the city's most influential citizens were involved. It developed into a most regrettable situation. Good friends became estranged. At the time I was telegraphing for the Associated Press on the *Herald,* but I was keenly aware of what was going on.

Late in 1921, a man named Hal Kelly was given a job on the *Herald;* it was remarked by some of the *Herald's* experienced men that Kelly learned amazingly fast. He became a member of the Klan and obtained a roster of its membership. I never knew for certain, but I always felt that Kelly had been planted in the *Herald* by the *Times.* When it became known that Kelly was a member of the Klan and that he had turned the roster of its membership over to the *Times,* he emerged as city editor of the *Times.* He was an extremely clever newspaperman. I knew him well. He made friends easily and was well liked. He left El Paso some years later, and I never knew what happened to him.

District Judge W. D. Howe, who, as a justice of the peace in 1895, had stood over the body of John Wesley Hardin and ordered that Old John Selman, Hardin's killer, be held for murder, impaneled a grand jury on November 6, 1921. The *Times* of November 7, 1921, quoted him as saying to the grand jury: "It is improper that an organization of the kind we are discussing, one that takes upon itself the conviction of persons without proper trial, should be permitted to exist." There is no record that any action was taken by the grand jury. The fight over the Klan waxed hot in El Paso for about three years, then it seemed to die out of its own accord. But it did considerable damage.

At one time, Editor Black of the *Times* had a police escort. In the School Board election of April 4, 1923, Mrs. Milton A. Warner, Mrs. John A. Wright, J. H. McBroom, and Wyeth Doak, all pledged to "end Klan domination in school affairs," were elected to office. The real Klan fight in El Paso took place in the 1923 municipal election when P. E. Gardner ran for mayor with the open support of the Klan. A parade was held in El Paso which he led. The *Times, Herald,* and *Post* all supported the ticket headed by R. M. (Dick) Dudley, who had served in the State Senate. Most of the fighting was done by the *Times.*

In a front page editorial, the morning of February 23, 1923, the *Times* called on the people of El Paso to reject the Klan:

> Tomorrow you decide the fate of your city. The eyes of the nation are on you. Sunday morning throughout the length and breadth of the land El Paso will be heralded as a Klan city or a city where American ideals prevail.
>
> If El Paso is stigmatized as a Klan city we may as well say goodbye to our hopes of a bigger El Paso for two years — or until our citizens, disillusioned by the bitter lessons that are certain to come from Klan rule, stamp it out forever.

The people of El Paso on Saturday, February 24, 1923, rejected the Klan; the entire Dudley ticket won.

In later years, known or suspected former Klan members declined to discuss the days of the early 1920s in El Paso. They preferred to let sleeping dogs lie.

Battle in The Newsroom

G. Allie Martin was managing editor of the El Paso *Herald* when I first came to El Paso in 1918. He was a hard worker, but he was tyrannical, and he made life miserable for the men who worked under him. He was well regarded in El Paso, a charter member of the El Paso Rotary Club, and district governor of Rotary in the early 1920s. This is a story of how his mistreatment of the men under him backfired and caused a fight in the newsroom. At the time I was working for the Associated Press and had a desk on the balcony overlooking the newsroom. The *Herald* was located where the Plaza Theater is now.

On New Year's Day, 1922, Martin as usual came into the *Herald* newsroom swinging his cane at 9:45. The regular city editor, the late Alden Evans, was on vacation, and H. W. Bierhorst, who somewhat resembled Ben Turpin but was an excellent newsman, was sitting in for him. Martin summoned Bierhorst to his office and demanded to see his New Year's Eve story. Bierhorst replied that he had not yet had time to prepare the story, whereupon Martin yelled at him, "You are a hell of a city editor." Bierhorst returned to his desk, brooded for a few minutes, and then returned and attacked Martin. I could see the whole encounter from my balcony. Martin was too strong for Bierhorst and chased him from his office, kicking him in the seat of the pants.

Shortly thereafter, Martin sent for Bierhorst, but he had left, and he never did return. For a while he operated a flower shop in El Paso, and later he left the city. He came back to El Paso during World War II and worked for the *Times* while I was editor; he served for a time as managing editor during the wartime manpower shortage. Martin left the *Herald* in 1924 and moved to California. He married while he was Rotary District Governor and published the story in the *Herald* with the headline, "Rotary District Governor Weds." He died in California in the 1950s.

El Paso Newspapers in The Mid-1920s

Captain H. D. Slater, publisher of the El Paso *Herald,* served his country in France in World War I. The *Herald* flourished during his absence under J. C. "Uncle Jimmy" Wilmarth as business manager, Ralph M. Henderson as advertising manager, Henry Fris as circulation manager, and G. Allie Martin as managing editor. I have always thought that Slater became jealous of those men.

After he returned from France they left one by one. Wilmarth retired in 1921, and it seemed to me that he was not too happy about it. Fris then left to join the Hearst organization; he was a first-class circulation man. Then Henderson left to take a job in the East. Martin quarreled frequently with Slater and often threatened to quit. One day in 1924 after such an encounter, Slater surprised him by accepting his resignation. Martin tried to stay on, reminding Slater of his long and valuable service, but Slater dismissed him curtly by saying, "You have been adequately paid."

Slater always favored the beautification of El Paso. He advocated a recreational park below what is now Rim Road and the replacement of the slum area known as Stormville on the rim with an exclusive residential development. He was a fighter and a dreamer; he had his faults, but I will always remember him as the man who gave me a job as a reporter in September, 1927, when the Associated Press wire was put into automatic machines.

The El Paso *Post,* established in August, 1922, was reputed to be the brainchild of E. W. Scripps himself, who contended that a newspaper could be started from scratch and earn its own way. Tom Sharpe was the first editor of the *Post* and F. G. Westberg was business manager. The *Post* had a hard time for awhile, selling on the streets for a penny. After a few years, it began to take hold.

Slater of the *Herald* in 1925 engaged in a bitter war with E. C. (Eddie) Simmons, youthful publisher of the *Times.* They even went to the extreme of publishing editorial cartoons on the front page. One cartoon on the *Times* front page showed Slater weeping huge tears because the *Times* was taking away his circulation. The *Times* of November 21, 1925, announced that Slater had bought out the newspaper from Simmons and his associates. Rumor had it that the purchase price was $300,000. Slater continued to publish the *Herald* and the *Times* as separate newspapers.

Slater had a succession of editors running the *Times,* with none lasting very long. Some of the men who worked for him on the *Times* were James S. Black, Hector McLean, Duncan Aikman, and J. C. (Uncle Jimmy) Wilmarth, temporarily in charge of the *Times* operation. I always thought Slater did very well in directing the editorial policies of the two newspapers. He was a staunch Republican and the *Times* continued to be a Democratic paper. The *Times* was on the wet side and the *Herald* was dry. In November, 1927, Slater decided that the *Herald* would join the *Times* in calling for the repeal of the Eighteenth Amendment. Slater wrote the editorial for the *Herald* and Duncan Aikman for the *Times.* They argued that prohibition had caused a breakdown in law enforcement and a loss of respect for the law. The local reaction was quick; ministers denounced the two papers from their pulpits.

In February, 1927, a ticket headed by R. E. Thomason and backed by the *Post* won over a slate headed by former Mayor Charles Davis and backed by the *Herald* and the *Times.* After the new officials took office, the Slater-owned newspapers continued their attacks on them.

In December, 1928, Slater sold the *Herald* and the *Times* to Dorrance D. Roderick and Lindsay Nunn.

A Prophecy

It had been known for some time in 1922 that Scripps Howard was considering starting a newspaper in El Paso. There was much discussion in the *Herald* newsroom. Men of the *Herald* staff, headed by Bud Rutherford, the news editor, began to obtain copies of the Cleveland *Press* and other Scripps-Howard newspapers. The idea grew that the Scripps-Howard paper was going to be something notable, and when the rag-tag El Paso *Post,* with its four pages and typographical errors, arrived in the *Herald* newsroom in August, 1922, a loud guffaw went up.

John Harm, a large man and something of a philosopher, was the pressroom foreman for the *Herald.* He later distinguished himself as production manager of the Chicago *News.* On the day when the roar of amusements rose in the *Herald* newsroom to meet the new El Paso *Post,* he said, "Don't laugh, boys. You might live to see the day the *Post* will absorb the *Herald.*" How prophetic he was. On April 2, 1931, the *Herald,* which had been bought by Scripps-Howard, was merged with the *Post* and appeared as the El Paso *Herald-Post.*

Good Newspapermen

It used to be said that there were two ways to meet the nation's top newspapermen; one was to go out on the highways and byways and meet them; the other was to stay in El Paso and they would come to you. Over the years there was a parade of topflight newspapermen through El Paso. The El Paso *Herald* and the El Paso *Times* seemed to attract them. Some stayed only briefly before continuing their journeys toward greener fields.

Poor health brought many excellent newsmen to the wholesome climate of El Paso, among them Chester Chope, Hector McLean, Bill Griffin, Marshall Hail, and Jim Halloran.

Easily one of the best newspapermen ever produced by El Paso was S. L. A. Marshall. I remember the day in 1923 he started on the *Herald* as a reporter. He caught on so rapidly that he was sent to cover the trial of Fred McClure, *Times* circulation manager, on a charge of murdering Miss Louise Frentzel. Marshall covered the trial with a pencil and paper, with copy boys picking up his stories and rushing them to the *Herald* city desk. He made an impressive reputation for himself in El Paso. His "Slam Bangs" attracted wide attention. When he left the *Herald* and went to the Detroit *News,* I took his place on September 7, 1927. He later became a brigadier general and, as historian for the Defense Department, continues to write on military subjects.

Two top men who were in El Paso more than 50 years ago were Reed Hayes and Gilbert Cosulich of the Associated Press. During the revolutionary days in Mexico in 1911, many Eastern newspapers, had representatives in El Paso. The story was told that once when in his cups one of these reporters for an Eastern paper sent off a story that the battleship Oregon had anchored off the port of Juarez to protect American interests, and the story was published.

In 1913 Norman Walker, correspondent for the Associated Press, journeyed south from Juarez to convince Pancho Villa to delay a scheduled attack on Juarez because the World Series then under way would divert the attention of American newspapers from his military exploits. It was that same Norman Walker who telephoned General John J. Pershing at Fort Bliss to break the news to him that his wife and daughters had died in a fire in the Presidio at San Francisco. Walker told me in later years, "There was silence on the other end of the line, then General Pershing said, 'Thank you,' and hung up." Walker left the newspaper business and became a partner in the McMath Printing Company. He died in the 1930s.

A Crucial Election

El Paso has had many hotly contested elections. Probably the most crucial, at least in modern times, was the election on February 11, 1927, in which Attorney R. E. Thomason defeated former Mayor Charles Davis for mayor of El Paso. This election was important because its outcome was the beginning of the end for the El Paso *Herald* and *Times* under the ownership of Captain H. D. Slater. As early as December 24, 1926, Slater laid the *Herald* and the *Times* on the line in support of Davis. The upstart El Paso *Post,* which had been in existence less than five years, supported the Thomason ticket.

The *Times* reported on its front page on that date that Mayor H. P. Jackson and leaders of the city-county political machine were becoming concerned over the possibility "that the usual solid machine vote south of the tracks will be split about 50-50 between Mayor Jackson and Charles Davis, [constituting] . . . a break in both city and county machines."

The *Times* of December 27, 1926, reported Charles Davis as urging the formation of a citizen committee to work toward obtaining a municipally-owned airport. On December 31, 1926, the *Times* printed rumors that Mayor H. P. Jackson might "withdraw from the race for mayor, leaving the field to Charles Davis;" and on January 5, 1927, the *Times* reported Mayor H. P. Jackson's announcement "that he had decided not to run for reelection. . . . Even the definite announcement of R. E. Thomason that he is in the race failed to halt the Davis stampede."

The *Times* of January 18, 1927, under the headline "Thomason 'Dignified' Mudslinging Is Started," carried the following:

> Christened with a spattering of mud, oozing vindictiveness, R. E. Thomason and his running mates launched forth last night on the stormy political waters on the main platform plank of Charles Davis — El Paso a greater convention city.

The *Times* of January 21, 1927, reported that the City Democratic Executive Committee had set the Democratic primary, which in those days in Texas was tantamount to election, for February 11.

Thereafter the campaign accelerated. A *Times* headline of January 25 proclaimed, "Davis asks Thomason if he was on Bitulithic payroll when speaker of the Texas House. Thomason charged Washington Park books kept in Roy Martin's office." The *Times* of January 28, 1927, told of a speech at Liberty Hall before a large audience by Tom Lea, Thomason's law partner, reviling Charles Davis and Captain H. D. Slater, editor of the *Times* and *Herald,* using the terms "lousy," "dirty," "vicious," "rot-gut," "make a pole cat sick," and "make a dog sick." Mr. Thomason and Mr. Lea, the report wryly concluded, were holding to their promise of "scrupulously avoiding personalities."

The *Times* of February 7 told that Joe Bennis, aldermanic candidate on the Davis ticket, knocked down Attorney W. H. Fryer in front of the Community Center. The *Times* of February 10 reported Davis as supporting civil service for city employees and Thomason as favoring the spoils system.

The *Times* on February 6 and February 11 predicted victory for the Davis ticket, but the issue of February 12 had this startling headline: "Thomason By 1,707." Thomason had received 7,214 votes to Davis's 5,507. Thomason's entire slate, composed of aldermanic candidates R. E. Sherman, A. B. Poe, R. N. Mullin, and Stewart Berkshire, was elected. A *Times* editorial had no word of congratulation for the new mayor, saying, "It was a fight of ideas. The 'Little El Paso Idea' triumphed over the 'Big El Paso Idea.' "

That election represented the swan song of the prestige of the *Herald* and *Times* under Captain Slater's ownership; it was never recovered while he owned them. Without a doubt, the *Herald* and the *Times* had not treated the Thomason ticket fairly in its news columns. On one occasion, Thomason talked about a high line from Elephant Butte Lake to bring water to El Paso. A *Times* reporter understood Thomason to say "pipe line," and ridiculed the idea, calling it a "pipe dream." As a reporter, I soon discovered that the *Herald* and the *Times* continued slanting the news even after Mayor Thomason took office.

Early newspaper days as city editor of the HERALD *in 1929.*

CHAPTER ·III·

On The Herald

Lindbergh's Visit

COLONEL CHARLES A. LINDBERGH, the first man to fly the Atlantic, visited El Paso on September 24 and 25, 1927. One of my earliest assignments as a *Herald* reporter was with W. G. (Bud) Roe to cover his arrival at the Fort Bliss Flying Field. We arrived on the scene early, and Roe commandeered the only telephone in the office of the flying field, established connection with the *Herald* and held it. Chester Chope, one of the *Post* reporters assigned to cover Lindbergh's arrival, complained to Major Hugh Shannon, in command of the Texas National Guard unit in control. Major Shannon instructed one of his officers, a Lieutenant Ferlet, who was with the telephone company in civilian life, to order the company to break the connection with the *Herald,* stating that he had to be in contact with the El Paso High School Stadium where other National Guardsmen were stationed. Then, without saying a word, Shannon turned the telephone over to Chope just as Colonel Lindbergh was circling the field.

Roe and I had to leap into an automobile and speed to the nearest telephone at a nearby water station to call the *Herald* city desk. Captain H. D. Slater, publisher of the *Herald* and *Times,* was incensed when he heard what Major Shannon had done. He instructed Roe and me to get ourselves arrested by the National Guard. We went to the High School Stadium, where Lindbergh was to speak, and shoved a few national guardsmen around, but they declined to arrest us.

The *Herald* of September 24, 1927, stated in a front page story:

> One of those tingling thrills that come just about once in a lifetime was experienced by thousands as Col. Charles A. Lindbergh turned the nose of "The Spirit of St. Louis" down and made the landing. . . . The din of auto horns was terrific.

The parade for Colonel Lindbergh led through Fort Bliss to William Beaumont Hospital along the paved road in the vicinity of the Municipal

Golf Course, and thence to the El Paso High School Stadium. Lindbergh's speech at the stadium stressed the necessity of an El Paso airport. Lindbergh learned belatedly that he was supposed to have stopped at the hospital to greet the disabled veterans. He returned later to the hospital and said repeatedly as he walked through the wards, "Boys, I would not have passed you up for anything." He appeared in a most favorable light at the hospital.

The *Herald* on September 26, 1927 covered the departure of Colonel Lindbergh. The lead of the story was:

> A huge silver bird against a sky of blue, dotted here and there with banks of white clouds. It hovered over the downtown district, sailed to the edge of Juarez and then headed northeast for Santa Fe. This was "The Spirit of St. Louis" in which Col. Charles A. Lindbergh left El Paso Sunday.

Later Lindbergh developed a dislike for newspapermen. He was rude to me and to other newsmen during a later visit he made to El Paso. I never liked him; I thought he was a conceited ass and a cold fish. I learned early in the newspaper business that the bigger a man is the more courteous he is. An Associated Press dispatch in the *Times* of June 2, 1928, said Gene Howe, editor of the Amarillo *News-Globe,* criticized Lindbergh as a victim of the "swell head" and, despite opposition from a majority of Amarillo's 30,000 people, stood by his guns and declared he had no apologies to make. I admired and agreed with his stand.

Battle of The Bridge

In 1927, El Paso was caught up in a free-swinging fight over whether the international bridge from Juarez was to be kept open until midnight or be closed at 6 p.m. At the weekly luncheon of the Board of Directors of the El Paso Chamber of Commerce on September 23, 1927, a resolution was introduced to request Washington to authorize the collector of customs to close the bridge at 6 p.m. when there was open gambling going on in Juarez and to leave it open until midnight when there was no gambling. I was sent by the *Herald* to cover the meeting, and we carried a modest front page story announcing that the Board of Directors had voted to postpone action on the proposed resolution for a week. The Foreign Relations Committee, it was reported, was composed of C. W. Croom, chairman, Lawrence Gardner, and Alfonso Martinez.

Then the "fun" began. The *Herald* of September 26 carried a headline reading: "Pastors 'Regret' Bridge Row." I covered for the *Herald* the meeting of the El Paso Ministerial Alliance held in the Church of St.

Clement. Dr. Floyd Poe, pastor of the First Presbyterian Church, predicted that the proposed resolution would be defeated. He was quoted as saying, "I feel like I have been betrayed. It is not the business of the Chamber of Commerce to meddle in religious or bridge closing questions." Dr. T. V. Neal, pastor of the First Baptist Church, said something about an agreement having been made, and adding, "And Bassett knows it." The *Post* that afternoon reported Dr. Neal was referring to C. N. Bassett, president of the State National Bank. He actually had meant Dr. George Bassett, pastor of the First Christian Church. Dr. Poe presented six resolutions which were approved by the Ministerial Alliance.

All week long, El Paso's newspapers published stories pro and con about the resolution. On September 28, the *Herald* reported the Women's Department of the Chamber of Commerce had entered the bridge row:

> Mrs. Max Mayer, chairman director, will appear Friday speaking the line that the department is strictly for maintaining the present hours for closing the bridge and therefore against the report of the Foreign Relations Committee specifying the midnight closing so long as there is no open gambling in Juarez.

Practically all of the Chamber of Commerce directors dodged the question when the *Herald* quizzed them about how they would vote on the report. The headline in the *Herald* of September 30 said, "Defeat Midnight Bridge." The story said the midnight bridge squabble ended when the Board of Directors of the Chamber of Commerce Friday noon unanimously adopted a resolution introduced late in the proceedings by J. W. Kirkpatrick calling on the government to appoint a commission to study present border regulations with a view of enforcing a uniform closing hour all along the line.

Thus ended the 1927 "Battle of the Bridge." This was not the last time, however, that the basic conflict dictated by El Paso's location asserted itself: the natural desire to be an average American city running into direct conflict with its inevitable involvement with Old Mexico.

To The City Hall

I was sent to cover the City Hall-Court House beat for the *Herald* on the first Thursday in October, 1927. In those days, the City Hall had no auditorium and the City Council met in the County Court Room in the Court House across San Antonio Street. Under Captain H. D. Slater's direction, the *Herald* and the *Times* had been at war with Mayor R. E. Thomason and his administration. Thomason had been elected the preceding February despite the vigorous opposition of the two papers. Even after the Thomason administration took office, the *Herald* and the *Times* continued their onslaught.

I had never met Thomason personally. I did not know how I would be received at the City Council session that Thursday morning, so I sat outside the rail. Thomason kept looking at me, and when the meeting was over, he invited me into the office of the county judge for a chat. "I see you are a reporter," he said, holding out his hand; "Thomason is my name." I gave him my name and explained I was representing the *Herald*, and also the *Times* on occasion. "I know your boss is not for me," Thomason said, "but that is no reason why you and I cannot be friends." I liked him from the first, and we have been friends from that day to this. I did my job as a reporter for the *Herald*. Thomason seemed to understand; he never spoke a cross word to me, despite the harsh things the *Herald* and the *Times* were saying about him.

Thomason had two successful years as mayor, and won reelection in 1929, this time with the support of the *Herald* and the *Times*. In 1930, he was elected to Congress, served 17 years there and then was appointed a federal judge by President Harry S. Truman. I am confident that I was among the first to know that Thomason was to become a federal judge. In April, 1947, I was in Washington, attending the convention of the American Society of Newspaper Editors, and I had invited Congressman and Mrs. Thomason to be my guests at the annual banquet in the Statler Hotel. In my room before going to the banquet, Thomason told me that President Truman had informed him that day that he was going to name him a federal judge. Judge Thomason installed me as potentate of El Maida Shrine Temple in 1948. At the age of 94, Judge Thomason is still my warm friend. He presented me a copy of his book, *Thomason: The Autobiography of a Federal Judge*, which is remarkably well done. Judge Thomason came to the *Times* newsroom on March 31, 1970, to attend my retirement party and to wish me well. He has received many honors from the people he loves so well, and he has deserved every one of them.

Note: Judge Thomason died in El Paso November 8, 1973.

Death in The City Hall

El Paso's City Hall was rocked by gunfire on January 5, 1928.

Dr. R. A. Wilson, who had been city health officer, went to the City Hall and, after talking with Mayor R. E. Thomason, created a disturbance in which he was shot to death. His death was ruled a suicide.

Said the *Herald* of January 5:

After making demands on Mayor R. E. Thomason that he be reinstated as city health officer from which position he resigned Jan. 1, Dr. R. A. Wilson Thursday morning entered the Health Department office at the City Hall, fired on Mrs. Louise McKeon, chief city nurse, then committed suicide.

Dr. Wilson went to Mayor Thomason's office accompanied by Dr. Willis Waite and Dr. G. Werley. He told Mayor Thomason that he had decided he was not too sick to fill the Health Department position and demanded he be reinstated.

The *Herald* quoted Mayor Thomason as saying:

I told him that I understood he had been accusing Dr. P. R. Outlaw, present city health officer, and Mrs. McKeon of trying to undermine him. I told him that I would not stand for that.

He left my office and Dr. Waite and Dr. Werley said they owed me an apology, that Dr. Wilson was evidently mentally deranged.

Dr. Wilson entered Mrs. McKeon's office where she was talking with Miss Kathryn Salyer, Dr. Outlaw's stenographer. Dr. Wilson produced a gun and she fled to the office of Willis Ransom, city registrar. Dr. Wilson fired at her and missed. She closed the office door and Dr. Wilson tried to force it open. He was grabbed from behind by Gammon Guinn, a city sanitary engineer. Guinn said Dr. Wilson apparently recognized him. "He struggled for a moment," Guinn said. "Then he turned around and looked at me. He could have shot me. I grabbed his gun. He quickly raised it to his head and pulled the trigger." Guinn had powder burns.

I arrived in the City Hall as Dr. Wilson was dying on the floor. Mrs. McKeon, Miss Salyer and Ransom were badly shaken up. I talked with Gammon Guinn later that day. He told me that, although Dr. Wilson could have shot him, he was not completely satisfied in his mind that the physician had actually intended to shoot himself, but the verdict was suicide and that's that. I was the City Hall reporter for the *Herald,* but the *Herald* story was written by Reporter H. Worth Jones, police reporter. As I recall, I got the quotes from Mayor Thomason which I gave to Jones.

Border Romance and a Will

This is the story of a wealthy Mexican girl, her marriage to an El Paso orchestra leader, her death, her will, the contest of the validity of the marriage, the unhappiness of the attorney for the girl's family, and a wrong picture.

It all came to light on February 17, 1928, when the will of Mrs. Carmen Gorrochotegui Johnson was filed for probate. A. W. Norcop was attorney for the Gorrochotegui family. He also was the attorney for the El Paso *Post,* and the paper was given advance warning that the story was coming. As court reporter for the *Herald,* I was not favored by Norcop's confidence. He waited until I had left the court house to write my stories before lunch and then filed the will and announced his intention to contest the marriage of Carmen Gorrochotegui to E. V. "Jerry" Johnson, former Hotel Hussmann orchestra leader.

I had left the *Herald* office and had entered Bolton's Cafe for lunch when something told me to go back to the court house. There I found Chris Aranda, Jr., wating for me; he said he had been sending brain waves trying to summon me back to the court house; he said he would believe in mental telepathy from then on. I checked the probate docket and saw the will had been filed.

I ran all the way to Norcop's office and found him just leaving for lunch. He somewhat reluctantly gave me the same background information he had given the *Post,* but he insisted that I get my story from the Gorrochotegui family.

There was no time left unless I was to be soundly scooped. I telephoned the *Herald* to clear the way for a good story and then hurried to write it, using everything Norcop had given me, with the city editor taking it out of my typewriter a paragraph at a time. The *Herald* account ran February 17, 1928. The next morning Norcop entered the *Herald* office and made a bee line for me. He was intercepted by *Herald* News Editor Robert Lepley and finally was persuaded to leave. He insisted I had violated his confidence; maybe I had, but it was either that or be badly beaten on a very good story.

Miss Carmen Gorrochotegui and E. V. "Jerry" Johnson were married in Las Cruces October 19, 1927. She had met him while staying at the Hotel Hussmann. She was taken ill and placed in Providence Hospital with a throat infection. She underwent an operation, and on her deathbed she told her mother of the marriage and had Norcop draw up a will leaving Johnson $2,000.

After the *Herald* and the *Post* came out on the afternoon of February 17, Chester Chope, *Post* reporter — and one of the best — and I waited a good while in the lobby of the Angelus Hotel where Johnson lived, hoping to get a picture of the girl. Finally I gave up and went home; Chope later obtained a picture which he thought was of the dead wife. The *Post* printed the picture the next afternoon, but it was a picture of Johnson's sister. On February 18, I obtained from my friend, Attorney W. C. Roche, a correct picture of the girl, and had an interview with Johnson in his office.

The *Herald* of February 18 quoted Johnson as saying:

Any attempt to invalidate the marriage between me and Miss Carmen

G. Gorrochotegui, which took place in Las Cruces Oct. 19, will be fought.

I didn't marry her for her money. It's not a matter of the will but a matter of recognition. She was of age, in fact she was two years older than I and knew what she was doing. The marriage was planned for at least seven months.

Mrs. Johnson in her will left the remainder of her estate in Mexico, said to total as high as $300,000, to her mother, Mrs. Carmen G. Vda. Gorrochotegui. Mrs. Gorrochotegui denied the validity of the marriage. The *Post* on February 18, 1928, quoted Johnson as saying his wife had purchased a trousseau and was planning a church wedding when she became fatally ill. Records in the office of the El Paso County Clerk show that the will of Mrs. Johnson was admitted to probate on April 10, 1928, and was confirmed by a district court order June 10, 1928.

Soda Pop Upheaval

A. B. Poe, prominent in El Paso politics for a long time and a member of the original R. E. Thomason City Council elected in 1927, was an astute businessman but somewhat thin-skinned. He was considered fair game for barbs by the *Herald* during Thomason's first term. One of Poe's campaign promises in the 1927 campaign was to reduce the price of soda pop at Washington Park from a dime to a nickel.

On the morning of March 13, 1928, I was covering the City Council meeting for the *Herald*. A discussion came up pertaining to the baseball season at Dudley Field, and the price to be charged for peanuts and soda pop was mentioned. I went back to the office and told *Herald* News Editor Robert Lepley what had been said. He wrote this story which appeared in the *Herald* that afternoon in a box on the front page:

Poe Puts Peanuts At Five a Bag In Pop Price Plank.

"Has Alderman A. B. Poe changed his idea about 10-cent soda pop?" was a question being asked at the City Hall Tuesday.

During a discussion at the City Council with representatives of amateur baseball concerning the refreshment concession at Dudley Field for the summer, Alderman Poe said: "I don't think the people would object to paying 10 cents for a bottle of soda pop and five cents for a bag of peanuts."

One of Alderman Poe's main planks during the campaign of last year was a promise to reduce the price of soda pop at Washington Park from 10 cents to five cents.

Tuesday he expressed willingness to permit the baseball team to keep the entire gate receipts provided the city has the refreshment concession.

No agreement was reached with the baseball representatives, but a written proposition will be submitted to the council later, it was announced.

The next morning when I went to the City Hall, Poe was so angry he was shaking. He demanded to know why I had treated him so shabbily.

Poe and I in later years became very close friends, both personally and politically. The *Times* supported him when he was defeated for mayor in 1937 by Marvin Harlan and he joined the *Times* in warmly supporting Congressman Ken Regan from 1947 to 1954.

Who Keeps Federal Fees?

A legal battle was waged for almost three years over whether Sheriff Seth Orndorff had a legal claim to money paid his office by the federal government for feeding federal prisoners in the county jail. A suit was instituted against Orndorff by the County Commissioners' Court for recovery of $67,500 of those fees. An Associated Press dispatch from Washington of March 19, 1928, and appearing in the *Herald* of that date, said that Orndorff and his sureties were refused a review by the Supreme Court of decisions of the state courts holding them liable to the County for fees approximating $67,500 received from the federal government for keeping federal prisoners in 1923, 1924, and 1925. The *Herald* explained that El Paso County had won a victory in the suit against Orndorff for fees which the commissioners charged were illegally retained by the sheriff.

That case ended the political power wielded for many years by Sheriff Orndorff in El Paso County. He tried unsuccessfully to make a deal with the Commissioners' Court in 1928 regarding the judgment against him. Orndorff was a member of a prominent pioneer family. The Cortez Hotel in El Paso was built by his family and was first named "The Orndorff." I knew Seth Orndorff well and always liked him; he lived in the Lower Valley; he died in the late 1960s.

A Matter of $9,435

Chief of Police Tom Armstrong was held in contempt of court by District Judge W. D. Howe on May 8, 1928, and sentenced to serve two days in jail and fined $200. That sentence was later set aside by the Court of Criminal Appeals in Austin.

The *Herald* of March 27, 1928, gave the background for the action against Armstrong:

> Chief of Police T. C. Armstrong must appear in district court at 10 a.m. May 7 and show cause why he should not be held in contempt and punished accordingly. Judge W. D. Howe handed down the order Tuesday following the filing of an affidavit by M. V. Ward, assistant district attorney, charging Armstrong failed to follow a court order to deliver to Los Angeles authorities $9,435 taken from William Cardone, Mrs. William Cardone and Eugene Brignola.

Ward charged the money was turned over to Cardone and Brignola in violation of a court order and that it was $6,000 short of the amount turned over to Armstrong when it reached Los Angeles.

Cardone and Brignola were charged with grand theft of $11,000 in Los Angeles. They were taken from a train here on request of the Los Angeles authorities. The money was turned over to the district attorney.

In habeas corpus proceedings, Judge Howe ordered the money and the two Cardones and Brignola into the custody of the chief of police to be delivered to Los Angeles authorities. Attorneys appealed the decision to the Court of Criminal Appeals. Brignola and Cardone on March 14 appeared before Judge Howe and said they agreed to dismiss the appeal. The suit to recover the money was dismissed. Ward delivered the money to Armstrong. Armstrong said Cardone and Brignola together opened the package given to Armstrong by Ward and each gave $700 to Attorney Tom Lea, as reported in the *Herald,* March 27 1928. The *Times* of May 8 said Armstrong had given the money back to the Cardones and Brignola. Brignola and Cardone were taken to Los Angeles and Mrs. Cardone was said to have gone to New York. According to the *Herald,* Brignola and Cardone failed to deliver the $9,435 to the Los Angeles authorities.

The *Times* of May 9 reported:

Chief of Police Tom Armstrong was freed on $200 bond after he was found guilty by Judge W. D. Howe on contempt of court charges and sentenced to two days in the County Jail and fined $200.

Armstrong filed a habeas corpus with the Court of Criminal Appeals at Austin immediately after Judge Howe passed sentence. It was in reply by telegraph from the Austin court that Armstrong was released on bond.

Chief of Detectives L. T. Robey was appointed to fill the position of Chief of Police by Mayor Pro Tem R. E. Sherman during Armstrong's detention by the sheriff.

Armstrong was a candidate for sheriff at the time, running mainly against M. V. (Buddy) Ward. The contempt of court charge against Armstrong was brought up a number of times during the ensuing campaign, but he won the election. The El Paso *Post* on June 29, 1928, said in a front page headline: "Court Of Criminal Appeals Upholds Armstrong." The court, in its opinion, said, "One could not be guilty of contempt for refusing to obey an order which was void or which the court had no authority or jurisdiction to make." M. V. (Buddy) Ward naturally accepted the court decision, but he still insisted there was a moral issue involved.

A New Industry

Good news was received in El Paso May 31, 1928. The *Times* on June 1 announced in big headlines: "Copper Refinery Comes Here." The sub heads said: "Council Agrees Not To Take Plant Into City For Taxation." "W. H. Burges Announces Selection After Message From Walter Douglas." The *Times* story said:

> El Paso has been selected for the $3 million copper refinery of Phelps Dodge.
>
> At a special session of the City Council late yesterday a resolution was adopted which virtually relieves the refinery from the possibility of municipal taxation, the resolution providing that the corporate city limits of the city will not be extended to include the refinery.

That was one of the biggest industries ever to come to El Paso. The *Times* added editorially under a heading "The Copper Refinery":

> The spirit of El Paso, which swiftly brought it from a border town to a flourishing city, is today in evidence. El Pasoans believe in their town, are proud of it, confident it is at the beginning of a new era of prosperity.

In the same edition, the *Times* said it was announced that the J. C. Penney Company had bought a site for a $150,000 downtown store at Stanton and San Antonio Streets.

In later years, the copper refinery and the Texaco and Standard refineries all were taken into the city limits. There was some discussion concerning the action of the City Council on May 31, 1928, but no serious objections were raised. The refineries had been caught in the middle when the cities of Ysleta and Ascarate were incorporated, only to be later dissolved. They seemed agreeable to being brought into the El Paso city limits.

Politics of 1928

The late spring and early summer of 1928 again found the *Herald* and the *Times* on one side of the political fence and the *Post* on the other. The *Herald* and the *Times* were charging that the city administration was trying to take over the Court House. The *Post* was supporting the city administration. The *Times* on June 12 said, "The city administration is backing a ticket to oust all county officers who opposed Mayor Thomason and his aldermen in the election last year."

District Attorney C. L. Vowell, candidate for reelection, opened the fireworks in Liberty Hall on the night of June 22. I covered that meeting. "Tom, tom, tom, tom, tom, tom," said Vowell. "Tom, tom, tom,—Tom Lea, Tom Armstrong and Thomason." "Vowell painted a graphic word picture of the assembling of the city hordes to the tune of 'Tom, Tom, Tom,' on the night of July 27, the night before the primaries," said the

Times of June 23. Vowell disparaaragingly called Alderman R. E. Sherman "X-ray Sherman," because he would fold his eyes inward.

Alderman Sherman responded a few nights later at a meeting in the Alta Vista School:

Charlie Vowell is known as the boy orator of the Rio Grande. We all know that the Rio Grande is only a few inches deep in places, but that it is a mile wide at the mouth.

I covered that meeting also. To this day I can almost see Ray Sherman smilingly cut C. L. Vowell to pieces.

Tom Armstrong was running for sheriff mainly against Buddy Ward. Ward attacked Armstrong and Attorney Tom Lea about the "stolen money," which he said Armstrong had returned to William Cardone and his wife and Eugene Brignola.

Tom Lea, who was one of the spearheads in the campaign particularly to elect Tom Armstrong sheriff and Stewart Berkshire district attorney, spoke in Liberty Hall on the night of July 9. Before a packed house, Lea said, "Here I am. Don't I look like a boss?" Then Lea made a terrible mistake: Buddy Ward had a slight curvature of the spine; Lea walked from the back of the stage to the front in a stooped position, while referring to Ward. On July 14, the *Times* quoted Lea as denying he had ridiculed Buddy Ward. He did; I saw him. But I have always thought that Lea did so unintentionally; he was a great criminal lawyer and he regularly acted his part before a jury; I thought he had unconsciously acted a part before that huge audience in Liberty Hall.

Then came the Democratic primary on July 27. The *Times* headline on July 28 announced Armstrong and Berkshire as winners. Dan Moody, who was running for governor, was reelected. The "Old Pro" W. D. (Bill) Greet, candidate for reelection as county clerk, was the sole survivor of all those candidates actually marked for defeat by the City Hall.

Thus ended another bitter political campaign with the *Herald* and the *Times* the losers; the *Post* was still on the rise in El Paso.

Buddy Ward was one of the finest men I ever knew. He also was a bushel of fun in a poker game. In those years there were a number of men in El Paso with keen wits. Among them were Attorney Walker Morrow, who later became president of the School Board, and Attorney John Penn, who for a time was connected with the district attorney's office. Anyone who played poker with Ward, Morrow, and Penn was in for a hilarious evening. The new Austin High School was dedicated in 1930, while Morrow was chairman of the School Board; as Mrs. Hooten, who was a teacher at Austin, and I went through the receiving line at the dedication, Morrow remarked to her, "That's a pretty dress you are wearing. Don't forget that I helped pay for it." He was trying to give her the impression that I had been lucky at poker.

Jimmie Walker Visits

Sunday, July 1, 1928, was a sort of red letter day in El Paso and Juarez. Mayor James J. (Jimmie) Walker of New York paid us a visit. I met him at the Union Depot with an El Paso delegation headed by Alderman R. E. Sherman, a strong supporter of New York Governor Alfred E. Smith, who had just been nominated for President by the Democratic National Convention in Houston. In a top head on Sunday, July 1, the *Times* said that "Mayor Jimmie Walker will be here today, according to a telegram received by Mayor Pro Tem R. E. Sherman, who invited him."

In its issue of Monday, July 2, the *Times* on its front page described the visit of the New York mayor.

> Lil' ol' New York came to El Paso and Juarez yesterday, at least the biggest part of it.
>
> Lil' ol' Jimmie Walker, himself mayor of Gotham — and before he left he could have been a triple mayor — mayor of New York, Juarez and El Paso.

The Elks Drum Corps cleared the way for Mayor Walker at the Union Station. Alderman Sherman introduced him to the crowd that jammed Hotel Paso del Norte. "It sounds more like home every minute," said Walker.

The group, growing by the minute, went to Juarez. First it stopped at the Central Cafe, where Walker surprised everyone by taking a bottle of water. The group then moved to the Mint Cafe, operated by the late Harry Mitchell, where lunch was served. Many toasts were offered. Sherman offered a toast to "the next President of the United States, Alfred E. Smith." Jimmie Walker proposed a toast to friendly relations between the United States and Mexico, another to General Francisco A. Martinez, in charge of the Juarez garrison, and still another to Harry Mitchell.

The *Times* reported, "Jimmie was the life of the party." "The Sidewalks of New York" was heard on several occasions. Then Mayor Walker wanted to see some of the night life in Juarez. The party went to a cabaret commonly called "The Bucket of Blood," located underneath the Big Kid's saloon on Sixteenth of September Street, where Mayor Walker danced the "Black Bottom" with one of the young women employed in the cabaret. The day had to come to an end and Mayor Walker and his large retinue departed. I asked one member of his party what he did; he answered, "Confidential to the mayor." The next day Alderman Poe expressed surprise to me that the mayor of New York would do the "Black Bottom."

Coming of Natural Gas

The coming of natural gas to El Paso was a big story — it still is. First indication that El Paso was to get natural gas appeared on the front page of the *Times* of August 14, 1928. Under a top head, the *Times* reported:

> According to Associated Press dispatches from New York yesterday, Houston interests, in cooperation with the Moody-Seagraves Corporation, are arranging plans to pipe natural gas to El Paso from Winkler County, Texas, and Lea County, New Mexico.
>
> Although the names of the Houston concern were not given in the dispatch, it is thought to be the same as that represented by Paul Kayser, a Houston attorney, who was in El Paso Friday and talked with Mayor R. E. Thomason.
>
> Mr. Kayser told Mayor Thomason he had been in New York on the matter of piping natural gas to El Paso and that he had already seen several large consumers here. He said he would return to the city some time this week, according to Mayor Thomason.

Nothing else happened until the City Council meeting of Thursday, September 27. I covered that meeting. Regular business of the meeting was conducted. Then Mayor Thomason asked if there was any other business to come before the council. A man, who had been seated outside the rail, arose and addressed the council. I had never seen him before. It turned out to be Paul Kayser. He said he wished to make application for a franchise to distribute natural gas in El Paso. He represented the El Paso Gas Utilities Corporation. Kayser deposited a check for $10,000 with the City as evidence of good faith. The occasion was reported in the *Herald* of September 27 and the *Times* of September 28, 1928.

The franchise, said Kayser, would be principally for the distribution of natural gas for industrial purposes, but would include domestic distribution provided an agreement could not be reached with the Texas Cities Gas Company, operators of the El Paso Gas Company. He said negotiations were going forward with the local distributor. The El Paso Gas Utilities Corporation was incorporated in Delaware and had a permit to do business in Texas. Officers were J. W. Colvin of Houston, president, and Paul Kayser and H. G. Frost, vice presidents. An office had been opened in the First National Bank Building.

On October 8, 1928, the County Commissioners Court granted the El Paso Gas Utilities Corporation a franchise to construct and maintain pipe lines and telegraph and telephone lines along and across public highways and streets and alleys in unincorporated towns over which the commissioners had control. It was revealed in the *Times* of October 16 that the Texas Cities Gas Company was negotiating with the El Paso Gas Utilities Corporation and other concerns for the purchase of natural gas at the gates of the city, but that it also had made arrangements to pipe the gas from Lea County, New Mexico, on its own initiative unless an agreement was reached. Quite obviosuly serious negotiations were under way.

The *Times* of November 2 said:

> The Texas Cities Gas Company's proposal of $1.02 as a basic or average rate for natural gas was accepted by the City Council.
>
> The company came down to $1.02 when the El Paso Gas Utilities Corporation reduced its gate rate to 34 cents per 1,000 cubic feet from 35 cents.
>
> Mayor R. E. Thomason and members of the City Council wanted a $1 basic rate but agreed to the $1.02 rate when H. L. Birney, president of the Chamber of Commerce, D. A. Bandeen, general manager of the Chamber of Commerce, and others urged the council to take action.

The El Paso Gas Utilities Corporation changed its name later to the El Paso Natural Gas Company. Today it is one of the largest corporations in the nation. Of most importance is that El Paso is its home city. The Company built a magnificent 18-story office building in Downtown El Paso, the tallest in the city at the time.

Here is a highly interesting paragraph from the story of the firm's first 25 years, as published in the *Pipeliner,* company publication, in its winter edition of 1953:

> In 1929, El Pasoans gathered outside in the hot June night to stare toward the east edge of town. There Mayor R. E. Thomason fired a roman candle igniting jetting gas into a giant flare. Flaming 60 feet into the night, it signaled watchers for miles around that natural gas was flowing from 200 miles away to serve El Paso's homes and industries.

Initial deliveries of natural gas were made to El Paso homes the next day, June 19. The *Pipeliner* continued:

> This gas flowed through the first all-welded steel pipeline ever built for natural gas. For the first time, the 16-inch steel tubes had been joined, by welding, into one continuous piece of piping, climbing and curving its way from field to city.

The *Pipeliner,* in its review of 40 years of progress, said in its October, 1968, issue:

> By the year 1943, the company was supplying the fuel requirements

for more than 42 per cent of the total new production of copper produced in the United States, plus a magnesium plant, two steel plants, 20 military installations, and 62 communities in Arizona, New Mexico, and Texas. (By 1968, El Paso Natural was to sell more gas each year than any other natural gas pipeline company.)

In 1946 authorization was received for a 1,200-mile line to California. In 1965, Howard Boyd became chairman of the board and H. F. Steen became president of El Paso Natural. Paul Kayser had served as El Paso Natural Gas Company's chief executive for 37 years.

I have always been proud of the El Paso Natural Gas Company. I am proud that El Paso is its home. I always felt I had a hand in its beginning because I covered that story on September 27, 1928, when Paul Kayser made his move in El Paso.

I have never understood why, but the late Drew Pearson, in his column "The Washington Merry-Go-Round," seemed to take a very unreasonable dislike for the El Paso Natural Gas Company. He wrote very unfair columns about it at times. Usually, I declined to publish those columns in the *Times* while I was editor. I saw no reason to allow Pearson to use the hometown newspaper of El Paso Natural Gas Company to try to pillory it.

El Paso at Sunrise

At 5:30 one morning in 1928, James L. Wadley, telegraph editor of the *Herald,* encountered on the roof of the newspaper building the publisher of the paper, Captain H. D. Slater. I never learned why each of the men happened to be on the roof of the building at that time of day. Slater seldom spoke to the men who worked for him. On the roof that morning Wadley remarked, "El Paso is beautiful at sunrise, isn't it?" Slater agreed and then he instructed Wadley to write him 500 words on El Paso at sunrise. Wadley was an excellent telegraph editor, but 500 words on El Paso at sunrise was something else again! He appealed for help from the *Herald* reporters and the essay was finally completed and delivered to Slater. It was never published. Slater probably just wanted to see whether Wadley could rise to such an occasion.

Hoover Versus Smith

The nation underwent an emotional bath during the presidential election contest between Republican Herbert Hoover and Democrat Al Smith. El Paso took that bath along with the rest of the country. While some chose to deny it, there was not the slightest doubt that Smith's Catholicism contributed voltage to the situation. Smith also was advocating repeal of the Eighteenth Amendment, and it was generally accepted that some of those who opposed Smith primarily because he was a Catholic pretended they objected to him because he was a wet. Herbert Hoover was a strong candidate; no one denied he was a man of high personal honor.

In El Paso, an organization was formed calling itself Democrats for Al Smith for President, under the chairmanship of Attorney Harris Walthall. An Independent Hoover Club, headed by J. T. McCullough, was formed to convert dissident Democrats into Hoovercrats. Many of El Paso's Protestant ministers were active in opposition to Smith. The Reverend George H. Bassett, pastor of the First Christian Church, Dr. T. V. Neal, pastor of the First Baptist Church, and the Reverend H. D. Tucker of the Asbury Methodist Church supported Hoover. The full story was told in the *Times* of November 4, 1928.

Election day brought surprises: The *Times* reported that Hoover carried Texas by 16,481 and New Mexico by 15,251. Hoover won in the City of El Paso by 438 votes, but Smith carried El Paso County by less than 100. Hoover won the presidency with an Electoral College vote of 444, reckoned by most observers as a landslide.

But hard times lay ahead. The stock market crashed in October, 1929, and the Great Depression followed; many people blamed Hoover, I think unfairly, for those developments.

The Story of a Bank Robber

Ace Pendleton, a notorious bank robber wanted in several states, was arrested in El Paso January 22, 1929. He came to El Paso and took up residence in the illegal red light district. It was not known how long he had been there, but one night while drinking he confided his identity to one of the girls, who promptly told Lucy Tims, later known as Lucy Stevenson, the "head woman" in the red light district. Lucy, who always tried to stay in the good graces of the police, passed the information on to Police Sergeant J. W. FitzGerald, who then informed Police Chief L. T. Robey. The police followed Lucy's advice that Pendleton be arrested without revealing they knew his identity, and he was jailed in routine fashion on a charge of vagrancy.

The next morning, Chief Robey gave *Herald* Police Reporter H. Worth Jones the privilege of telling Pendleton they knew who he was. As the City Hall-Court House reporter, Jones and I frequently met on our beats. Jones opened the slot in the cell door and said, "Hi, Ace." Pendleton did not change his expression, but asked for a cigarette. He insisted the police were trying to frame him, but fingerprint records quickly proved he was bluffing.

Pendleton was the head of a daring band of bank robbers. He used aliases of Edgar Murphy and Ed Bailey. He was 32 years old at the time of his El Paso arrest.

The *Times* of January 25, 1927, reported:

Ace Pendleton, bank bandit wanted in several states, is believed to be on his way back to Shreveport, La., under guard of Chief of Police L. T. Robey and Sgt. J. W. FitzGerald, who arrested him here early Wednesday.

About 3 p.m. yesterday, Robey and FitzGerald hustled Pendleton out the back door of the City Jail, placed him in an automobile and set out for an unknown destination.

Pendleton is wanted in Shreveport in connection with holding up a bank and wounding the bank cashier.

The *Times* reported that a $5,000 reward was offered in Shreveport for the arrest and conviction of Pendleton and his two confederates. I heard later that Pendleton escaped from Shreveport police and headed back to El Paso to get even with Lucy Tims, but was taken from a freight train at Van Horn and rearrested. I do not know what finally happened to him.

New Day in El Paso

As I have already written, Captain H. D. Slater sold the *Herald* and the *Times* to Dorrance D. Roderick and Lindsay Nunn in December, 1928. The new arrivals made this announcement on the front page of the two papers on February 1, 1929:

With their editions of today, the El Paso *Herald* and *Times* pass to new ownership and new management. The history of the *Herald* and *Times* has been a glorious one and both have made great contributions to the growth and development of El Paso and the Southwest. During the past five decades, many men of prominence in the life of El Paso have been associated with them in the many phases of the great tasks of city building.

The new owners are not unmindful of the responsibility and accept the *Herald* and *Times* as a great public trust. We, who now control the future of these newspapers, will constantly strive to improve and strengthen the work they have done.

The *Herald* and *Times* will not be interested in the fortunes of any political organization or to exploit any special interests. They will not seek nor accept political favors or do anything to restrict their liberty. As papers dedicated to the public good, the *Herald* and *Times* will express the thought and life of the community as fairly and accurately as humans with honest intentions can do. The *Herald* and *Times* will be ready and eager to publish all sides of any question in a fair, equitable and tolerant manner.

Your newspapers stand ready to fight for the right, as it is given us to see the right and to develop and express an informed and intelligent public opinion. The *Herald* and *Times* will continue to be useful members of the community. Their columns will be kept clean for news, entertainment and instruction and things of vital interest to every member of the family.

The *Herald* and *Times* are dedicated to promote the happiness, prosperity and well-being of all the people they are privileged to serve.

Dorrance Roderick was only 28 years old at the time. Obviously, the new owners of the *Herald* and *Times* meant what they said. A new day dawned on the newspaper horizon in El Paso. Sound business methods were used in the business office, news columns were devoted to news and the editorial pages to opinion and discussion. When I retired March 31, 1970, as editor of the *Times*, I was the last member of the old *Herald* staff still with the paper who stood up in the newsroom February 1, 1929, and met the new owners of the papers.

Immediately after the new owners took charge, there was considerable speculation among the newsmen as to who would be appointed editor. H. S. Hunter had been assistant to the editor under Slater. *Herald* News Editor Robert Lepley also had his eye on the job. In an effort to impress Roderick, Lepley asked me to get some timely news from Mayor Thomason. Thomason told me that there was talk of giving the city firemen a raise, and I wrote an editorial suggesting that the city firemen were entitled to a raise. Lepley put his own name over my editorial and submitted it. The pay raise for the firemen came through. But Hunter was appointed editor of both papers on February 7. It was an excellent choice.

Hunter was well acquainted all over the Southwest and was highly respected. He continued as editor of both papers until the *Herald* was sold to Scripps-Howard and merged with the *Post* on April 2, 1931. Then he served as editor of the *Times* until he died in the *Times* newsroom of a heart attack on October 20, 1940. He had a distinguished newspaper career. Lepley was fired by Roderick and Hunter later that year; he was not even permitted to clean out his desk. Complaints had been made to Roderick by Charles Gibson, auditor of the papers; that much was known, but it was not revealed exactly why Lepley was summarily discharged.

The *Herald* and *Times* took their proper place in the community and things went well. Control of the two papers was gained by an Amarillo group headed by Gene Howe of the Amarillo *News and Globe.* They sold the *Herald* to Scripps-Howard, which merged it with the *Post* to become the El Paso *Herald-Post,* and Roderick became owner and publisher of the *Times*; but more on that later.

The Peyton Divorce

One of the most sensational divorce cases in El Paso history occurred early in 1929. Judge Ballard Coldwell, in whose 65th District Court the action was brought, always had a nose for news. On the day the hearing was to come up, he told *Post* reporter Gerald Daily and me he had a case coming up that would make us a good news story if he let it run. We asked him to let it run. That was on December 28, 1928, when Mrs. Mary M. Peyton filed for divorce against J. C. Peyton, founder and president of the Peyton Packing Company, asking for a division of community property estimated at $300,000. I covered that case from beginning to end.

The *Herald* and the *Post* printed full details of the proceedings.

The story developed into skirmishing between Peyton and Mrs. Peyton. The real sensation came on February 25, when the *Herald* reported that Peyton had filed suit in 34th District Court to annul the marriage, charging that Mrs. Peyton was already married to another man when she married him. On February 26, Mrs. Peyton, said the *Herald,* filed an application in 65th District Court for $600 a month alimony from J. C. Peyton. The hearing began in 65th District Court February 27.

On one occasion an altercation developed between Peyton and Eric Bruhn, a socially prominent El Pasoan, whose name was linked romantically with that of Mrs. Peyton, and shots were fired at the Peyton home at 2919 Federal. The *Herald* story on February 27 quoted Mrs. Peyton as saying that, at the time the shots were fired, Bruhn was with her. She said she and Bruhn in company with other people had been to Juarez. After they returned to El Paso Bruhn took her home, insisting that she was ill and that she call a doctor.

> I told him I was all right, but that I wanted to take my temperature. I told him to come in. It was about 11:30 p.m. A large police dog which I have acted very nervous and I said someone was outside. I looked outside and someone appeared. I said, "Who are you?" and he said, ". . . I'll show you who I am." He then pointed the pistol at me and fired. The bullet didn't miss me two inches. Eric jumped off the porch and grappled with Mr. Peyton for a few moments. Mr. Peyton said, "My God, I nearly killed you," and I said, "That's what you almost did, Joe."

Peyton testified to his belief that Mrs. Peyton married him for his money, that she held no affection for him, that she had represented herself as much younger than she was, and that she was married to another man when she married him. Mrs. Peyton testified that she had married Loch Sawyer, but had divorced him nine months before she married Peyton.

Attorney Walker Morrow, representing Peyton, contended that Mrs. Peyton could not account for the years in her life from 1907 to 1913 because during that time she was married to Robert Maxwell. Mrs. Peyton testified that she was a small girl at that time. A baptismal certificate, purporting to be that of Mrs. Peyton, was introduced; if it was hers, which she denied, she would have been 43 years old at the time. Judge Coldwell awarded Mrs. Peyton legal expenses and $250 a month alimony, until such time as the pending suit was adjudicated.

On March 7, 1929, the entire action was dropped by Mrs. Peyton and Judge Coldwell dismissed the suit. On that same day, District Judge W. D. Howe in 34th District Court declared the marriage null and void, and Mrs. Peyton got no settlement. The court records show that Mrs. Peyton's name was changed in the action to Maxine W. Sawyer.

The former Mrs. Peyton and Eric Bruhn were married five hours after Judge Howe granted Peyton the anulment. The *Herald* of March 8, over a picture of the former Mrs. Peyton, said:

> Mrs. Maxine Sawyer Peyton whose marriage to Joe C. Peyton was annulled by Judge W. D. Howe in 34th District Court Thursday at 3 p.m., and who became the bride of Eric Bruhn of El Paso in Alamogordo at 8 p.m. Thursday. The ceremony was performed by a justice of the peace. Friends of the couple said that they plan to return to El Paso Sunday.

Revolution in Mexico

War clouds hung over Mexico early in March, 1929. General Jose Gonzalo Escobar, former commander of the Juarez garrison, was chosen by a group of generals to head a revolution against the government in Mexico City, of which Emilio Portes Gil was provisional president, and General Plutarco Elias Calles, former president and secretary of war, was the strong man. That government had been in power since 1920, when the de la Huerta-Calles-Obregon revolt swept President Venustiano Carranza out of office.

I was assigned to the Douglas *International* when the 1920 revolution broke out. I put the flash on the Associated Press wire that the State of Sonora had seceded. Adolfo de la Huerta was the provisional president of Mexico after the revolt. Later Calles was elected president. General Alvaro Obregon was elected president to succeed Calles, but he was assassinated in Mexico July 17, 1928, before he could take office. Early in March 1929 numerous battles were reported in the interior of Mexico. Juarez was on pins and needles as General Marcelo Caraveo of Chihuahua joined the revolution. An attack on Juarez was expected momentarily. I was one of the reporters for the *Herald* assigned to cover events as the revolution unfolded.

The federal commander of Juarez, General M. J. Limon, and Mayor Agustin Gallo were being pressured to join the Escobar forces; tension could be felt in our neighbor city. A rebel army was reported approaching Juarez day by day. On March 6, rebel troops were reported at Samalayuca. One afternoon a shot was heard at one end of Sixteenth of September Street; someone cried, "Caraveo!" and the whole city panicked, with business houses closing and people fleeing in the streets, but it turned out to be a false alarm.

The *Herald* reported the attack on Juarez early March 8. Reporters for the El Paso newspapers took refuge in the home of Harry Mitchell, operator of the Mint Cafe. From the windows of that home we could see what was going on. I recall seeing a cavalry charge down Sixteenth of September Street.

Late in the morning there was a lull in the fighting and *Herald* Reporter H. Worth Jones and I, with our interpreter Richard North, ventured into the street and walked down Sixteenth of September to the Rio Bravo Hotel, then the headquarters of rebel officers General Jose de la Vega and General Miguel Valle. General de la Vega informed me that his forces were in command of the city. I walked down Avenida Lerdo to the Rio Grande where I saw the federal army. It had taken refuge behind the banks of the river. If the rebels shot at them, the bullets would go over their heads into El Paso. I walked across the Stanton Street bridge and telephoned the *Herald* office what General de la Vega had said.

At the United States customs house I saw the commander of Fort Bliss, Brigadier General George Van Horn Moseley, flanked by his entire staff, including Major Alexander Day Surles, chief of G2 of the First Cavalry Division. General Moseley was highly incensed because a number of El Pasoans had been shot. He asked me if I knew where the opposing generals were in Juarez. I pointed to General Matias Ramos (seated on a black horse on the river levee about 100 yards from the Mexican customs house), the federal commander who had been flown to El Paso and taken across the river the night before. He had taken command of the Juarez troops from General Limon. I told General Moseley that General de la Vega and General Valle were at the Rio Bravo Hotel.

General Moseley was so angry he was hitting his leg with his riding crop. He and his staff crossed the Rio Grande at 11 a.m. He asked me if I would tell General Ramos that he wanted to see him and he dispatched a taxi driver to the Rio Bravo Hotel to fetch one of the rebel commanders. As I walked along the river levee to get General Ramos, a Mexican federal soldier who talked English suggested that I get down off the levee or I might get shot.

I told General Ramos that General Moseley wished to see him. I walked beside his horse as he rode to the customs house. Just as we approached the place where General Moseley and his staff were standing, General Valle came dashing up, standing on the running board of a taxicab. As General Ramos dismounted, General Valle approached him, trying to embrace him. I was told the two had attended Chapultepec together. Ramos turned his back and spat on the ground, saying he would not embrace a traitor.

General Moseley immediately called a conference, with Emmett Hines of El Paso as interpreter. General Moseley told the Mexican commanders that the fighting had to stop, that El Pasoans had been shot, and that he had moved a number of artillery pieces mounted on flat cars to the border. General Ramos demanded of General Moseley that, since our government recognized his government, he be permitted to reassemble his forces on the United States side and there be furnished with arms and ammunition. General Moseley replied that any Mexican soldier crossing to the United States side would be interned. General Ramos left the conference and came to El Paso to confer with the Mexican consul general and to get instructions from Mexico City.

General Moseley congratulated General Valle on his success thus far and hoped he would be generous. Valle replied that his superiors had instructed him to be very careful that no rebel soldiers fired into El Paso. The shooting stopped. At sundown, the Mexican federal army, with the honors of war, with their flags flying and their drums rolling, marched across the Stanton Street bridge and on to Fort Bliss, where they were interned.

Major Surles, whom I mentioned as being chief of staff of G2 of the First Cavalry Division, went on to become a major general and chief of Army Public Relations in Washington during World War II. The rebels took command of Juarez; the churches were opened and their bells were rung. Among those killed in the battle was a rebel colonel. His body lay in state in the Juarez City Hall; thousands of Juarez residents, mostly women, walked by his bier. A company of rebel soldiers marched from the garrison on the hill to act as his honor guard.

General Marcelino Murrieta was sent to Juarez to take command. Escobar visited Juarez a number of times during the month the rebels held the city. He was visited twice that I know about by General Moseley. The *Times* reported on March 26 that General Escobar was delayed in Juarez while he completed $30,000 worth of purchases in El Paso for his rebel army. Rebel officials said no arms or ammunition were obtained in El Paso and that the neutrality laws were strictly observed. The *Times* reported on April 1 that the rebels were massing an air fleet in Juarez for an attack on federal forces to the south. Nine planes from the United States side were reported assembled at the Juarez airport. The *Times* also reported that the 325 federal soldiers interned at Fort Bliss had been taken to Naco, Arizona, where they crossed into Sonora and helped defeat the rebel forces.

Things were going from bad to worse for the Escobar forces in the south; federal troops under General Juan Andreu Almazan were driving them northward. On April 2, the *Times* reported that General Escobar with five troop trains loaded with men and cavalry horses had arrived in Juarez. Trucks and taxicabs were purchased in the city. That same day, General Escobar's troop trains left Juarez by way of the Mexican Northwestern Railroad for Pulpito Pass and on into Sonora. General Caraveo, according to the *Times* of April 10, 1929, came to Juarez with a rag-tag troop train. Anyone who never saw a Mexican troop train during that period missed something. Women and children were on top of the box cars while the soldiers were inside. Some rebel soldiers took livestock, chickens and any other food they could find. Caraveo moved out of Juarez later that same day, taking the Mexican Northwestern Railroad through Pulpito Pass into Sonora, where he joined Escobar.

Juarez was left without any authority. As I recall, a wounded federal soldier took command in the name of his government. The Mexican consul general in El Paso appointed temporary city officials for Juarez. Order was quickly restored and a number of federal officers who had been in Juarez when the city was attacked soon reappeared.

The day the rebels left Juarez, April 9, was the day the Sheldon Hotel caught fire in downtown El Paso. I recall writing the Juarez story in the *Herald* newsroom and looking across to the burning Sheldon. I saw Reporter H. Worth Jones walking along the Sheldon roof with flames leaping into the air; he was looking for Fire Chief John Sullivan to get some facts about the fire.

The following weeks were hectic in Juarez. One day a rebel sympathizer tried to escape across the railroad bridge into the United States. He was shot dead and his body was left lying in the middle of the railroad bridge. The *Herald* sent another reporter and me to the Santa Fe Street bridge, which was then under construction, to get the story. We could see the man's body lying in the middle of the railroad bridge; we decided not to go out on the bridge for a closer look, and that proved sensible because, somewhat later, the army officer who had shot the fleeing rebel asked me why I had not walked out on the railroad bridge so he could shoot me. He knew me by sight and I apparently was not one of his favorite people.

The rebels were defeated on every front. General Almazan and his troops came to Juarez for a brief stay. Some of the Almazan troops were seen on the streets of El Paso. General Escobar fled to the United States and then to Canada.

Mexico was one of our staunchest allies during World War II, guarding our back door in marked contrast to World War I, when a hostile Mexico kept thousands of our troops tied down along the border.

The Escobar revolution was the last in Mexico.

The Unwritten Law

The *Herald* on April 15, 1929, committed a serious blunder when it published the wrong picture of an El Paso family in connection with the killing of a young El Paso man in an unwritten law case. On the night of April 14, 1929, A. F. LaFon, 41, 1116 Wyoming Street, left his home early in the evening ostensibly to go to work. A short time later he returned and found his wife gone. He found her around the corner in an automobile with Charles Titus, and there he shot and killed Titus.

The next morning *Herald* Reporter H. Worth Jones and I went to the LaFon apartment, to which we were admitted by the landlady. I picked up from the dresser a picture of LaFon and his wife and their small child and tried to take it with me, but the landlady objected. Before putting the picture back, I noted the name of the photographer; from the *Herald* office, News Editor Robert Lepley called the photographer, who agreed to make us a print. He did so and the picture appeared on the front page of the *Herald* that afternoon. It was of the wrong people. The man, wife, and child shown were a highly respectable El Paso family. The *Post* had the correct picture of the LaFons and their child.

The next day, April 16, the *Herald* published the correct picture of the LaFon family with this apology over it:

> Through an error, pictures furnished yesterday by a photographic studio as being those of Mr. and Mrs. A. F. LaFon and baby and so published by the *Herald,* were not those of the persons they purported to be. The *Herald* deeply regrets the mistake in identification however unintentional and takes this means of expressing sincere apologies to the estimable family whose pictures were confused with those of the LaFons.

The young couple whose picture had been mistakenly published by the *Herald* went to Mayor R. E. Thomason, who also was one of El Paso's leading lawyers. The *Herald,* under its new ownership, had switched its support to Mayor Thomason. I am convinced that had nothing to do with it, but Mayor Thomason told me in the City Hall that he felt sorry for the *Herald.* He could have made it rough on us, but he did not. Obviously we had damaged the couple. *Herald* and *Times* Publisher Dorrance Roderick handled the difficulty beautifully. The *Herald* paid the money the young couple owed on their automobile, and the incident was closed.

On the front page of the *Herald* of April 15, Mrs. LaFon was quoted as saying, "It's all my fault. I got him into this." She testified for her husband at his trial, and he was acquitted.

I was in Silver City with a Good Will group from the El Paso Chamber of Commerce in 1939. We went to a night club called the Casa Loma on the edge of town. There I struck up a conversation with a woman at the bar and invited her to dance with me. She told me that she was Mrs. LaFon and that her husband was the bartender; without further comment, I delivered her back where I had found her. Records in the office of the sheriff in Silver City show that Amos LaFon was tried and acquitted in 1941 in the murder of D. D. (Dixie) Owens. I have no idea what happened to the LaFons after that.

Law Firm Wiped Out

An entire El Paso law firm was wiped out May 31, 1929, and the killer later committed suicide in El Paso County Jail under mysterious circumstances. El Paso Attorneys Frank J. Lyons and Herbert D. Oppenheimer were in their offices in the First National Bank Building, where they operated under the firm name of Lyons and Oppenheimer. Jose Marin, a 64-year-old Spaniard, walked in during the noon hour and opened fire, killing Oppenheimer first. Lyons, upon hearing the shots and some of the conversation, had taken refuge under his desk; Marin pursued him, and shot him there. When I got there, I found that District Attorney Stewart Berkshire was in command. I talked with Marin at the county jail and he told me that the State of Texas owed him a bounty. He expressed absolutely no regrets.

This appeared on the front page of the *Times* June 1:

Charges of murder were filed against Jose Marin, 64-year-old Spaniard, who shot and killed Frank J. Lyons and Herbert D. Oppenheimer in their offices shortly after noon yesterday. Marin was being held in a cell alone. The district attorney had given instructions that no one could see him.

Marin had not engaged counsel.

Dr. S. Haffna and Dr. Celestino Ortiz said they had treated Marin for a nervous disorder for two years. They expressed the opinion that he was a psychopathic case.

After the shooting, Marin walked across the hallway into the office of the Fruit Dispatch Co., and proffered his gun to W. O. Smith, an employe. Marin asked that officers be summoned.

Mayor R. E. Thomason and his law partner, Tom Lea, were among the first to reach the slain men.

The *Times* said that information was received by the district attorney that Marin had shot and seriously wounded his business partner, Jose Lago, in Sostenes, Chihuahua, in 1903. The *Times* also reported that United States Public Health physicians announced that Marin had been declared mentally normal within the last six months. Then it was discovered that Mrs. Leonora Rios, wife of Rosendo Rios of Juarez, was in the law office paying a fee and had been an eyewitness to the shooting. The *Times* said that Marin claimed self-defense, that he shot only when the lawyers had made threatening moves. The *Times* of June 18 quoted Marin as saying his conscience was clear, as the June 24 date of his trial drew nearer. Before District Attorney Berkshire clamped on the rule that no one could see Marin, the killer told me that a disagreement over a mine had developed between him and Lyons and Oppenheimer.

On June 23, the day before Marin was scheduled to go on trial, his body was found in his cell by Walter W. Whitehead, turnkey, on his routine visit bringing breakfast. "We thoroughly examined every article before it reached his hands," said E. S. Bache, chief deputy sheriff. An autopsy showed that Marin had died of poison that he had apparently concealed in his belt.

Kills Wrong Man

A most regrettable incident occurred in Juarez June 18, 1930. A young El Pasoan, W. J. (Jeff) Meers, through an error in identification, shot and killed Antonio Visconti, a Juarez bartender, in the Owl Saloon. He mistook Visconti for Manuel Villareal, sought in El Paso for the slaying of Meers' father during an attempted payroll holdup several years previously.

The *Times* of July 22, 1930, reported that Meers was being taken to Chihuahua City for trial; he was convicted and sent to prison. He was released after a few years and returned to El Paso, and then he dropped from sight.

I recall Meers asking me in the *Herald* newsroom to show him a picture of Villareal. He impressed me as a sincere young man interested in apprehending the alleged killer of his father, and I asked the person in charge of the *Herald* morgue to show Meers the picture. I have always wondered whether or not Meers had already spotted Visconti in Juarez. Anyway, the incident resulted in a dead man in Juarez followed by long imprisonment of a young El Pasoan in Mexico.

Thomason for Congress

Mayor R. E. Thomason made his successful bid for Congress in the Democratic primary on July 26, 1930. The Sixteenth Congressional District at that time was the largest in area in the United States, comprising 38 counties and extending almost to San Antonio.

Thomason in his book THE AUTOBIOGRAPHY OF A FEDERAL JUDGE wrote that Houston Harte, publisher of the San Angelo *Standard-Times,* telephoned him in the spring of 1930 and told him that Congressman Claude B. Hudspeth had just announced he would not be a candidate for reelection. Harte wanted to announce Thomason's candidacy in the morning paper, but Thomason told Harte he needed a little time to think about it. Harte said he was going to announce him anyway, which he did. C. C. Belcher, of Del Rio, announced the next day, but he withdrew from the race a month later. E. E. (Pat) Murphy of San Angelo and M. L. Birkhead of El Paso also announced. Thomason stumped the district and conducted a successful campaign. Murphy was very active also, but Birkhead was somewhat inactive.

The coverage of Thomason's campaign for Congress in the El Paso *Herald* and *Times* was in sharp contrast with their coverage of Thomason's campaign for mayor of El Paso in 1927. On January 18, 1927, the *Times* said on its front page:

> Christened with a spattering of mud, oozing vindictiveness, R. E. Thomason and his running mates launched forth last night on the stormy political waters. . . .

On July 23, 1930, the front page of the *Times* reported:

> A remarkable demonstration of affection and esteem which the community holds for R. E. Thomason, mayor and candidate for Congress, was given last night when 406 El Pasoans and a number of guests from Juarez attended a testimonial dinner arranged by the women of El Paso in Hotel Hussmann's Crystal Ballroom.
>
> Speaker after speaker was introduced by Mrs. A. F. Quisenberry.
>
> Mayor Thomason, telling funny stories of his campaign to cover his embarrassment at the flattering things that had been said about him, also referred to the importance of voting.
>
> "I won't talk politics on this occasion," said the mayor, "but after this marvelous demonstration here tonight, after all the wonderful things that have been said about me, wouldn't it be just too awfully bad if I were to get beaten? You folks won't let that happen, will you?
>
> "Your votes Saturday will record your convictions."

The *Times* said on its front page of July 25:

For the second time within a week, El Paso citizens gathered to give an ovation to their chief executive, Mayor R. E. Thomason, who made his last appearance last night at Cleveland Square in his campaign for a seat in Congress from the 16th Congressional District.

The crowd was fully as large as any that has gathered in El Paso during the present campaign.

When the mayor was introduced by Joseph Nealon, his former law partner and friend for 20 years and now a partner of Claude B. Hudspeth, retiring congressman, the crowd arose as one man and cheered while the mayor beamed with his sunny smile and bowed his thanks for the friendship and cordiality extended him.

The *Times* headline of July 28 said: "Thomason Almost Sure To Win Without Runoff." The story said latest available figures gave Thomason 19,323; Murphy 13,447, and Birkhead 1,250. In El Paso County, Thomason had 8,088, Birkhead 858, and Murphy 650. In addition to El Paso County, Thomason carried Brewster, Culberson, Ector, Glasscock, Hudspeth, Jeff Davis, Martin, Midland, Pecos, Presidio, Reeves, Val Verde, Ward, and Winkler Counties. Tom Green County (San Angelo) gave Murphy 3,180 and Thomason 1,596. On July 29, the *Times* said:

Mayor R. E. Thomason is the next representative from the 16th Congressional District. His chief opponent, E. E. (Pat) Murphy of San Angelo, yesterday evening sent telegrams to Mayor Thomason and the *Times* conceding the election.

Thus began 17 years in Congress for R. E. Thomason.

A Lesson Learned

In the newspaper business we sometimes learn lessons the hard way. I hope newspapermen will always strive for a good story. Without such an incentive, the profession would be dull indeed.

When I was city editor of the old *Herald* in 1930, a grandmother came to the office and talked with me for a long time about finding a home for a small granddaughter. The father had deserted them, and neither the mother nor the grandmother was financially able to care for the child. We published a picture of the beautiful blond-haired, brown-eyed little girl of 18 months, trying to find her a home.

A childless El Paso physician and his wife fell in love with her and took her home with them; the doctor's wife even furnished a room for the little girl. Soon it was noticed that the child did not respond to the attention and affection showered on her by the doctor and his wife. An examination showed the child to have syphillis. The grief-stricken doctor and his wife, so I was told, were at a loss to know what to do.The last I heard the little girl was in a Salvation Army home.

The lesson learned was to leave child adoption in the hands of the proper authorities, who through training and experience have a way of finding the best solutions.

A New City Editor

My career as a reporter ended in September, 1929, when I was named city editor of the *Herald.* Lynn C. Townsend had replaced Robert Lepley as news editor of the *Herald;* he will be remembered in El Paso Little Theater circles as the founder of the Townsend Players. Down through the years I have always sought to remember something that was attributed to William Randolph Hearst. It went something like this: "No newspaperman no matter how high he rises, should ever forget that, first of all, he must be a good reporter." I thoroughly enjoyed my years on the beat, and, to this day, I still enjoy writing a story.

The job of city editor did not offer the excitement or the fun that the reporter enjoyed. That I had made many good friends while covering the City Hall and the Court House was plainly evident at my first Christmas as city editor, when my friends on the beat remembered me with many presents. It was while I was city editor of the *Herald* that I learned about typography. The printers were my instructors, teaching me how to select type, and how to dummy a page and arrange heads attractively. That training was valuable to me during the remaining years I had in the newspaper business.

In the 18 months while I was city editor of the *Herald,* control of the two papers was gained by an Amarillo group headed by Gene Howe. That Amarillo group sent Henry Ansley to El Paso as managing editor and Magner White as assistant editor. Men in the *Herald* newsroom smiled and chatted together in the wash room when Ansley, writing a column under the heading "Old Sapp," patterned after Gene Howe's column "The Tactless Texan" in Amarillo, wrote that he was trying to eat a quail a day, and White, also writing a column, went on an orange juice diet. H. S. Hunter, the editor, was writing in his column "Around Here" about the nutritiousness of *frijoles.* The *Herald* and the *Times* were prospering. Business was good and the *Herald,* which had challenged the *Post* under Dorrance Roderick's direction, instead of ignoring it as Slater had done, was gaining circulation.

Then came that fateful day, April 2, 1931, which was the last date of publication of the El Paso *Herald.* The Amarillo group had sold the *Herald* to Scripps-Howard, which combined it with the *Post* and began publishing the El Paso *Herald-Post.* Roderick became owner and publisher of the *Times.* I remember very well the last gloomy day at the *Herald,* with men sitting around who would be without jobs. The *Herald* and *Times* editor, H. S. Hunter, had given the *Post* editor, Wallace Perry, a list of the men the *Times* was not keeping. Chester Chope, *Post* managing editor, telephoned me that he needed two topnotch reporters. I recommended Marshall Hail and Lester Sutcliffe, and agreed to send them over. Hail, for a long time considered the best reporter in El Paso, stayed with the *Herald-Post* until his retirement in 1969; he died in 1971. Sutcliffe left the *Herald-Post* and went to the Phoenix *Gazette.*

Thus ended the old El Paso *Herald.*

It had its up and downs, but it was a great newspaper. I always thought that if Dorrance Roderick had been given his way and the *Herald* and the *Times* had continued publication together, the *Post* would eventually have been in serious trouble. But that was not in the cards.

At the time of the merger, Magner White, who was to become managing editor of the *Times,* told me that I could either go with the *Herald-Post* as assistant city editor or be city editor of the *Times.* In the smartest decision I ever made, I unhesitatingly chose the *Times.*

Dorrance D. Roderick and Charles Guy were my close associates during my years with the TIMES. *They presented me "The Best News Hound Award" in my office in April, 1956.*

CHAPTER ·IV·

The Times Under Roderick

New Newspaper Battle

EL PASO SAW the stage set April 3, 1931, for the beginning of another community newspaper battle. That battle was fought on clean, competitive lines, with little or no mudslinging. The struggling El Paso *Times,* under Dorrance Roderick's ownership, began the uphill fight against the powerful El Paso *Herald-Post.*

On the front page of the *Times* April 3, 1931, Roderick made this announcement.

With this issue, the El Paso *Times* passes to my control. Because the operation of a newspaper exerts such widespread influence in a community and because a newspaper derives its strength and well-being from the confidence readers have in it and because I am not unmindful of the fact that publication of the *Times* is a public trust and that its success is dependent upon public acceptance, I take this opportunity to state as fully and clearly as possible the policies under which the *Times* will be operated henceforth.

The Times will be a constructive newspaper. It will be a thorough newspaper in every sense of the word. With its full Associated Press membership and the exclusive night wire of the United Press, it will bring to El Paso the news from every corner of the world. As fully as the resources and local support will permit, it will fill the local morning and Sunday newspaper field on an adequate scale.

These things, I realize, cannot be done without the confidence, respect and support of the citizens and the business men of El Paso. The *Times* intends to merit their cooperation by publishing a good newspaper.

We will not hedge on any important issue. Instead, according to our lights and best judgment, we will back to the limit any project which seems to us for the best interest of the community as a whole. We will take the same attitude in local politics, preserving our integrity, our absolute freedom of expression, and independence at all costs.

I feel I have been fortunate in associating with me for the production of this newspaper men and women who make their homes in El Paso. Many of them have been identified with El Paso all their lives. Their loyalty to their home city and its institutions is beyond question. Naturally, this fact will have a profound influence on the newspaper with which they are identified — which is exactly as I would have it.

The *Times* will forego "bells and hullabaloo" for constructive, forward-looking action. We do not intend to be trivial, or to be led astray by the superficial.

A newspaper's operations are limited to the support it gains for itself by reason of its policies and its functioning as a community institution. This we will not lose sight of.

We will do our part, knowing that if we perform our journalistic duties faithfully, El Paso, appreciative and still motivated by the spirit of fairness characteristic of this great Southwest, will make our efforts worth the ambition, the energy and the sincerity which we shall put into them.

I was only the city editor of the organization Roderick had put together. He had such men as H. S. Hunter, Val Lawrence, Mayo Seamon, C. B. McCauley and others to help him make the *Times* a success. On April 3, 1931, the *Times* had 11,500 circulation, and the *Herald-Post* had an unduplicated circulation of 28,000. It takes no imagination to see what an uphill battle faced the *Times.*

To make matters more difficult, the Great Depression was closing in on the nation. Roderick applied sound business methods; if he had not, the *Times* would surely have hit on evil times. Even as it was, we had many difficulties. It was necessary to cut salaries, as other business concerns were doing. In that terrible depression, hardly a day passed without unemployed newspapermen applying for jobs to the *Times.* It became so bad that at one point I contemplated asking Publisher Roderick to put cots on the fifth floor of the Times building and give the jobless a night's lodging, a free shower, and one day's work, but it never came to that.

In October of 1931, Magner White discovered he did not like to work for Editor Hunter. He quit as managing editor and Hunter gave me the job. Soon, White started publication of the El Paso *Digest,* which was somewhat critical of local conditions. It did not last long, and White moved to California.

Even during the depression, the *Times* circulation continued to increase. To get ahead of my story, the *Times* overtook the *Herald-Post* by 1937 and passed it in 1939.

The Newspaper Printing Corporation was formed in September, 1936, by which the *Times* and the *Herald-Post* had one business office. The *Times* was in the black at that time, but I was told on good authority that the *Herald-Post* was not.

I am extremely proud of the part I was permitted to play in the building of the *Times*. Roderick was only 30 years old in April, 1931, and he had a tremendous responsibility. He also had a loyal, hard-working, competent staff of men who put their hearts in their work. One of his mainstays was Hunter, the editor, who knew every wide place in the road in the Great Southwest. He had made many friends while writing the column "Around Here" on the old *Herald.* He moved "Around Here" from the *Herald* to the *Times* on April 3, 1931. It had a wide following, and continued in the *Times* until Hunter's death of a heart attack in the *Times* newsroom on October 20, 1940. One month later Roderick announced that I had been made editor of the *Times.*

Gambling in Juarez

Under Roderick's ownership and Hunter's editorship, the *Times* in May, 1931, quickly declared war on open gambling in Juarez, which was draining the resources of El Paso at a time when its economy was already strained. The *Times* attacked the problem by suggesting that the bridge from Juarez, then being kept open until midnight, be closed at either 9 p.m. or 6 p.m. That was a rather difficult decision to make because El Paso was competing for conventions, with Juarez as a strong selling point. Prohibition was still in effect and saloons in Juarez were doing a land office business. Gambling also had its attractions. It was against Mexican federal law to operate open gambling, but exceptions were being made by the Mexican government along the border.

The Tivoli was the main gambling hall in Juarez. The *Times* opened its attack on it. Ingeniero Andres Ortiz was governor of Chihuahua and Mrs. Georgia Burlingham Carmichael was his representative in El Paso. When news came that gambling was being suppressed in other parts of Chihuahua, but being permitted in Juarez, the *Times* said editorially:

> Why gambling is an intolerable evil elsewhere in Chihuahua, but can be tolerated in Juarez is understandable. It is the sucker money from the north side of the Rio Grande that is attracted to open gambling in Juarez and money is always useful.

The *Times* and Editor Hunter were receiving support from growing numbers of El Paso businessmen. A group of downtown store owners had circulated a petition requesting early closing of the bridge. The petition was sent to Washington. Sentiment was increasing to close the bridge at 6 p.m., rather than 9 p.m., which had been previously suggested. On August 21, the *Times* reported that the Baptist Workers' Conference of the El Paso Baptist Association, representing 4,000 Baptist workers, approved a resolution reading:

> We unanimously endorse by vote the vigorous fight of the El Paso *Times* to close the international bridges at such hours as to prevent persons from going to Juarez to gamble at night.

The Chamber of Commerce had polled its membership on the early closing of the bridge. The results of the poll showed 368 to 91 in favor of "asking our government to change the hours of closing the international bridge." A majority of the members favored 6 p.m. closing, the hour which the *Times* had been urging.

On August 26, Wallace Perry, editor of the *Herald-Post,* took up the fight and wrote that,

> "Instead of bickering over bridge hours and weakening our appeal to conventions — instead of attempting to use a club to force Juarez to operate as we think it ought to operate — the *Herald-Post* insists that we . . . ought to capitalize on other advantages."

Thus the *Times* and *Herald-Post* locked horns under the "New Deal" in newspapers in El Paso.

The *Times* conducted a straw vote on open gambling in Juarez. The poll also sought opinions on the best closing hour for the bridge. A total of 5,470 votes was cast, of which 4,549 favored the 6 p.m. closing hour, 305 favored continuing the midnight hour; 22 favored permanent closing of the bridge. The rest of the votes expressed a variety of opinions.

The El Paso Chamber of Commerce adopted a resolution favoring 6 a.m. to 7 p.m. bridge hours unless the Tivoli gambling hall was closed, whereupon the Juarez Chamber of Commerce notified the El Paso Chamber that its Foreign Relations Committee had been eliminated. The *Times* said editorially on September 9:

> In other words, the Juarez Chamber of Commerce is severing relations with the El Paso Chamber of Commerce.
>
> But let us not too much blame the Juarez Chamber of Commerce. The voice is the voice of the Juarez C. of C., but the hand is the hand of Ortiz.

The *Times* of September 12, in an Associated Press dispatch from Mexico City, said:

> A political blow was dealt Gov. Andres Ortiz tonight when the National Revolutionary Party appointed a new provisional executive committee for its Chihuahua party, including federal congressmen inimical to the governor.

El Paso labor entered the controversy, by asking bridge hours from 10 a.m. to 6 p.m., saying there were 7,000 idle American citizens in El Paso.

The *Times* of September 11 had pointed out that,

> Alleged irregularities in connection with gambling conditions in Juarez have been added to charges which Gov. Ortiz of Chihuahua must face before the general assembly of the National Revolutionary Party in Mexico City.

The *Times* then reported that the hearing in Mexico City was in a "friendly manner." Officials said any action taken by the party necessarily would be limited to a disciplinary nature and any move to depose Ortiz would be taken by Congress.

Assistant Secretary of the Treasury Seymour Lowman was sent to El Paso to report on the bridge situation. He turned thumbs down on either a 6 or 7 p.m. closing, but left the door open to a 9 p.m. closing. The Mexican national holiday, September 16, found a number of Mexicans throwing stones at American automobiles at the Juarez end of the bridge. Regrets were expressed by the Mexican officials.

The *Times* was continuing daily editorial blasts at the Tivoli. It quoted one unnamed El Pasoan as saying "more money was thrown away in Juarez Saturday night than was spent in El Paso all last week." The Tivoli requested the central government in Mexico City for a 50 per cent reduction in taxes. The *Times* on October 2 said editorially, "There is a fairly definite rumor that the Tivoli is soon to close. In fact, according to reports from Mexico City, it will close Saturday."

On October 3, the *Times* reported in an Associated Press dispatch from Mexico City:

> Congressional investigation of the practice of granting gambling concessions hastening a concentrated attack on the Ortiz Chihuahua administration was believed imminent tonight after a conference between Chihuahua senators and deputies and President Ortiz Rubio.

On October 31, the *Times* said, "Chihuahua deputies ask Mexico City to remove Gov. Ortiz." On November 2, the *Times* said, "Col. Roberto Fierro was given a rousing ovation in Chihuahua City as the new state governor."

The *Times* said editorially November 3, "Closing of the Tivoli is expected," but it stayed open. Another gambling casino was to be opened in Juarez, the *Times* said on its front page, under the direction of Theo Elson. A new Juarez mayor, Jesus Quevedo, was sworn in January 1. The Tivoli was still running. The *Times* had conducted a persistent and lengthy editorial campaign against the Tivoli. Probably the *Times* campaign might have had something to do with the removal of Governor Andres Ortiz, but even that could not be proved. Ortiz had gotten into trouble with his state's agrarians and with the federal deputies. The Tivoli was to close later in 1932, due partly to effects of the depression in the United States. Our Mexican friends are "funny" about yielding to pressure from our side of the border. They have been known to bow their necks.

Of utmost importance, however, was the fact that the *Times*, under the ownership of Dorrance Roderick and the editorship of H. S. Hunter, had demonstrated its courage. It was not afraid to tackle any project which it considered to be best for the community. The battle against the Tivoli brought prestige to the *Times*, and many new friends were made.

Albert Bacon Fall

Albert Bacon Fall, secretary of the interior in the Harding Cabinet, was taken from his home in El Paso in 1931 to begin serving a sentence of a year and a day in the New Mexico Penitentiary at Santa Fe, following his conviction of accepting a $100,000 bribe from E. L. Doheny, oil magnate, for leasing oil reserves during the Harding Administration.

The *Times* in a Santa Fe dispatch May 8, 1932, said that Fall, to be released from the penitentiary on Monday, was expected to be taken to his home in El Paso. Upon his release, he went first to his Three Rivers Ranch in New Mexico, and then came to El Paso. An editorial in the *Times* of May 8 seemed to reflect the thinking of millions of Americans:

> So the Department of Justice is trying to get the court that convicted A. B. Fall to fix the thing up so the elderly victim of Republican politics may not be held in prison any longer.

Dr. David H. Stratton, professor of history at Washington State College, published No. 15 in the SOUTHWESTERN STUDIES of Texas Western Press in October, 1966, called "The Memoirs of Albert B. Fall." Dr. Stratton wrote that Doheny in 1925 furnished financial backing to Mark B. Thompson, a Las Cruces lawyer, to help Fall write his story. During the summer of 1925 at Fall's Three Rivers Ranch, Thompson worked with the former secretary's correspondence, newspaper files and government documents. Fall, who was financially poor at that period, was also involved in some kind of employment arrangement with Doheny.

Before he was sent to prison, Fall worked with Magner White, managing editor of the El Paso *Times,* in writing 15 syndicated newspaper articles giving his side of the oil controversy. In 1931, Fall, an old man in ill health, was sent to prison in Santa Fe in an ambulance. I remember going to his imposing home in Golden Hill Terrace with Magner White, who was working on his series of articles. I cannot say I was personally acquainted with Fall, but I saw him on a number of occasions.

Fall became the only American cabinet officer ever to be convicted while in office. Oddly enough, Doheny was acquitted of giving the same bribe that Fall was convicted of accepting. Fall died in El Paso November 30, 1944, in Hotel Dieu; he is buried in Evergreen Cemetery. I was always very fond of Fall's daughter, Mrs. C. C. Chase. My father-in-law, C.

E. Bull, went to Las Cruces in 1895 to publish Fall's newspaper, the Las Cruces *Democrat.* Fall in those days was a Democrat.

Closing of First National

El Paso was dealt a severe economic blow September 4, 1931, when the First National Bank closed its doors. Although El Paso had two banks left, the State National and the El Paso National, the closing of the First National, the city's largest financial institution, put an icy grip on the business life of the community.

The *Times* top head on the morning of September 5 quoted the bank's president, F. M. Murchison, "May Reopen First National, Says Murchison."

The closing of the bank was decided upon just 10 minutes before the customary 10 a.m. opening hour.

"In view of the whispering and rumors and resultant fear on the part of the people," Murchison said, "we decided it was best to close to protect the depositors. Withdrawals have been more or less continuous due to rumors."

In an editorial October 31, following efforts to raise money to assist in the reopening of the First National, the *Times* reported that only $212,000 more was needed of the $1 million necessary to reopen the bank.

A mass meeting was called to discuss efforts to reopen the bank. It was reported that approximately $150,000 was yet to be subscribed of the $1 million needed by November 5. The *Times* reported on November 15 that a total of $1,019,000 had been raised to reopen the bank. On November 17, the *Times* reported that the bank might be reopened in 30 days; and on December 19 it was explained that $1,400,000 must be received from accounts of over $500. Every effort to reopen the bank failed.

The First National's failure did more to bring the depression home to the people of El Paso than any other thing. Two payments on deposits made by the receiver helped a great deal, and the State National and the El Paso National made valiant efforts to help stabilize the economy, but the First National was gone. El Paso, along with the rest of the nation, was in the depths of the Great Depression.

A Great El Pasoan

I want to pay tribute to R. E. Sherman. He was elected on the original R. E. Thomason City Council in February, 1927. He was a power on that council, serving as mayor pro tem. Long before entering politics, Sherman had established himself as an orator of great ability. His speech on "My Home Town" won first place in a Texas-wide contest in Houston in

1923. Sherman's speech has been widely quoted; I have used it in my writing and in speeches down through the years. I have not seen it printed in full in more than 45 years. I think it should be preserved for posterity. Here it is, as Sherman delivered it:

In the words of Paul of Tarsus at Jerusalem, "I am a citizen of no mean city."

More than a hundred years ago Humboldt prophesied that there would some day spring up on the Mexican border a great metropolis. Growing from a cow town on the plains to a city of a hundred thousand people in 20 years, El Paso fulfills that prophecy. El Paso is the workshop of the new Southwest, the back door of Texas, the front door to Mexico, the side door to New Mexico and Arizona, the ground floor of opportunity and the skylight to Heaven — the last spot kissed by the setting sun on Texas soil and the first that will be reached by the return tide of Pacific Coast immigration; Mexico fought to retain it, it was twice taken from California, and Texas, holding it her own, contests to this good hour New Mexico's boundary claim that would wrest it from her. El Paso has the largest undisputed trade territory of any city in America. With hardly a frame building in it, it has the lowest fire insurance key rate in Texas and has been called the best built city of its size in the world. It has the largest irrigation dam in the world, the second largest custom smelter in the world and is located on the only river that is wet on one side and dry on the other.

Placed by the hand of Destiny at the lowest trans-continental pass in America through the Rockies, six railroads converge at its gates and a prosperous and beautiful city has risen at the very edge of the desert in a region once so barren that the conquering army of Cortez could not subsist upon it.

Under irrigation the desert has been made to blossom and the one-time cactus plain is now green with verdure. Stately in her glory, proud in her might she stands sentinel on the shores of the silvery Rio Grande, the city of Destiny and of Prophecy. Within her fertile valleys the wonders of Nature's laboratory may be witnessed and from out its elemental labors come forth annually treasures richer than those from the mines of the Incas, treasures indeed the richest that may exist except those of that type that we are advised to lay up.

Where moth and rust do not corrupt,
Nor thieves break through and steal.

Time will not permit me to more than sketch to you my city's advantages. It has 329 sunshiny days a year, abundance of pure water, where water is a precious thing, is parked and paved, sewered and guttered from end to end, a city that has never had a boom or a panic, where good people love to live and from which only criminals flee.

I can tell you only briefly of our parks and churches, schools and colleges, boulevards, scenic drives, stadiums, skyscrapers, libraries, public buildings and playgrounds. I cannot more than mention our industries, from factories and smelters to mines and cattle. These things, or similar things, exist in every city; but I want to tell you of an industry in which we take the greatest pride, which is that of building homes and making men. For the need of today is not factories and shops and mines and gold, Aye, but men —

Men who can dream but not make dreams
their master,
Men who can think, but not make thoughts
their aim.

Cities, like individuals, build character through the years; we are not ruled by sordid aims of commerce or the sodden power of gold, but by those warmer impulses of the human heart that cause one to hold out a welcome to the stranger and the friendless, and the man who comes with a hectic flush upon his cheek finds parks and sanitariums, civic centers and resting spots.

Out where the Santa Fe Trail of the red man, broadened by the hand of the white man, marks the portals of the Last Frontier, El Paso typifies the land of Tomorrow, the Spirit of Today. We who live there, who have there our hopes and our all, love it for its present, believe in its future and honor its traditions. We know that it has come up against formidable odds. We know that the courage and labors of an earlier generation have made life there pleasanter and sweeter for us today — for I say to you with utmost earnestness, that it has taken blood and it has taken lives to build El Paso.

Such, briefly, is El Paso — my city — my home — for whose recognition and in whose name I contend with more than the pride of Cato. Born of strong men's hopes, it is the pioneer's dream city come true, a realized vision at the desert's pass, a castle in the air that God let stay — the City of the Lily in the Valley of the Rose.

Sherman first ran for mayor on his own in the February, 1931, Democratic primary against Jack Burke. The *Times* quoted Burke as admitting that he had run for county tax collector as a Republican in 1924. Votes counted on February 21, 1931, showed Sherman had won 5,257 to 1,398.

The depression was closing in. The *Times* quoted Mayor Sherman May 24, 1932: "The City of El Paso faces the most serious situation since the day it was incorporated in 1873." The *Times* headlined May 26: "Deluge Of Protest Due To Greet City Aldermen On Budget Paring Plan." On June 1, a *Times* headline said, "Announce 10 Per Cent Salary Cut Ordered For City Employes."

During those years, the City Schools were dependent upon the City Council for their money. The School Board members and the school administrators would appear with hat in hand before the City Council asking for operating money. That money and a per capita from the State was practically all the money the School Board had; Federal money in those days was practically unheard of. In later years, the school districts were separated from the City Administration. Today, the El Paso Independent School District levies its own taxes to support a larger annual budget than that of the City of El Paso, and the Ysleta Independent School District also is in the El Paso city limits. In 1932, the Sherman City Administration was forced to cut the appropriation for the schools. The *Times* headline of June 5 said, "66 Teachers Lose Jobs; 661 On List."

There had been a great deal of discussion concerning retention of married teachers. Louis A. Scott, president of the School Board, was quoted by the *Times* as saying:

> No married woman was dropped solely because of her marriage. However, in the case of a few of the El Paso public school teachers who demonstrated they preferred husbands to their jobs, it was different.

It required a fine line indeed to separate teachers on such a basis, but a number of married teachers did lose their jobs.

There cannot be the slightest doubt that Mayor Sherman saved the credit of the City of El Paso. He had the courage to say "No" when it was necessary; many city employes and schoolteachers were unhappy with him, but he did what he knew he had to do.

One of Sherman's problems during his first administration was the arrival in El Paso of Southern California's "Bonus Army" on its way to Washington. The *Times* of June 24, 1931, reported an army of 800 men led by Royal W. Robertson stopped at El Paso on commandeered trains. With colors flying and band playing, it continued its journey to Washington. The army caused little trouble in El Paso, but the city authorities were on pins and needles and did not give them the run of the city. Everyone heaved a sigh of relief when those 800 men were on their way.

Sherman permitted a zone of tolerance to operate in a number of South El Paso hotels. One Sunday evening in 1932, while wandering on South El Paso Street with Raymond Stover, one of the most capable men the *Times* ever had, we noted "the ladies of the evening" sitting in the second-story windows and on the steps of the hotels propositioning men passing by. I returned to the office and wrote a story about it. The next day, Chief of Police L. T. Robey told me he was glad I had written the story, and that the situation had been deteriorating for some time. The "district" was moved lock, stock, and barrel to Ninth and Mesa.

Mayor Sherman did not object when liquor was served by the drink in El Paso bars and slot machines were operated under a purported federal injunction. Sherman was reelected in 1933 without opposition, and shortly thereafter he declared war on gamblers in El Paso, fighting them tooth and toenail. In 1935 Sherman had two opponents, Lawrence A. Lee and P. D. Lowry, and that campaign soon developed into a vigorous affair. The high man would win without a runoff.

El Paso gamblers, headed by Dave Lawson, operator of the Knickerbocker Club, rallied behind Lowry. Sherman appointed Walter G. Clayton, local insurance agent, as his campaign manager and adopted a campaign slogan of "Honesty Plus Service." Lee and Lowry both launched sharp attacks on Sherman. Sherman opened his campaign in Liberty Hall on February 2 before a crowd of 1,200, The *Times* reported, favoring separation of the schools from the city. Lowry fired back with charges that city employes were being assessed for the Sherman race, and he promised that open gambling would be barred in El Paso, but the *Times* reported a Sherman charge at a meeting attended by 1,700 in Liberty Hall on February 22 that the gamblers were backing Lowry.

The *Times* headline on February 24 said: "Sherman Victor By 247 Votes; Lowry Threatens Investigation; Thompson And Levy On Council." Sherman thus had a split council; two of Lowry's aldermanic candidates, Don Thompson and Ben Levy, were elected. The other two aldermen were Oscar Allen and W. E. Casteel. Sherman retired from politics in 1937. His business in El Paso was real estate and insurance. He died April 30, 1947.

The Lindbergh Baby

El Paso played a part in the terrible tragedy that befell the family of Colonel Charles A. Lindbergh when their baby son was kidnaped from his crib in the Lindbergh home in Hopewell, New Jersey, on March 1, 1932. A trip to El Paso figured in the trickery that accompanied efforts to find the baby. Gaston B. Means, former Justice Department investigator, obtained $100,000 from Mrs. Edward B. McLean, wife of the publisher of the *Washington Post,* on false reports that he could obtain the child from the kidnapers, who, as related in the *Times* of May 6, 1932, had fled to Mexico. Mrs. McLean, accompanied by another woman, came to El Paso to meet Means. Means was later tried and convicted in Washington.

The *Times* reported on April 26, 1932, in a Chicago dispatch that Al Capone had offered to post bail and endeavor to return the baby to his parents. On May 13, the *Times* published a dispatch from Hopewell, New Jersey, announcing that the stolen baby son of Colonel Lindbergh was found murdered in the Sunland Hills of New Jersey. On May 14, the *Times* said Dr. John F. Condon, the "Jafsie" who figured in efforts to obtain the release of the child, said the abductor demanded $70,000 in cash. The baby was dead when "Jafsie" paid the $50,000 ransom to the kidnaper's agent.

Bruno Richard Hauptmann, a German-American carpenter, was arrested when he tried to pass one of the bills from the ransom money. More of that money was found concealed in his home. Hauptmann went on trial January 2, 1935; he was convicted February 13, 1935, and he died in the electric chair for the baby's murder. Thus ended one of the saddest chapters in modern American history.

County Politics of 1932

Since the advent of the radio and particularly television, much has gone out of political campaigns. In the old days, the candidates made speeches in school houses, on street corners, in parks. In El Paso practically every major candidate had his big rally either in Liberty Hall or Cleveland Square. Today most of the candidates confine their politicking to personal contact and to television time. My mind goes back to the rousing speeches that used to be made by men like R. E. Thomason, R. E. Sherman, C. L. Vowell, Tom Lea, W. H. Fryer and in 1932 by Chris P. Fox. In the July 23, 1932, Democratic primary in El Paso County, the voters had an opportunity to select their choices among 261 candidates for the various congressional, state, county and precinct offices.

The *Times* headlined on June 7, 1932, "Jackson's Entrance Throws Bombshell Into Local Politics." Former District Judge Dan M. Jackson, then with the Federal government in Washington, had announced for Congress opposing R. E. Thomason, then serving his first term. In his book AUTOBIOGRAPHY OF A FEDERAL JUDGE, Thomason wrote that "some disappointed politicians in El Paso encouraged and induced Judge Dan M. Jackson to announce against me." I knew at the time that two of those El Pasoans who were after Thomason's scalp were County Clerk W. D. (Bill) Greet and Attorney W. H. Fryer. George Simpson, who usually was in the same camp with Greet, declined to go along with them.

Bob Chapman, veteran *Times* reporter, said in his story of June 7 that Jackson's main plank was a popular vote on the repeal of the Eighteenth Amendment. The head over a *Times* editorial that morning asked: "Jackson For Congress, Why?" The comment ran,

> Thomason has made a splendid record in Congress as the people of this district well know.
>
> Jackson wants us to prove ourselves completely unappreciative and ungrateful by turning Thomason out of office and putting Jackson in.

Jackson had enjoyed a splendid reputation in El Paso as a trial lawyer and was elected judge of the 34th District Court. Thomason conducted a vigorous campaign. He was quoted in the June 8 *Times* as agreeing with Jackson on the proposed popular vote on the Eighteenth Amendment. He also said that Jackson's home city was listed in Washington as Richmond, Virginia. Thomason soundly whipped Jackson, carrying every precinct in the Sixteenth Congressional District.

The spotlight on the local front was quickly centered on the attempt of Chris P. Fox to unseat Sheriff Tom Armstrong, who was seeking his third term. That race developed into a debate between Fox and Attorney Tom Lea, a former mayor of El Paso, who was given the credit for breaking the so-called "Kelly Ring" years before. The *Times* of July 15 quoted Fox as saying at the Bailey School:

> Tom Armstrong invested $16,000 in three years while his salary totaled $22,000, and he has a beautiful Lincoln car and a motorboat on Elephant Butte Lake, yet he says he is broke.

Bailey School was located where the Central YMCA is now. On July 17, the *Times* said, "Fox launches an attack on Tom Lea, who announced yesterday he will take the stump in support of Tom Armstrong."

Then came the two big nights in Cleveland Square. I attended both rallies; for sheer entertainment, they could not be beaten. Armstrong had his rally on the night of July 19. The *Times* reported it was the largest crowd ever assembled in Cleveland Square. Tom Lea was the main attraction. The *Times* reported that Lea had removed his tie, turned down his collar and had one leg over the front railing of the bandstand. Lea said he "would not hurt the heart of Mrs. Fox" and would not say insinuating things. But he proceeded to refer to Fox as a loose jointed fellow with a big nose and questioned his business ability, referring to court action involving the Chris P. Fox Transportation Company. In closing, Lea had Armstrong come forward and stand beside him. He praised Armstrong to the sky, saying Armstrong was "as clean as a hound's tooth." Armstrong, who could not make a speech, merely bowed and sat down.

Fox had his big rally in Cleveland Square the next night, July 20. The *Times* reported that the crowd was quite as large as the one attending the Armstrong rally the night before. The *Times* said the crowd "cheered, applauded and at times rocked with laughter as Chris P. Fox matched wit and oratory with Tom Lea and ended up by calling the El Paso attorney the Mussolini of the Border." Mimicking Lea's move in having Armstrong come forward and stand beside him, Fox praised a certain person warmly, talking about honesty, virtue, support, friendship and sheer grit, and then he asked his mother to come forward and stand beside him. That made a big hit.

The *Times* made a tactical error in that campaign. Attorney Joseph McGill was running against County Judge E. B. McClintock. The *Times* supported McClintock, the only local candidate to receive its endorsement, since it considered other local candidates to be about evenly matched. McGill opened a strong attack on the *Times;* at his big rally in Cleveland Square July 8, he really let us have it. *Times* Reporter Bob Chapman, who covered that meeting, persuaded me to let him write the type of story he wanted to. The *Times* headline said: "Reporter Dozes At Political Meeting, Writes 'Opera' Then Wakes Up, McGill Was Speaker." Chapman reported that McGill talked for an hour. He told about his dream while he slept. I was foolish to agree to such a report; when McGill made another major speech July 22, the *Times* gave full coverage to what he had to say.

Other main races in that election pitted Attorney Roy D. Jackson against District Attorney Stewart Berkshire and former City Clerk Herman "Heinie" Rosch against County Tax Collector R. D. (Del) Richey. There were other races hotly contested, but those two, along with the Fox-Armstrong duel, attracted most attention. The *Times* headline of July 25 reported that Fox, McGill, Roy D. Jackson, and Rosch had won. Said the *Times.*

Of all the candidates in the field, Joseph McGill was the one to emerge with the greatest majority over his opponent. In the 50 boxes, McGill established a lead of 3,181 votes over Judge E. B. McClintock.

The *Times* was supporting County Judge McClintock for reelection.

It was an election long to be remembered. The *Times* and the *Herald-Post* had refrained from indulging in a slugging match.

Josephus Daniels

If I were asked to name my favorites among the men I met while in the newspaper business, high on the list would be Josephus Daniels. Daniels was owner and publisher of the Raleigh (N.C.) *News and Observer.* My family took his newspaper in my early days. Daniels was secretary of the Navy in the administration of President Woodrow Wilson and during World War I. A young assistant to him was Franklin D. Roosevelt. It was Josephus Daniels who "dried up" the Navy. To this day, liquor is not served on our ships at sea. It is plentiful at Navy clubs on shore, but not on ships. When Franklin D. Roosevelt was elected President of the United States in 1932 and took office March 4, 1933, one of his first acts was to appoint Josephus Daniels ambassador to Mexico.

Daniels had been secretary of the Navy when our forces had occupied Vera Cruz during the first administration of Woodrow Wilson. On his way to Mexico City, Daniels came through El Paso. I attended a small dinner given in his honor in the Hotel Paso del Norte, and made myself known to him. After the dinner, he accompanied me back to the *Times* office and went all over the building shaking hands. I shall never forget his pancake hat and string bow tie. I saw him in Washington several times in later years while I was attending conventions of the American Society of Newspaper Editors. He always referred to me as his "Tar Heel editor."

I was privileged to talk several times with Daniels in Mexico City in December, 1946, when I was there as a guest of the Mexican government, along with E. M. Pooley, editor of the El Paso *Herald-Post,* attending the inauguration of Miguel Aleman as President of Mexico.

I'll always have a warm place in my heart for Josephus Daniels. He was a gracious gentleman of the old school. He had strong convictions and courage to back them up.

Nude Dead Woman Found

Early in November, 1933, El Paso and the Southwest were treated to a murder mystery that was to draw national and international attention. On November 7, 1933, a cowboy riding the range just east of Van Horn ran across the nude body of a woman. The *Times* reported on November 8 that the police thought it was the body of a woman hitchhiker. Then a woman's bloodstained silk shirt, partially burned, was found behind the stock pens at Kent, 38 miles east of Van Horn. Officers felt they were on the trail of the persons who had killed the unidentified woman. The *Times* of November 9 said the garment was sent to District Attorney Roy D. Jackson in El Paso by Sheriff Albert Anderson of Van Horn.

The *Times* on November 10 printed an artist's drawing of what the dead woman was supposed to have looked like in life and suggested she might have been a hitchhiker whose first name was Ramona. The next day, the *Times* had a news report from Las Cruces that the body had been identified as that of Mrs. Lee Hirt, dramatist and lecturer, but Mrs. Hirt turned up in Tucson, very much alive. The *Times* on November 17 said that Ruth Ingram, a dancer whose professional name was Ramona Warren, was found safe in Healdton, Oklahoma. On November 16, the *Times* published a picture of the dead woman made from a photograph taken in Kaster and Maxon's Funeral Home.

On November 23, charred and bloodstained bits of a woman's clothing were found in a culvert near Barstow. They were identified as having belonged to a woman whose nude body was found near Van Horn November 7. Identification was made by matching the button found pressed into the woman's cheek with one on the dress found in the charred parcel, said the *Times* of November 23.

On December 1, the *Times* announced in a big headline: "Van Horn Murder Victim Identified." The story said:

> The nude body of an American woman found near U.S. Highway 80, nine miles east of Van Horn Nov. 7, was identified last night by Cleveland, Ohio, relatives as Mrs. Irene DeBolt, 28, a widow.
>
> Concurrent with the identification, which came as a climax of 23 days of driving investigation by Sheriff Chris P. Fox, orders were issued for the arrest of Arthur C. Wilson, 28, of Cleveland, on a charge of murder.
>
> Examination showed that the woman had been slain by several heavy blows near the base of the brain, probably with a blunt instrument. A left forefinger was cut and broken where she had evidently thrown up her hand to ward off a blow.
>
> A long piece of twine had been jerked tightly about her neck.

Then began a long, painstaking search for Wilson. Most of the credit for identifying Mrs. DeBolt's body and the later arrest of Wilson and his return to El Paso must go to Sheriff Fox. I can testify he did a magnificent job of detective work, because I watched the DeBolt story develop from its beginning.

The *Times* revealed that Wilson had become a member of the crew of a Canadian steamship traveling to ports in the Caribbean Sea. A shipmate saw his picture and notified Sheriff Fox in El Paso; a reward of over $1,000 had been offered for Wilson. Six months after the murder of Mrs. DeBolt, Wilson was arrested in British Guiana, and District Attorney Roy D. Jackson and Sheriff Albert Anderson of Culberson County went to Port of Spain and brought Wilson back to El Paso. Jackson told me Wilson had at first affected a cockney accent and denied his identity.

On December 13, 1934, Wilson was found guilty of murder and given a life sentence; the *Times* reported on December 14 that a lone juror saved him from a death sentence. Wilson, according to the evidence in his trial, accompanied Mrs. DeBolt on a trip to California and back east after she had received $4,000 in insurance proceeds when her husband died. She was robbed of the remaining money and murdered. Part of the evidence which convicted him was a dry cleaning check discovered in a Pecos tourist court made out to A. C. Wilson, Cleveland.

The *Times* of November 8, 1950, carried the headline, "Arthur Wilson Freed." The story said that Wilson received a full pardon, carrying restoration of civil rights, for reasons I never learned. There was a storm of protest, particularly from El Paso, but Wilson was a free man. I never heard any more about him.

Fight for City-County Merger

A valiant effort was made in 1934 to bring about a merger of the city and county governments in El Paso through the submission of a county home rule charter. The *Herald-Post* spearheaded that movement. Its editor, Wallace Perry, pulled out all the stops in that newspaper's campaign to have the charter adopted by both the city and the county. Under the law, to become effective the proposal had to be accepted by the voters of the city and also by the voters in the county outside the city. The *Times* played a coy game; its editor, H. S. Hunter, saw the advantages of the home rule charter and supported it, but he did not want the *Herald-Post* to have the credit.

Attorney Joe Bennis was chairman of the charter commission. The *Times* reported on March 27, 1934:

> Nine of the County Home Rule Charter Commission of 14 met last night and officially approved the document.
>
> Absent were R. E. Cunningham, who has announced he will oppose passage of the charter, W. J. Moran, who opposes some of its provisions, Joseph E. Morgan, who was out of the city, and L. N. Shafer. Walter Scott arrived too late to sign the document.
>
> Voting to approve were Chairman Bennis, D. L. P. Duke, M. Scarborough, H. B. Hardin, S. J. Isaacks, William Rosing, C. H. Leavell, L. L. Fuller and K. B. Ivey.

The *Times* said editorially April 7:

> The report that J. G. Bennis might be entered by the *Herald-Post* as a candidate for mayor against Mayor Sherman was declared unfounded yesterday by Mr. Bennis. . . .
>
> A good decision this. Because even if he could be elected, no matter how good a mayor he might endeavor to be, all his actions would bear the brand in the public mind of *Herald-Post* domination. That would be an exhausting ball and chain to drag around.

In an editorial April 18, the *Times* said:

> County officials are quoted in the newspapers as believing the home rule charter will not pass, the wish being father to the thought.
>
> If the charter is not approved in the county, it will be because of farmers' fear of city domination, higher taxes and the city tax load. These fears are largely groundless, but they exist.
>
> If the charter fails in the city, it will be because of suspicion that a newspaper is planning to put a man-Friday in office as county executive and tell him what to do. After which he could proceed to run the county as it has never been run before — from a standpoint of bossism.

Two developments in the charter campaign are worth reporting. First, the *Times* of April 28 said School Superintendent A. H. Hughey warned city principals to prevent home rule charter propaganda in El Paso schools, saying that the schools were no place for politics and partisanship. Second, *Times* Reporter Raymond J. Stover had a front page article on April 29, reporting that the names of L. E. Saunders, Benjamin Sherrod, E. L. Haynes, J. M. Taylor, George O. Payne and Walter Kohlberg had been used in support of the charter without their consent.

The *Times* of May 13 reported that Valley voters defeated the charter on home rule. In the city there were 3,389 votes for the charter and 2,086 against; in the county there were 761 votes for and 1,690 against.

There is renewed talk today of combining the city and county governments. Herbert Schwartz, president of the Popular Dry Goods Company, served as chairman of a study committee. I heard him talk on the subject before two El Paso service clubs. I look forward to another vote on the subject.

A Border Dope Story

One of my favorite newspaper stories began in 1934.

I was getting ready to leave the office of the *Times* on San Francisco Street for dinner when a man came in and said he wanted a private conversation with me. I took him to the office of Editor Hunter, who had left for the day. He told me his name was Holliday, an American Airlines pilot, grounded for drinking, and he wanted to sell me a story. He had exhausted his resources, including borrowing on his life insurance, and a week before two men approached him in a cantina in Tijuana and asked him if he wanted to make some money. They gave him some money and told him to go to Juarez and report to the chief bartender in a certain cafe, who would give him instructions about flying narcotics across the border in a Boeing pursuit plane then concealed south of Juarez.

Holliday told me he was dead broke, but he had not sunk low enough to smuggle narcotics; he wanted to sell me a story for enough money to get out of town. I told him I had a better idea: I proposed that he make a deal with the United States government, telling him that an informant under such conditions would receive half the sale price of the plane and its contents. He agreed to meet with federal narcotics officers in his room in the Hilton Hotel at 2 a.m. A deal was made for Holliday to land the plane in Salt Lake City, regardless of what he was told to do by the narcotics smugglers. The airport at Salt Lake City was to be kept under surveillance.

Days went by and nothing happened. I checked repeatedly with the

Hilton Hotel, and Holliday's luggage was still there a month later. I could draw no conclusion other than that the underworld had been watching Holliday and that his body probably would be found some day south of Juarez, or that he had gone through with his deal with the underworld and had flown the narcotics to the destination they had named.

The story does not end there. In 1945, when the *Times* had moved to Kansas and Mills and I was editor of the paper, that same fellow came into my office. He said his name was Holliday and that he wanted to sell me a story. He said he had been ferrying planes across the Atlantic and began showing me pictures of sinking ships and naval engagements. Looking him straight in the face, I said: "Don't you remember me? What about that deal you made with the federal government in 1934 about the Juarez plane and narcotics?" Holliday dashed from the office and was away before anyone could stop him. I have not seen him since. I am still wondering about what happened in 1934. Was Holliday trying to pull my leg to get a little money, or was there actually the traffic in narcotics across the border that he so vividly described? I am inclined to believe the latter.

Rosch Beats Lowry

In the Democratic primary of 1934, the *Times* supported J. U. Sweeney, former mayor and county judge, in his effort to unseat County Judge Joseph McGill, and County Tax Collector Herman "Heinie" Rosch in his battle with County Tax Assessor P. D. Lowry for the combined office of tax assessor-collector.

McGill started the fireworks early. At Cleveland Square, said the *Times* on July 8, he called on Sweeney to explain a $3,600 city warrant made in his favor April 28, 1920, on the date Sweeney resigned as mayor of El Paso. Sweeney replied that the money was to reimburse him for expenditures.

On the front page of the *Times* July 12, Raymond J. Stover wrote:

> Let us take a look at the record of County Judge Joseph McGill as reflected by reports of the county auditor and see just how much money, if any, he has saved the county since he took office Jan. 1, 1933.
>
> The general fund overdraft Jan. 1, 1933, was $252,146. A year later it was $278,392, representing an increase of $26,246 since the last year E. B. McClintock was in office.

The *Times* said editorially July 13, under a heading, "More Amusing Vaudeville:"

> Paul Lowry's accusation that editorial criticism of his administration

was at the instigation of "some of the paper's big advertisers" doubtless is amusing to these same "big advertisers" who know how baseless it is. It is equally amusing to the *Times.*

In an editorial July 15 the *Times,* pointing to Sweeney's excellent record as county judge and mayor, said Sweeney would make a better county judge than McGill. On July 20, McGill and Lowry were accused by the *Times* of making an attack on the paper and Editor Hunter. The *Times* reported July 24 that "Rosch and Lowry hold 'debate' in Cleveland Square. The assessor talks for 35 minutes, his opponent, Rosch, is allowed 15 minutes."

The *Times* in that primary also supported State Senator Clint Small of Amarillo for governor, editorially, saying about him on July 25: "This is a man with the full mental stature of a governor." Small came to El Paso and was given emphasized front page coverage by the *Times.* Members of his campaign committee from other points in West Texas also were here. The rally was held in Cleveland Square.

The primary was held on July 28. The *Times* on July 30 reported that Rosch had received 6,863 votes to 6,449 for Lowry.

McGill defeated Sweeney 9,521 to 3,958.

Jimmie Allred won the race for governor, but Small carried El Paso County.

Good Appointments

Two young Mexican-Americans whom I promoted and encouraged on the *Times* have brought me much gratificatiion. In 1936, while I was managing editor, I made a reporter of Ramon Villalobos, who had for five years been a copy boy. His English might have been a little shaky, but he made up for that in native intelligence and a burning desire to be a newspaper reporter. He caught on rapidly, and he soon was covering Juarez for the *Times.* He gained prestige rapidly in Mexico, even as far away as Chihuahua City. Officials there soon learned that he was a reporter for the *Times.* When President Lazaro Cardenas visited Juarez in 1937, he took a liking to Villalobos, even giving him a scoop.

On April 1, 1938, Villalobos had a narrow escape from death. He was a good friend of Mayor Jose Borunda of Juarez. During the day a package had arrived in Borunda's office. Early in the evening the Mayor asked Villalobos to accompany him to his office while he opened the package, but Villalobos was delayed by other duties. The package contained a bomb that killed Borunda and wrecked his office. Several arrests were made, but the case was never solved. Mayor Jose Borunda's nephew, Teofilo Borunda, became mayor of Juarez, and later became a power in the National Revolutionary Party. He and Villalobos remained staunch friends through the years.

Villalobos served our country with distinction in military intelligence during World War II. Today he is immensely valuable to the *Times* as a veteran newspaperman who knows his way around anywhere.

A second Mexican-American of whom I am proud is Villalobos' cousin, Balta Alvarez, who also was a copy boy. He joined the Air Force and saw combat during World War II. He was shot down over Germany and found his way back to the American lines. He could not speak French, but found that his knowledge of Spanish was helpful. After the war, he was made librarian at the *Times.* Today I would compare Alvarez's library with that of the best to be found. His morgue is of extreme value to the paper. He keeps needed information at his fingertips.

Chamber of Commerce Work

My association with the El Paso Chamber of Commerce was most enjoyable. It began in March, 1934, when I accompanied a Good Will automobile trip sent into the territory, in the hope of marking the end of the Great Depression. I accompanied many other Good Will trips; I was chairman of the Chamber of Commerce Good Will Committee for eight years. In the late 1930's we began traveling in buses; by that time Lloyd P. Bloodworth, assistant manager of the Chamber of Commerce, was going on the trips and making the arrangements.

The Bluebonnet Square Dance Team, headed by Mr. and Mrs. Herb Greggerson, now living in Ruidoso, accompanied us in 1938. They danced in the streets of the various communities. On that same trip in 1938, some of us pulled a practical joke on District Attorney Roy D. Jackson who was on the trip and was a candidate for reelection opposing Justice of the Peace Clarence M. Wilchar, Jr. We decided to hold a straw vote on the bus, and Joe Evans and I framed it. As he read out the names on the ballots, Evans sang out "Wilchar," regardless of the name written. Jackson did not get the joke for awhile. Of course Jackson was favored in that group by at least 10 to 1.

One of the leaders of those Good Will trips was Jack Chaney, manager of Hotel Paso del Norte, who later became president of the Chamber of Commerce. A few of the regular Good Will trippers were Herman Liebreich, Marshall McCrea, Allen Bruce, Bowen Leonard, Joe Evans, Dusty Waller and Bob Williford. Roy Jackson was reelected in 1938 and later became a district judge; his death while delivering a commencement address at Texas Western College was reported in the *Times* of August 29, 1955.

I was elected a director of the Chamber of Commerce in April, 1944. At the organization meeting of the directors, Hope Smith was chosen first vice president and I was named second vice president. The next year, Smith decided he did not want to be president of the Chamber and resigned. Chris P. Fox, general manager of the Chamber, told me that if I were elected first vice president in Smith's place, I would be in line for the presidency my final year on the board, and he asked me if I wanted it. I did not think an editor should be president of the Chamber, and I still do not. I nominated C. M. (Boots) Irvin for first vice president. He became president the next year and, after serving as his first vice president, I went off the board.

One of my pleasant memories in connection with service on the Chamber of Commerce had to do with the placing of markers at historic spots in El Paso. Early in 1941, a committee consisting of Fox, the late C. D. Belding, and me, was named to look into that situation. The first spot we picked was in front of the Hilton Hotel in Pioneer Plaza where a replica of the old newspaper tree stood. The original of that tree was used by early residents to post signs and news bulletins. Our committee had a suitable marker made and inscribed. It was dedicated on Labor Day, September 1, 1941. A platform was erected in Pioneer Plaza and Fox did the talking. When World War II came along, our committee ceased functioning. After the war, the State National Bank took up that project and has done a wonderful job.

In the summer of 1941, Captain E. H. Simons, general manager of the Chamber of Commerce, became ill and Sheriff Chris P. Fox was selected by a committee to take his place. Fox did not know much about running a chamber of commerce, but neither had he known much about being sheriff when he was first elected to that office. The Chamber of Commerce soon came to resemble a three-ring circus.

Captain Simons was a real pro in the chamber of commerce business. One day, while still confined at William Beaumont Hospital, Captain Simons came to the *Times* editor's office to see me. He was a man of few words; he stopped just inside the office, pointed to a picture on the wall of the late H. S. Hunter, and said, "That man would not stand for what is going on today at the Chamber of Commerce," and turned and left. He died the following June. He was a friend of mine and I have nothing but praise for him, but I must say that Chris P. Fox was a huge success as general manager of our Chamber of Commerce. His work in promoting and handling the Fort Bliss Centennial in 1948 was a masterpiece, with important men from all over the United States coming to El Paso for that occasion. Fox is now vice president and public relations officer of the State National Bank.

Today, the El Paso Chamber of Commerce is a flourishing concern. It has a new home office near the El Paso Civic Center. The old Chamber of Commerce building on San Francisco Street was razed to make room for that center.

Dillinger's Death

A headline in the *Times* of July 23, 1934, said in bold letters: "Dillinger Slain By Federal Officers." John Dillinger, at the top of the list of the most wanted men in America, was killed in Chicago by FBI men as he left a theater. R. C. Suran, later special agent in charge of the El Paso FBI office, was in on the killing, and he told me about it.

The *Times* of July 23 told in a dispatch from Tucson that Arizonians were pleased that Dillinger was dead, because he had sworn to return to Tucson and "get" the officers who had captured him and members of his gang in spectacular raids.

On January 30, 1934, Dillinger spent half an hour at Airmail Field in El Paso, said that day's *Times,* on his way to Crown Point, Indiana, heavily manacled, and was accompanied by Indiana officers. In an interview with a *Times* reporter, Dillinger was highly critical of Tucson officers. "They railroaded me out of jail in Tucson," he said. "Several officers dragged me out of my cell. I wanted to be taken back to Wisconsin. There is no death penalty there." Dillinger later escaped from jail by bluffing a jail guard with a fake pistol. He had been at liberty only briefly when he was shot to death in Chicago. His death was among the last of the Public Enemies Number One.

Newspaper and police files and those at the FBI in Washington are filled with the accounts of the war the FBI conducted against the "bad men" of those days, among them "Machine Gun" Kelly, "Baby Face" Nelson, and "Pretty Boy" Floyd. I was always a friend and supporter of J. Edgar Hoover. His death was a great loss to the country, and I fear we will never find an adequate successor for him.

In December, 1946, I attended a reception in the United States Embassy in Mexico City for the inauguration of President Miguel Aleman. The group included those above: Stephen Aguirre, Josephus Daniels, myself, and E. M. Pooley.

CHAPTER •V•

The Late Thirties

The Lorius Case

ONE OF THE GREAT MYSTERIES of the Southwest came to be known as "The Lorius Case." Lynwood Abram, writing in the *Times* of May 21, 1955, under the heading "Mystery 20 Years Old," told the story of the disappearance of Mr. and Mrs. George M. Lorius of East St. Louis, Illinois, and Mr. and Mrs. Albert A. Heberer, of Du Quoin, Illinois, as they journeyed toward a California vacation. Their car was seen in Albuquerque May 22, 1935; police believed they headed for Springerville, Arizona, on Highway 60. They were last seen at a service station at the small town of Quemado, New Mexico. Their car was found in Dallas, almost 1,000 miles away from where the police believe they were murdered.

On May 23, the day after the disappearance, the Lorius car was overturned near Socorro, New Mexico, by a young man with a tattoo on his left arm, but he was not detained. The same night, a young man with much baggage using the name of James Sullivan spent the night in a small El Paso hotel. He was very nervous, one guest said, and he paced the floor all night. The next morning, the young man cashed traveler's checks under the name of Lorius and then headed for Dallas. He was questioned at Fort Hancock by a customs official but was released. He cashed more traveler's checks and he proceeded to Dallas. On reaching Dallas, he had another wreck, but it was minor and there was no police action. Soon afterward he abandoned the Lorius car, and when the police found it, a search for the missing couple started. They were never found. Twenty years later, Abram wrote:

> The man with the tattoo on his arm is free today. No one has ever reported seeing him again.
> And the bodies sleep on.

I remember when the Lorius car was brought to El Paso under FBI jurisdiction, and placed under guard in the Plaza Garage. A tremendous search was conducted by New Mexico authorities; at one time, the National Guard was called out to assist. In 1958, New Mexico State Police Chief Joe Roach said the FBI, which had entered the case because of the Dyer Act (crossing a state line with a stolen car) had withdrawn. The statute of limitations had run out and the Lorius Case was left in the hands of the state police. Roach said in a pamphlet issued by his department that the young man presumably was a hitchhiker, and it was believed that he murdered the two middle-aged couples and hid their bodies in the New Mexico desert, probably tossing them into a crevice and covering the bodies with sand. It looks as though the Lorius Case will never be solved. Thirty-eight years is a long time. The young man with the tattoo on his left arm would be pushing 65 years of age now.

The NPC is Formed

Dorrance D. Roderick, *Times* publisher, began negotiations with Scripps-Howard in the summer of 1936, with the general idea in mind of establishing a publishing agreement in El Paso similar to the one being so successfully operated in Albuquerque. I did not know about those negotiations. I was managing editor of the *Times* and had only indirect contact with the business office. I have written before that the *Times* by that time had worked and struggled its way into a strong position since that eventful day, April 3, 1931, when it started out on its own under Roderick's ownership. The *Times* was making money, although perhaps not much, and I have been told on good authority that the *Herald-Post* was losing money; but even so, the *Herald-Post* had unlimited resources behind it.

On August 30, 1936, the *Sunday Times* announced that the *Times* and the *Herald-Post* "have arranged, effective immediately, for the joint printing, sale, and distribution of their newspapers, and for the sale of advertising, without affecting the ownership of either party." That was the beginning of another new era in the newspaper business in El Paso. As a working member of the news department, I did not much approve of this arrangement. I did not like the idea of getting that close to the opposition, the *Herald-Post.* I also felt that it would put an end to the competition between the two papers insofar as extras were concerned.

Under the new arrangement, the *Herald-Post* had control of the mechanical departments from 6 a.m. to 6 p.m. and the *Times* from 6 p.m. to 6 a.m. I recall very well the first day the *Times* began publication in the former *Herald-Post* Building at Mills and Kansas. That Sunday afternoon, for some reason I have never understood, the printers questioned whether or not they had a contract, and for a while they refused to work.

It took the combined persuasion of Roderick and T. M. Pepperday, of Albuquerque, publisher of the *Journal* in that city and Scripps-Howard representative for the Rocky Mountain Region, to get the printers back to work. Finally, everything was worked out satisfactorily and the *Times* came out.

The Newspaper Printing Corporation was formed with Roderick as its president, and he still is. Since those early days of the NPC, I have realized what a mistake I made in not seeing the wisdom of the new arrangement. It strengthened both newspapers, enabling them to publish better products. I have been told by advertisers that they preferred the NPC to the old arrangement because they had only one business concern to deal with.

Since the beginning of the NPC until I retired March 31, 1970, I saw many improvements in both papers. It may have been a toss-up whether the *Times* or the *Herald-Post* had the larger circulation when they combined their circulation departments in 1936, but the *Times* soon forged ahead and has steadily increased its lead. I know, of course, that distribution favored the morning paper, but the readers seemed to share my prejudice that the *Times* put out a better paper. The *Times* had a daily lead of some 2,400 over the *Herald-Post* and some 2,500 lead on Sunday when I became editor November 19, 1940; and on March 31, 1970, when I retired, the *Times* had 60,000 daily and the *Herald-Post* 43,000. The Sunday *Times* circulation was 88,000.

The growth of the city has had a great deal to do with circulation increases; there would have been something radically wrong if the paper had not grown. The *Herald-Post* always strove to get the lead in local circulation since the NPC was born, but the *Times* enjoyed a healthy lead. The *Herald-Post* had the larger street sales, but the *Times* had more home-delivered circulation. Today, El Paso has two strong newspapers, both of which strive to fill a community need. I see a great future for both of them.

Speaking of extras, there was a time when the newspapers published extras, or special editions, to announce a big event. When the *Times* and the *Herald-Post* started their competition in 1931, we fought hard to get extras on the streets first. Today that function is performed by radio and television. In my opinion, the most unusual and most discussed extra in El Paso's history was issued in 1923 by G. Allie Martin, then managing editor of the *Herald*, with the headline: "El Paso World's Biggest Oil Field." Some wildcat drilling was going on in the area and Martin had talked to some of the promoters. Tongues wagged over that one, but the headline still has to be proved 50 years later.

The *Times* made a heartbreaking blunder in issuing an extra on the night of February 13, 1935. Bruno Richard Hauptmann was on trial for the murder of the Lindbergh baby and a verdict was expected momentarily The *Times* ran off three stacks of extras of 500 copies each, one saying, "Hauptmann Gets Death," another saying, "Hauptmann Gets Life," and the third saying, "Hauptmann Acquitted." We stationed one man standing over the Associated Press machine, another in the hallway leading to the mailing room, where he could plainly see the man in the wire room, and M. T. "Shorty" Pomar, street circulator, over the extras with his boys ready. The man at the AP machine was to signal which extra to use, holding an arm straight up if the verdict was death, straight out if it was life imprisonment, or down if it was acquittal.

The mix-up began in the courtroom in New Jersey where the AP had an arrangement with a member of the jury to give a signal in advance as to what the verdict was. The AP some way through error flashed that the verdict was life imprisonment. Our man at the AP machine gave that signal, which was relayed to Pomar, and we hit the street with the wrong extra. The AP straightened it out in a few minutes, saying the verdict was death, but the damage already had been done. We tried vainly to round up our wrong extras and we put out a correct one, but we were never permitted to forget the error that we had made.

L. A. Wilke, who came to the *Herald-Post* as city editor from the Cleveland *Press,* taught all of us a lesson in putting out an election extra. In the 1935 City Democratic Primary, he had *Herald-Post* carrier boys go to the polls when they closed at 7 p.m., and telephone the latest figures to the *Herald-Post* city desk. Their extra had many more figures than ours did. That never happened again because we did the same thing from then on.

Competition in extras between the *Times* and the *Herald-Post* vanished with the birth of the Newspaper Printing Corporation, but the *Times* continued to put out election night extras until the advent of television. I have fond memories about extras; they brought excitement to the newsroom as nothing else did.

A. B. Poe Vs M. A. Harlan

The *Times* and the *Herald-Post* did not lose much time after the formation of the Newspaper Printing Corporation in demonstrating their editorial independence. Early in 1937, the *Times* lined itself up behind the candidacy of A. B. Poe for mayor and the *Herald-Post* was stoutly in the camp of M. A. Harlan. Poe was a successful business man who had seen much public service on the City Councils of El Paso. Harlan was a disabled veteran drawing a federal pension. Another candidate for mayor was Don Thompson, operator of a sporting goods store, who had been on the City Council of Mayor R. E. Sherman. He had been elected from the P. D. Lowry ticket of 1935.

The *Times* of December 29, 1936, stated the three mayoral candidates agreed to conduct the campaign on issues, avoiding personalities and mudslinging. A. B. Poe announced first, opposing any move that would "bring about bitterness and disrupt this fine community," and Alderman Thompson and Harlan echoed these sentiments. But this expressed desire for lilac and old lace did not last long. Poe outlined ten points for city progress on January 3, 1937, but Thompson, said that day's *Times,* attacked Poe as a machine politician, indicating the prospect of a rough and tumble campaign, with few holds barred. Thompson was quoted as saying in that same issue that his election along with Alderman Ben Levy two years previously "threw a great big monkey wrench into the political machine which for ten years had been slowly throttling El Paso, and that Poe had for many years directed that city machine from the sidelines."

A *Times* editorial on January 4 compared the platforms of Poe and Thompson, with warm praise for Poe and dismissal of Thompson as "vague." The *Times* of January 12 reported Harlan as making a bid for the votes of El Paso's schoolteachers, promising complete restoration of teacher salaries. The *Times* reported Poe on January 18 as proposing a popular vote on the proposition of increasing the $1 city school rate to $1.15.

The *Times* asked editorially January 20: "Where Is The Machine?"

In a radio address, M. A. Harlan, candidate for mayor, said, "I am not a machine politician; if my ticket is elected the old political machine will have no control over us."

This is an assurance which could have been taken for granted. It needed no statement.

The other two candidates could say the same thing. Because for officials to be machine controlled, there has to be a machine. And where is it? Certainly it is not in the City Hall now. Never has El Paso been so free of machine politics as it is at the present time.

Poe, on February 2, charged Thompson with filing misdemeanor complaints against two Poe employees involving loans of poll tax funds. Woolford F. Swanson, sales manager for the A. B. Poe Motor Company, and Goode Renfro, manager of Evergreen Cemetery, were released on $200 bond each pending a preliminary hearing before Justice of the Peace Clarence Wilchar. Tom Lea was defense counsel. Attorney W. H. Fryer, as political adviser for the Thompson ticket, counseled submitting alleged poll tax buying charges to the county attorney, said the *Times* of February 2. In the preliminary hearing on the charges of irregularities in the payment of poll taxes, *Times* Reporter Steve Barker and *Herald-Post* Reporter Marshall Hail were called to testify. The *Times* of February 5 stated Swanson was freed for insufficient evidence, but Renfro was held under $250 bond, and Attorney Fryer was fined $5 for contempt of court following an argument with Justice Wilchar. The *Times* was in the hassling on the side of Poe and the *Herald-Post* on the side of Thompson.

Harlan on February 7 aimed an attack at the electric and gas utilities at a rally in Liberty Hall and said he would restore a $4 million cut in valuations. The *Times* quoted him as saying on February 16 that a city power plant would save El Paso $977,445. The *Times* stated on February 10 that Thompson was dividing his attacks between Harlan and Poe.

El Paso teachers, said the *Times* on February 11, tried to pin down all three candidates on the teachers' pay controversy. The *Times* said editorially February 12:

> Evidently, the El Paso Teachers Association is not to be wooed and won by the glamorous promises of M. A. Harlan, candidate for mayor. Or by the more restrained promises of the other candidates.
>
> Before making up their minds whom to support, the teachers want to get down to brass tacks.

The *Times* reported on February 15 that Poe told the teachers he would not mislead the small home owners on tax problems.

On February 21, following the primary, the *Times* said: "A. B. Poe and M. A. Harlan will oppose each other for mayor of El Paso in the runoff March 13." Poe received 4,385 votes, Thompson 2,686, and Harlan 4,727. Don Thompson freed his backers for the runoff election.

But a surprise change had taken place: Wallace Perry, hard-hitting editor of the *Herald-Post*, was fired by Scripps-Howard just before the runoff election. The new editor, Edward M. Pooley, was quoted in the *Times* of February 27 as saying the *Herald-Post* would continue its political campaign, with no change planned. The *Times* continued its support to Poe. The *Times* reported that El Paso Contractor R. E. McKee spoke for Harlan on March 12 at a Liberty Hall rally attended by 2.000.

The headline in the *Times* of March 14 said, "Harlan Wins Mayor's Race By 1,859 Votes." The results: Harlan received 6,853 votes and Poe 4,994. The *Herald-Post* had won a big election, and the editorial independence of the two papers had been definitely established.

It was a bitter defeat for A. B. Poe. He had wanted to be mayor for years. Probably no one but Poe himself knew how much the 1937 election cost him, for it was no secret that Poe had bet heavily on himself to win. The *Times* stuck by Poe in that campaign when many of the community's leaders left him. He continued to be active in the community life of El Paso.

Harlan's Two Years

Marvin A. Harlan took office as mayor of El Paso with two strikes against him. Apparently he had made commitments during the campaign which would be exceedingly difficult to keep. He made a poor choice in appointing a chief of police. He got at cross purposes with the Civil Service Commission. He had made promises to the schoolteachers which he could not keep. He became embroiled with the underworld, with consequent charges of police favoritism in enforcing gambling laws.

The *Times* on April 20, 1937, said on its front page:

> The first swift blow of the Harlan Administration against El Paso's underworld came suddenly Monday evening when city detectives, acting on orders from Chief of Police L. T. Robey, seized 12 slot machines and one marble board in 10 raids on establishments throughout the city.

The *Times* on April 21 said:

> El Paso's new City Fathers are confronted with the task of finding $55,500 additional for budgets of the Police and Fire Departments as the result of a bill signed at Austin by Gov. James V. Allred.
>
> Chief of Police L. T. Robey said nine men must be added to meet the requirements of the new law.

On April 22 the *Times* reported Harlan's consolidation plans under which he said some city employees would lose their jobs.

El Pasoans were treated to welcome news on May 4. The *Times* said:

> Negotiations looking toward a tunnel for railroad tracks through the downtown section to eliminate grade crossings and relieve traffic congestion were started with Southern Pacific Railroad officials Monday by Mayor Marvin A. Harlan.

A *Times* editorial of May 5 said of the track depression proposal:

> An estimated cost of $2 million to be paid partly by the railroad company and partly out of federal grade separation funds. No cost to El Paso.

No wonder that the *Times* was encouraged. Nothing came of that discussion.

The *Times* quoted Harlan on June 2 as disclaiming a rumor that Thomas G. Lackland, retired Army major, would replace Chief of Police L. T. Robey. Lackland was appointed chief of police June 3; Leonard

Butchofsky was named night chief of police. The *Times* of June 6 reported Harlan's orders to eliminate El Paso rowdyism. The *Times* said June 8 that Harlan had clamped down on Chinese lotteries after a conference with Lackland and Butchofsky. Then on June 10, Harlan said he was ready to order a halt to theater bank nights in El Paso.

The *Times* of June 13 stated that City Treasurer Ben Carroll refused to sign a check starting the release of $54,000 of Water Department funds to be used in restoring teacher pay cuts. On June 15, mandamus action was brought against Carroll to force him to sign the $54,000 check. The June 29 *Times* said Harlan was confident that El Paso schoolteachers would receive their $54,000 salary restoration despite an adverse ruling by Judge P. R. Price in 41st District Court. The Eighth Court of Civil Appeals later upheld Judge Price's ruling, and Harlan was unable to keep that campaign promise.

On June 22, the *Times* reported that officers had raided downtown gambling games while others were being permitted to operate without trouble. *Times* reporters saw poker and roulette played in two places. A *Times* headline said June 28, "Mayor Harlan takes hand to curb activities of the gamblers in El Paso. Issues orders against favoritism." The *Times* reported June 30 that Justice of the Peace Clarence Wilchar was ready to call a court of inquiry into gambling conditions. *Times* reporters continued paying visits to clubs and reporting gambling in progress; as managing editor of the *Times*, I assigned the reporters to that task. The *Times* reported July 8, "Bond denied in gambling injunction; restraining order against the Knickerbocker Club stands until September." On July 11, a *Times* headline said: "37 El Paso Policemen Raid 22 Places; Knickerbocker Closed; Annex and Plaza Harmless."

The Reverend W. H. Mansfield, pastor of Trinity Methodist Church, entered the fray on July 12. He extended a drive against vice in El Paso to include the restricted district. He was to preach many hard-hitting sermons on the subject.

Then came Mayor Harlan's split with the Civil Service Commission headed by Chairman Gowan Jones. A *Times* headline said: "Harlan Defies Civil Service Commission." The Commission had ruled that Police Chief Lackland and Night Chief Butchofsky had been illegaly appointed. The *Times* quoted Harlan as telling members of the Police Force that Chief of Police Lackland and Night Chief Butchofsky would continue in office. *Times* headlines July 18 said: "City Employes Split With Mayor Harlan; Condemn His Stand Toward Civil Service Body; Chairman Jones Refuses To Quit On 'Invitation.'" The *Times* headlined July 20: "Mayor Harlan

Says Gowan Jones Is Fired." Jones was quoted as saying, "Mayor Harlan has about as much right to remove me as he has to remove the governor of Texas."

Charges ranged back and forth. Jones retained Attorneys W. H. Burges and R. F. Burges and said injunction suits would be filed against Harlan and the City Council to prevent their interference with the Civil Service Commission. The *Times* of July 22 said the Central Labor Union refused a vote of confidence to the mayor, 19 to 10. The newly appointed Police and Fire Department Civil Service Commission approved the provisional appointment of Lackland and Butchofsky. The new members of that commission, named by Harlan and reported in the *Times* on July 23, were Earl Maxon, Charles Windberg, and Dr. Ralph Homan.

The *Times* headline of July 28 stated: "Harlan Haled To Court By Civil Service." Then followed a lengthy court hearing before Judge P. R. Price in 41st District Court. The *Times* headlined August 18, "El Paso Mayor's Authority To Oust Civil Service Commission Upheld By Price In Refusing Injunction." Said the story:

> Mayor M. A. Harlan, supported by the City Council, has the legal authority to remove members of the five-man City Civil Service Commission or any other appointive official at will, according to a ruling by Judge Price.

Judge Price's ruling was appealed but it was later confirmed by the Texas Supreme Court. Harlan had his way, but he was in for more trouble.

Times Reporter Martin O'Neill, one of the best El Paso has known, was covering the Police Station. Police Chief Lackland took a disliking to him and the two of them got into a feud. O'Neill ridiculed Lackland's new set of rules for the Police Department and dubbed him "The Dean of Men." Lackland ordered that O'Neill be denied access to police reports, but O'Neill's friends in the Police Department took care of him.

Harlan inherited the zone of tolerance at Ninth and Mesa and did nothing about it for a while. On December 26, 1937, one of the women from the zone died of jaundice in the City Jail, and a storm of criticism arose over her treatment by police. Justice of the Peace C. M. Wilchar, as a coroner, conducted an inquest into the woman's death, with spicy but inconclusive findings that led to a raid on the Ninth and Mesa area. On December 29, the *Times* reported the arrest of 40 women and 11 men. Wilchar expanded his court of inquiry to include gambling, and the city was treated once again to a ride on that merry-go-round.

Chief of Police Lackland's regime in the Police Department did much damage to Harlan's administratiion. In his race for reelection, Harlan was able to persuade only one of his aldermen to run with him. He was opposed by City Tax Assessor-Collector J. E. Anderson. Harlan was thoroughly repudiated by the people of El Paso at the polls on February 18, 1939. The count was Anderson 8,130, Harlan 2,759. Aldermen Dan Duke, Brooks Travis, Harris Walthall, and J. Francis Morgan went into office with Mayor Anderson.

Harlan left El Paso, and later fell ill in Houston, and wrote to a number of El Pasoans from there, asking for loans. In one of his letters to me, he mentioned the death of his wife and intimated that the way the *Times* had treated him had something to do with her early demise, and that I must accept some of the blame. I resented that deeply; I had always thought I had treated Harlan fairly, and he always seemed to like me. I prefer to think that brooding over his misfortunes warped his judgment a bit. I thought he had the potential of being a great mayor; he was a good organizer and he made an impressive speech. Perhaps he reached his level of incompetence.

About Edward M. Pooley

Much has been said and written about Edward M. Pooley, who was editor of the *Herald-Post* from February, 1937, until he retired in February, 1963. Pooley was sent to El Paso from Houston to be editor of the *Herald-Post* when Scripps-Howard fired Wallace Perry during the bitter campaign for mayor between A. B. Poe and Marvin A. Harlan. The *Times* was supporting Poe and the *Herald-Post* was in Harlan's corner. Some people thought that campaign had something to do with Perry's discharge, but actually it did not. Perry had for some time been crosswise with a number of El Paso businessmen who deeply resented some of his editorial campaigns, and his discharge was a culmination of those things.

The first thing Pooley did when he became editor was to announce that there would be no change in the *Herald-Post's* politics. He continued to support Harlan, and helped elect him mayor. Pooley and I engaged in some knock-down-drag-out editorial fights down through the years; I will tell about them in detail in later chapters, but some general comments appear in order here. Two of Pooley's main political targets were Ken Regan, who served as our congressman from 1947 to 1954, and Colonel John E. (Ned) Blaine, who represented us in the State Legislature for 16 years, retiring in 1970. Pooley unleashed his editorial big guns on those two men in every campaign in which they took part, conducting a vigorous — if not vicious — campaign against them. Pooley had other pet peeves also, but Regan and Blaine were at the top of the list.

Pooley and I never permitted our editorial differences to enter our personal relations until the bitter campaign between Raymond Telles and Tom E. Rogers for mayor in 1957. We stopped speaking to each other during that heated contest. Pooley won, as the record will show, and we soon got over our differences.

Pooley leaped to personal popularity in some quarters early in 1938, when he had been in El Paso less than 11 months and Mayor Harlan had been in office nine months. Justice of the Peace C. M. Wilchar, Jr., opened a court of inquiry into gambling conditions in El Paso, and subpoenaed Pooley as a witness on January 5, 1938. I was one of the newsmen in Wilchar's court room when Pooley took the stand. Wilchar asked Pooley if he knew Dave Lawson, operator of the Knickerbocker Club, and Pooley replied that he did. "How much has he paid you to . . . ?" Wilchar began a question, but before he could complete his question, Pooley reached up from the witness stand and slapped Wilchar hard in the face. Wilchar's spectacles were sent spinning across the floor. Wilchar came down off his bench and he and Pooley began to slug it out. Finally they were separated, mainly by Constable Dan Brungardt. Retrieving his glasses and resuming his seat on the bench, Wilchar said to Brungardt: "Lock him up, Dan." Brungardt insisted upon a commitment from the court, which Wilchar wrote out. Pooley was held in contempt of court and fined $25, and he and Brungardt left the court room together.

I felt it would not do for a newspaper editor to be put in jail; I rushed to the nearest telephone and called *Times* publisher Dorrance Roderick, and he came to the court house immediately. Pooley was in the sheriff's office, not yet in jail, and he was quickly released. That case was handled satisfactorily to all. The *Times* published a picture on January 8, 1938, showing Pooley and Wilchar shaking hands in the court room. Pooley immediately became a hero to the sporting element of El Paso. That night I was in the home of Joe Kennedy, who operated Duffy's Tavern on Missouri Street, and who was entertaining a few of his favorite newsmen. Pooley was not present, but a couple of *Herald-Post* men were. Kennedy told me there that Pooley easily had become the most popular man in El Paso by slapping Wilchar.

Pooley set tongues to wagging again on another occasion 17 years later. He had been editorially criticizing the official conduct of County Judge Hugh McGovern and the Commissioners Court, and he and McGovern had discussed matters personally. Late in December, 1954, Pooley attended, in a group of prominent El Pasoans, the coronation of the Sun Queen in the Coliseum. McGovern stopped at the table where Pooley was sitting and began to argue. Pooley asked McGovern to leave the table because that was no time or place to argue political differences, but McGovern persisted. Pooley picked up a whiskey bottle from the table and broke it over McGovern's head. I did not witness the incident, but this is the way it was described to me.

There was no newspaper publicity given that incident. The *Herald-Post* did not publish it and I, as editor of the *Times*, felt our paper could not publish it for the simple reasons that it was only hearsay and that no complaint of any kind was filed. Nevertheless, news can travel by word of mouth, and there was widespread talk.

In one of the *Herald-Post's* campaigns against the reelection of Congressman Ken Regan, a large newspaper ad was purchased by more than 400 El Pasoans. The *Herald-Post* would not publish it, but the *Times* did. I will tell about that in a later chapter.

On the whole, Pooley and I maintained cordial relations. I do not mean to infer that we were close friends, for we were not; I suppose the right term would be that we were "correct." We went to Mexico City together twice. The first time was in December, 1946, for the inauguration of President Miguel Aleman. We were picked up at the El Paso Airport early in the morning by a special plane from California which was carrying Governor Earl Warren, his daughter, Mayor Bowren of Los Angeles, Sheriff Biscailuz, and a number of movie stars. Pooley and I were the guests of the Mexican Government. We were given an automobile and chauffeur with "Diplomatico" on the windshield and we went to the functions together and thoroughly enjoyed ourselves. The same thing happened in December, 1952, when we went to Mexico City, also as the guests of the Mexican Government, for the inauguration of President Ruiz Cortines. Congressman Ken Regan also was in Mexico City for that occasion; he and Pooley were polite to each other. I went with Pooley on several Good Will trips into the Southwestern territory. I also saw him in Washington for conventions of the American Society of Newspaper Editors. We always got along well together.

Ed Pooley died in June, 1968. I attended his funeral with his successor, *Herald-Post* editor Robert W. (Pete) Lee. I have fond memories of the tough campaigns Pooley and I waged, and I have the deepest respect for his newspaper ability. He fought hard, asking no quarter and giving none. He was fearless. The people of El Paso saw some rough and tumble political and newspaper fights during the Ed Pooley era. Opinion is sharply divided about him: some sing his praises while others insist he hampered the progress of El Paso. I will have to say that he was one of the best shirt-sleeves newspapermen I ever saw.

The Frome Murders

On March 30, 1938, El Paso and the Southwest stirred to a story of murder that chilled the bones. Reporter Art Leibson, in a series of articles beginning in the *Times* of March 27, 1958, wrote of that horrible case 20 years after it happened:

Twenty years ago Sunday, a mother and daughter were tortured and killed in a murder that for grisly brutality made the Loeb-Leopold case pale into a mercy slaying.

Mrs. Hazel Frome and her unmarried daughter, Nancy, socially prominent in Berkeley, California, stepped out of Hotel Cortez and into their new Packard on another leg of a cross-country pleasure trip to Paradise Island, North Carolina. Hours later their bodies lay sprawled in a sandy waste near Van Horn where Nancy's death agony was read in her frantic clawing of the ground.

When their bodies were found four days later, the sadistic killer had left a cold trail. He and his woman companion eluded a man hunt spurred on by the nature of the slaying and by at least $10,000 reward money.

Leibson wrote:

When Jim Milam, a truck driver, led a posse to the spot where he had remembered seeing the Packard a few days earlier, he sounded an alarm that touched off screaming headlines from coast to coast.

The following morning, the *Times* carried an account written by *Times* Reporter H. Worth Jones:

A story of bestiality never before equalled in the Southwest was unfolded Monday morning in Peak-Hagedon's Mortuary as Dr. W. W. Waite performed autopsies on the bodies.

Miss Frome was tortured by placing the live ends of cigarettes or cigars on the knuckles of her right hand. She had a total of eight burns on the back of her hand She also had been jumped up and down on, apparently while she lay on her stomach, with such violence that her diaphragm was ruptured.

Both victims had been shot after being beaten into insensibility.

The 46-year-old mother had been smashed on the side of her head with a blunt instrument and a large chunk of flesh had been gouged out of her right arm before a bullet of German make put an end to her suffering.

It developed that the husband and father, Weston G. Frome of Berkeley, an executive of the Atlas Powder Company, had won the new Packard on a 50 cent chance in a Community Chest raffle at Wilmington, Delaware, while attending a convention there and had given it to his daughter Nancy.

The Frome case broke on a Sunday afternoon. The Frome women had just been reported missing, when their bodies were found a hundred feet or so off the highway just east of Van Horn. *Times* City Editor Raymond J. Stover telephoned me at home, and we put out an extra. Stover, who was the only man on duty at the *Times* at that time who could take pictures, was dispatched to the scene of the crime. He returned in time for us to put out a sunrise edition with full details and with pictures taken at the scene. Sheriff Chris P. Fox of El Paso, with the cooperation of other Southwestern officers, including Sheriff Albert A. (Ab) Anderson of Culberson County, set up a bureau in El Paso in an effort to solve the case. The State of Texas detailed Rangers Pete Crawford and Hugh Pharies to work on the case. The Frome automobile was found abandoned near Balmorhea, but their baggage has never been located. There was wild speculation about the case: that the Fromes were victims of a wrong identification; that narcotics played a part; that another Packard carrying two women went through El Paso that same day; that if robbery had been the motive, then why was valuable jewelry left at the murder scene?

The Frome murders remain unsolved to this day. A veteran officer told me years ago that somewhere, sometime, somebody would drop a word in a back room that would lead to the solution of the Fromes murders; but it has been 35 years.

Another Lesson Learned

I learned another lesson about the newspaper business in 1938 when I was managing editor of the *Times.* Just before Christmas I told Martha Mueller, a very talented young blonde reporter, to find El Paso's neediest family. She took her assignment to heart and soon reported that she had found the neediest family, and we published the story. The response was beyond expectations, but something was wrong: the "neediest" family was accepting groceries, clothing, and other assistance at the front door and carting it out the back door. They were just plain deadbeats, and we had been "taken." El Paso's trained social workers overlooked no opportunity to tell me what a mistake we had made. The lesson learned was that it is far better to work through the established charities, which have records showing needy cases and can prevent duplication and weed out imposters.

A Real Close Election

One of the closest elections in the history of El Paso occurred in the Democratic runoff primary August 27, 1938. The *Times* said on its front page of August 28:

> P. D. Lowry, veteran political campaigner, Saturday defeated Mrs. W. D. Greet for the county clerk's office by the narrow margin of nine votes in the Democratic runoff primary that called out a record vote of 10,241.
> Lowry led by but two votes in the tabulations in Liberty Hall when the final precinct — No. 34 at Tornillo — came in. A tense crowd broke into a roar as the final tally was posted: Lowry 4,933; Greet 4,924.

Mrs. Greet was the widow of the veteran County Clerk W. D. Greet, whom I had known well. Greet told me that once when he was captain of police, he had ordered Wyatt Earp to leave El Paso, and the famous man had done so. The encounter had occurred in the Gem gambling hall; Greet approached Earp and told him it would be better if he left El Paso. Greet said Earp left his seat at once and departed, and was not seen again in El Paso.

Mrs. Greet's campaign was managed by her nephew, Mayo Seamon, circulation manager of the Newspaper Printing Corporation and a very dear friend of mine. The County Democratic Executive Committee certified Lowry the winner. Seamon contested the case before Judge P. R. Price of the 41st District Court, but he was unable to upset the election count and Lowry took office as county clerk.

An Alarming Situation

What could have turned into a most serious situation occurred on the *Times* in June, 1939. Editor H. S. Hunter wrote an editorial commenting on Generalissimo Francisco Franco's regime in Spain which brought on the displeasure and disapproval of Most Reverend A. J. Schuller, S. J., Roman Catholic Bishop of El Paso. Here is the editorial which appeared June 19, 1939:

> Wreaking Vengeance in Blood.
> The savage ruthlessness with which the Franco Government of Spain is putting to death all those of the Loyalist faction who had any conspicuous part in the war, whether in battle or behind the lines, is without parallel save in Soviet Russia following the overthrow of the czarist regime.
> How can such a murderous gang as the Francoites dare commit the sacrilege of calling itself Christian?
> One also wonders what effort His Holiness, the Pope, is making toward putting a stop to the butchery.

Bishop Schuller prepared a pastoral letter which was read in all the Catholic churches in the diocese the following Sunday, June 25, urging Catholics to discontinue taking the *Times*. Editor Hunter was out of pocket that Sunday; I don't know where he was. I had driven to Cloudcroft to take a son to camp, but when I returned I was told some prominent Catholic laymen, including the late J. E. Morgan and the late E. C. Heid, wanted me to try to find Hunter for them. Finally, Hunter was found, and he went into conference with Bishop Schuller and a number of prominent Catholic laymen.

Hunter returned to the office and wrote this editorial, which appeared in the *Times* Monday, June 26:

When Good Will And Tolerance
Prevail, Misunderstanding Ends

An incident occurred yesterday which demonstrated anew the fact that when misunderstandings arise out of divergent points of view they may readily be adjusted by men of good will and tolerant spirit by a meeting of minds in a friendly conference.

Such a misunderstanding has arisen concerning certain editorial expressions of opinion in the *Times* regarding Generalissimo Franco's course in Spain subsequent to the end of the civil war.

These expressions were regarded as offensive to the Catholic Church and a letter to the congregation from the Most Rev. A. J. Schuller, Bishop of El Paso, delivered yesterday, set forth that viewpoint.

The misunderstanding quickly was erased last night in a meeting of Bishop Schuller and the *Times* editor. . . .

As a matter of record and not merely of opinion, the *Times* has been, through a long period of years, on friendly terms with Bishop Schuller and the clergy and the laity of the Catholic Church, as we have tried to be with all churches. This newspaper has commended the good works of the Catholic Church and has endeavored to be helpful in support of its undertakings, both through the news columns and editorially, and many have been the expressions of appreciation from the Bishop, the clergy and leading laymen for those cooperative services.

It naturally follows, therefore, that the *Times* has held the Catholic Episcopate and the church in general in high regard and continues to do so. Also to erase any possible vestige of misunderstanding, it should be stated that in editorially suggesting the mediation of the Pope in Spain to end the policy of executions the question was sincerely stated in the conviction that His Holiness is famed for being a prelate animated by a desire for peace and good will and there was no thought of implying that the Pope was responsible for this or any other phase of such policy. . . .

Bishop Schuller, in conference with the editor, expressing the point of view of the church, commented as to the cooperative attitude of the *Times* now as in the past and in this new understanding agreed to instruct the clergy and people in accordance therewith.

Bishop Schuller also signed the following statement:

After a conference with the *Times* editor, I am happy to say I am perfectly satisfied with the explanations he has given. Again, to know all is to forgive all.

I shall today instruct the clergy and people of my diocese to continue uninterrupted the spirit of mutual good will and cooperation that has existed between the *Times* and my people during all the years of my Episcopacy.

Most Rev. A. J. Schuller, S.J. D.D.,
Bishop of the Diocese of El Paso.

The Spanish civil war had brought on extremely delicate relations with France, England, and the United States. Hitler's Germany and Mussolini's Italy were openly aiding the so-called rebels, headed by General Franco. Communist Russia definitely had a foothold in the Loyalist camp; some said the Loyalist government was communistic. A number of Americans went to Spain to fight on the side of the Loyalists. With Franco's victory, the Roman Catholic Church again was the clerical power in Spain, as there is no separation of church and state in Spain. Roman Catholics the world over were loyal to their church and felt deeply about the situation in Spain. As a matter of record, Editor Hunter told me, the day that his peacemaking editorial appeared, that he checked with the circulation department to see how many cancellations had been received, and he was told one person had stopped taking the *Times*. But it is clear that, if the situation had been permitted to snowball, great harm could have resulted. All of us on the *Times* were greatly relieved when the problem was solved.

At my request, Andy Sparke, a former *Times* newsman, now with the Bureau of Information of the Catholic Diocese of El Paso, sent me Xerox copies of Bishop Schuller's pastoral letters of June 23 and June 28, 1939. The copies were not very legible, due to the age of the original documents. In the first letter this appeared:

You and they and all of us are justified in canceling our subscriptions to the paper until such time as the management will change the policy of the paper. We want no favors, we will stand no more unjust and offensive remarks.

Read this letter to your congregations and your commentaries and urge them all to stand united.

This appeared in the second pastoral letter:

I was the more willing to accept the editor's explanatory remarks since for so many years there had been a uniform, personal, mutual good understanding and good will between him and myself. I hope that the memory of the unpleasant incident will be completely erased from the minds of our people and that our relations with the *Times* and its editor will in the future be as pleasant as they have been in the past.

Your Reverence will therefore disregard the instructions of the letter of June 23rd.

From that day to this, relations between the *Times* and all churches, including the Catholic Church, have been most cordial, for which I am thankful.

The TIMES *editor with the publisher, Dorrance D. Roderick, on December 24, 1956.*

CHAPTER ·VI·

Editor of The Times

A New Editor And a Blackout

TIMES PUBLISHER Dorrance D. Roderick announced on the front page of November 20, 1940, that I had been named editor. I had been doing the work of H. S. Hunter since he died of a heart attack in the newsroom October 20, and Roderick had given me to understand that no one would be brought in and put over me; he made it official November 19. The day the announcement appeared in the *Times*, the editor's office was filled with flowers from well-wishers and I received many telegrams and telephone calls. On that day I embarked upon a career that was to last almost 30 years. My life was filled with successes, failures, heartbreaks, good fortune, bad fortune, high hopes, high ideals, and bitter disappointments.

I was overwhelmed at the assignment given to me; I knew what a great editor Hunter had been, and I was being called upon to follow in his footsteps. The responsibility was somewhat frightening. I was 40 years old at the time. I would not trade those nearly 30 years for anything that I can think of. I had an experience that few men enjoy: I had the number one ringside seat to watch and help a newspaper and a community grow and attract an ever-increasing amount of national attention.

I proceeded carefully for the first few months I was editor. Then, without realizing fully the potential of the idea, I hit upon something that caught on like wildfire and brought El Paso nationwide attention. On March 8, 1941, I wrote this editorial, which I did not even place at the head of the editorial column:

Why Not Blackout El Paso?

The first blackout test in the United States was to have been conducted in Seattle last night. That city of nearly 400,000 population was to have been darkened for 15 minutes.

Without alarming the people of El Paso in any way, it would seem logical to conduct such a test here. This is the largest city on the southern border of the United States. We have nothing to fear from our friends in

Mexico, but it is not beyond the realm of possibility that an attack could be launched on the United States from the south by foreign planes and pilots smuggled from a potential enemy of this country.

The first city which would be bombed, if such an attack came, naturally would be El Paso, which is a railroad center, with yards in the center of the city. It also is on transcontinental highways leading to the north and east and west. It has a good airport, and a large number of troops are concentrated here.

That may sound farfetched, but it is not. This is a day of quick attack from the air without warning.

Airplanes and antiaircraft units are now stationed at Fort Bliss. Why should not El Paso take advantage of that and ask the Army to show our people how best to protect themselves against air attack? Other countries have been conducting such drills for some time.

The United States is in the midst of a gigantic national defense program. Why not include blackout tests all over the country?

That editorial caught fire immediately. It was announced on the front page of the *Times* March 10, "Police To Be Ready For El Paso Blackout; 30 Officers To Guard Downtown Section During Period." In that same edition, a small article appeared that was to be the forerunner of a community hassle. The *Times* said:

Rev. John H. Crowe, pastor of Trinity Methodist Church, in his sermon Sunday night indicated opposition to the proposed blackout of El Paso at 11 p.m. April 7. Mr. Crowe expressed the belief that the move was not necessary and would add to the feeling that war is close to the United States.

Mr. Crowe would not make a statement for the press.

Also in the edition of March 10, I had an editorial which said:

Blackout Idea Growing

The idea of holding a blackout in El Paso has taken hold and indications are that it will be a huge success as a fitting climax to the Army Day celebration April 7.

Fort Bliss commanders and city officials expressed approval and promised every cooperation between the Army and civilians.

The experiment would be a fine, foresighted drill in preparedness, Mayor Anderson said.

"In such an experiment the interest and cooperation of every man, woman and child is necessary," said Brig. Gen. Oliver L. Spiller, commander of the Antiaircraft Center at Fort Bliss, "and the idea really is not a crazy dream because in modern warfare anything can happen."

Brig. Gen. Innis P. Swift, commander of Fort Bliss, pledged his wholehearted support. . . .

There may be some citizens opposed on the ground that such a drill tends to make our people war-minded. That is not the right way to look at it. It simply will be a drill in self defense, which certainly is advisable in a world gone mad with war lust.

The blackout spirit moved across the Rio Grande to Juarez. On its front page March 11, the *Times* said:

> Mayor Teofilo Borunda and Gen. Jaime Quinones, military commander, Monday night announced that Juarez will stage a blackout test in conjunction with El Paso's experiment.

The proposed blackout was discussed at the Chamber of Commerce meeting March 10. The *Times* reported March 11 that E. C. Heid, chairman of the Chamber's Military Affairs Committee, said a blackout proposal for El Paso originated with me. He said he had been informed that Juarez would cooperate to make it a complete blackout on the border. The time for the blackout had been moved to 9:30 p.m. April 7.

Of course, we had some fun along the way; on the front page of the *Times* this appeared:

> El Paso Quip of the Week:
> Stay up for the blackout so you won't be able to see anything.
> In Juarez, they say: "Estaremos pendientes del 'Obscurecimiento total' para ver nada."

The *Times* reported March 13 that steps would be taken to provide fire wardens, anti-looting squads, and other necessary protection measures during El Paso's April 7 blackout. Those chiefly concerned in the blackout plans were invited to a Friday luncheon in Hotel Hilton by E. C. Heid, chairman of the Military Affairs Committee of the Chamber of Commerce. On March 14, Roy S. Nelson, president of the El Paso Electric Company, was named by Mayor J. E. Anderson as chairman of the El Paso Home Defense Unit assigned to supervise the city's part in the Army Day blackout. The following Saturday morning the *Times* had a big picture on its front page showing the Heid luncheon in the Hilton. The caption said: "Gen. Swift Tells How To Stage A Blackout."

El Paso and Juarez dignitaries were in attendance. Heid called on me first to tell what I had in mind, and I did. Then Heid called on General Swift, a man after my own heart because of his ability and forthrightness. General Swift, who always was salty, exclaimed. "G—D—! Hooten is right!" He said there was nothing remote about the possibility of an air attack on El Paso.

> We should stage this thing seriously or not at all. No attention need be paid to long-haired men and short-haired women who oppose such things as this blackout. . . . [The] jittery people, morons, misfits and pacifists who oppose it because it may create war hysteria do not run El Paso.

The *Times* of March 16 said Radio Commentator H. V. Kaltenborn "debunked" El Paso's Army Day blackout from Los Angeles, but El Paso officials promptly retorted that the NBC news analyst was "misinformed and should not be sticking his nose where it doesn't belong."

I had been waiting for the reverberations from General Swift's remarks, and they were not long in coming. The *Times* said March 17:

> While two El Paso preachers hotly criticized the El Paso blackout experiment scheduled for 9:30 p.m. April 7 as a special feature of Army Day, members of the American Legion Sunday unanimously supported the test and offered their services.
>
> Rev. E. J. Bohmfalk and Rev. John H. Crowe scorchingly told their congregations the blackout was indicative of war hysteria. The main target of the ministers' verbal blasts was Brig. Gen. Innis P. Swift, commanding general of Fort Bliss, who at a blackout organization meeting Friday had said no attention should be paid to opposition from "long haired men and short haired women, jittery people, morons, misfits and pacifists."

Apparently someone sent General Swift's remarks to the War Department in Washington, for Major General Robert C. Richardson, former commander of Fort Bliss, was sent to El Paso to investigate. It looked as though General Swift might be in trouble. The next Sunday morning, Dr. W. D. Brown, Methodist district superintendent in El Paso, came by my office and discussed what was going on.

"You don't really want to get General Swift in trouble do you?" I asked him.

"No, I do not," he replied.

"Then, let's go to Fort Bliss and see General Richardson," I suggested, and we did so. General Richardson received us in General Swift's home. I couldn't prove it, but I always thought that General Richardson, whose nickname was "Nellie," secretly was amused at the uproar. General Richardson later became a lieutenant general and distinguished himself in the Pacific in World War II. No further criticism of the blackout was heard. On March 17, I wrote in my column "Everyday Events" that El Paso should be very grateful to Radio Commentator Kaltenborn for the national publicity given to the El Paso and Juarez blackout. I wrote, "Mr. Kaltenborn showed a shocking ignorance of facts and called the whole thing 'silly,' nevertheless he told millions about the two border cities."

The *Times* on March 19 said the El Paso blackout organization was taking form. Street lights would be turned off, streetcars and buses would cease operating during the 15-minute period during which sirens and whistles would warn pedestrians to get out of the streets, motorists to stop, and persons at home to prepare to pull down blinds and turn off lights. No master switch would be pulled to plunge the city and valley into darkness. On March 20, it was announced that a master switch would be pulled in Juarez and that city would be in total darkness.

The *Times* said March 22:

> Mayor J. E. Anderson Friday issued a proclamation inviting the co-operation of the people of this community in the practice blackout to be held in El Paso and Juarez at 9:30 p.m. April 7 in observance of Army Day.

H. C. Horseley was named assistant blackout director. The *Times* said March 23 that Houston was to have a blackout within six weeks emulating El Paso. The front page of the *Times* March 26 said that instructions were given to the people on what to do in the blackout. Whistles would blow at 9:25 p.m. On the American side, the blackout would extend from Las Cruces to Fabens. It was revealed April 1 that lights at El Paso's Municipal Airport would be extinguished during the Army Day blackout. On April 5 it was said that "enemy raiders" would drop flares on El Paso during the blackout.

The *Times* announced April 8 that "Practice Blackout Successful; People Acclaim Cooperation By Almost All; Army Day Banquet Draws Over 1500 At The Country Club." With the area blacked out, Army planes flew overhead and giant searchlights sent their beams skyward. One downtown merchant, Will Shutes, forgot and left a neon sign burning and an overly zealous patriot threw a stone and broke the light; the next day Shutes offered a reward to that person if he would come forward, but no one did. The blackout was a huge success and a great experience: The power of the press is still with us.

Secretaries to The Editor

During the almost 30 years I was editor of the *Times*, I had a number of secretaries. The ones to whom I was most devoted were Loraine Baldwin, Elsie Hooker, and Del Barton. Mrs. Baldwin's husband "Doc," a naval officer, died of a heart attack during World War II; later she married Tim Williams and she is now a widow living in El Paso. Mrs. Hooker was of great assistance to me for a few years; she died of cancer. Mrs. Barton, who was my beloved secretary for 17 years, was my faithful friend to the end of her life. She was my secretary when I retired; she died of cancer in 1971. I want to pay a special tribute to those three women in my life.

An editor's secretary has trials and tribulations. One day in the early 1940s, a man named Botello announced his candidacy for the School

Board. He was opposed to School Superintendent A. H. Hughey, and I wrote an editorial challenging him. The next day he dashed into my office, banged his fist on my desk, and announced to all within earshot:

"Mr. Hooten, you are a s.o.b."

I stood up as calmly as I could and said to Mrs. Baldwin, "Loraine, call the police." Botello left. The next day, he and I rode down the Newspaper Building elevator alone together, and everything was peaceful. Botello was not elected to the School Board.

Another time, a man dressed all in black, wearing a big black Texas hat and carrying a saw, came to my office. He said he had gone into various communities and had written a series of articles which local newspapers had published. He wanted to do the same thing for us. After inspecting his scrapbook, I told him I was not interested. Looking me straight in the face, my caller said he was going to cut off my head with his saw. I grabbed a long pair of scissors from my desk and prepared to defend myself as best I could. Just then, Mrs. Baldwin, who had been to lunch, returned and opened the door to my office to find out what was going on. My caller left with his saw.

Mrs. Barton became an expert on weeding out visitors whose business was with the city desk anyway, but she had to learn. One afternoon early in our experience together, I told her I was going to write and did not wish to be disturbed. She took me at my word. The governor of New Mexico called, but she would not let him in. Later she learned exactly what to do.

I lost two wonderful secretaries when Elsie Hooker and Del Barton died. The day she came to work, Mrs. Barton wanted me to understand clearly that she was a full-blooded Seneca Indian — as if that would make any difference. I used to think of her as the Indian who guarded my door; she always was a source of comfort to me.

Trip Into Territory

Soon after becoming editor I began to write a daily and Sunday column for the *Times* which I called "Everyday Events." It was patterned more or less after the column "Around Here" which H. S. Hunter began writing for the old *Herald* as he traveled around the vast Southwest. Later when Scripps-Howard bought the *Herald* and merged it with the *Post* and Hunter became editor of the *Times* alone, he transferred "Around Here" to the editorial page of the *Times,* where it remained until his death. I derived much pleasure from my column down through the years. A small section of "Everyday Events" was devoted to the canine world; I imagine

I established some sort of record for finding lost dogs and finding homes for puppies.

I discontinued writing the column for seven weeks in September and October, 1941, while I traveled the Southwest gathering material for the annual Harvest and Resource edition published by the *Times.* During those seven weeks, I visited just about every wide place in the road between Douglas, Arizona, on the west; Midland, Texas, on the east; and Carrizozo, New Mexico, on the north. I found a survivor of Billy the Kid's gang near Lincoln. He was an old Mexican-American whose home the Kid went to after killing Deputy Sheriff Ollinger and another officer in his wild escape from the Lincoln Court House. A picture of that old man and the accompanying story appeared in the Harvest and Resource edition. That was a highly interesting and educational seven weeks. I put close to 10,000 miles on my car and talked with many people.

I recall eating dinner in the Scharbauer Hotel in Midland with Bill Collyns, who at that time was secretary of the Midland Chamber of Commerce and now is editor of the Midland *Reporter-Telegram.* Rancher Clarence Scharbauer, known all over the Southwest, came in and shook hands with us. He asked me how I was getting along. I replied that I was getting old (I had just turned 41). Scharbauer responded, "Bill, when your mind makes a date your body can't keep, you're over the hill." I never remember seeing him again. I also visited with a few of the surviving old Southwestern cattle barons, including Lucas ("Luke") Brite of Marfa.

World War II was in progress and Phelps-Dodge was installing a huge project at Clifton and Morenci. I journeyed to Clifton and talked with Phelps-Dodge officials there, but they declined to give out any information; the project was some sort of a secret, and thus my trip was wasted. In the little, old fashioned hotel in Clifton where I stayed, I saw a printed sign on the wall instructing patrons how to get hot water with which to shave: they were to go to the kitchen after it. I brought that sign home and still have it.

Pearl Harbor Day

As history records, the Japanese sneak attack on Pearl Harbor, December 7, 1941, produced severe shock waves in the United States .On that eventful Sunday, I was sitting at my desk writing editorials for Monday's *Times.* Someone telephoned me and said the radio had announced that the Japanese had attacked Pearl Harbor. I asked him if he were certain of what he had heard. He insisted he was. I immediately telephoned the

Associated Press office in Dallas. One man was on duty, and he said he had heard nothing of the attack. But very quickly things began to happen.

I called the *Times* entire staff, and we went to work. Four extras that Sunday afternoon hit the streets off the *Times* presses. Their headlines told the story:

JAPAN ATTACKS U.S.; ARMY VESSEL SUNK; MANILA, HONOLULU HIT

JAPAN DECLARES WAR ON U.S. AND BRITAIN; OKLAHOMA SET AFIRE

CONGRESS TO RECEIVE FDR MESSAGE ON JAP ATTACKS AGAINST U.S.

WAR IS DECLARED ON U.S. BY JAPS

For the next few days it looked as though every piece of artillery, every tank, truck and other equipment that we had was being moved through El Paso on flat railroad cars on the way to the Pacific Coast. It was obvious that we feared a direct Japanese attack on the West Coast. Prior to Pearl Harbor, a large tract of land had been purchased for the expansion of Fort Bliss, largely through the efforts of Congressman R. E. Thomason and the Chamber of Commerce. Biggs Army Air Base came to life in a hurry. The war was slow in bringing changes to El Paso. For a while we continued much as we had been, but then came the wage, price and rent freeze, which caused much resentment among El Paso property owners, as I am sure it must have done all over the nation.

During the war, the cooperation between United States and Mexican military authorities was unprecedented. Fort Bliss maintained military police in Juarez to see that United States soldiers behaved themselves in that city. General Jaime Quinones was one Mexican general who could not do enough to show his cooperation with the United States. My secretary at the time was a very good-looking young woman. She told me she had met General Quinones at a party in Juarez and that he had been paying attention to her. She said when she started to work in the morning, a car and chauffeur representing General Quinones were in front of her home. A day or two later I came to work and there was General Quinones talking to my secretary. He arose and gave me an *abrazo,* which I thoroughly appreciated because I held him in the highest regard. I told my secretary she would have to solve that problem by herself.

During World War II, the *Times* newsroom experienced great difficulties The *Times* publisher, Dorrance D. Roderick, went off to war on September 14, 1943. One by one, most of our top men left for war service. LeRoy Nigra joined the Air Force. Steve Barker and Sports Editor Wilbur Bentley joined the Army. City Editor William I. (Bill) Latham, a reserve officer, joined his division. Managing Editor Raymond J. Stover somewhat later joined the United States Information Service. He was in charge of German newspapers operating after the war, with headquarters in Frankfurt. The "home front" was staggering under its "casualties." We had great difficulty in replacing Stover. For several months, I acted as managing editor and editor. Veteran *Times* Reporter Bob Chapman sat in on the city desk until he came down with a bad case of shingles. We had six girl reporters, a girl telegraph editor, and even a girl police reporter. They did the best they could but we needed experienced men.

I look back at those days with at least one pang of regret and sorrow. A very fine man named Davenport was working in the *Herald-Post* newsroom. We met one day in the washroom and he told me his wife was a fine newspaperwoman if I would not mind having an employee whose husband was on the opposition paper. I hired her promptly. She sat in on the city desk and handled copy most efficiently; she was a gem. One day she came to me and said she had to have surgery, but that she could wait a couple of weeks, and I asked her to do so, not realizing the seriousness of her condition. She waited the two weeks, then she had the surgery and the poor lady died. That was a terrible blow to me.

After repeated advertisements in *Editor & Publisher* and through every connection we had in the newspaper field, we finally hired Bicknell Eubanks from the United Press in New Orleans and he came to the *Times* as our managing editor. Needless to say, that was a great relief to me. I think we put out a creditable newspaper, even with our handicaps.

Breakers Ahead

It seems that there must be rapids in almost every stream. I ran into such rapids early in my editorship. In the summer of 1942, J. Francis Morgan, a man whom I have always liked and admired, was president of the Central Council of Social Agencies. He was leaving El Paso for war duty and called on me and asked me to take his place on the Central Council. He joined the Corps of Engineers July 4, 1942. Morgan said there had been some difficulties, but that everything had been smoothed out. I agreed to accept. As is the case with practically all new or young editors, I thought it was necessary for me to do a certain amount of public relations work. On the day I was to be installed as president at a luncheon in Hotel Cortez, Attorney A. W. Norcop telephoned me that the difficulties had not been solved and recommended that I not take the presidency. It was too late then; I went ahead and was installed.

The trouble was that the Roman Catholic Church objected to the treatment being given the Planned Parenthood Center, which some called a birth control group. An index was maintained by the companion organization of the Central Council of Social Agencies to prevent duplication in charity cases. The Catholic Bishop, the Most Reverend S. M. Metzger, who had recently come to El Paso, was insisting that the birth control records be opened or the Planned Parenthood Center be dropped by the Central Council of Social Agencies. Both Morgan and Norcop were highly respected members of the Catholic Church.

In an effort to arrive at some sort of agreement, I asked Attorney Joe Bennis, a member of the Board of Directors of the Central Council, and also a prominent Catholic layman, to go with me to visit Bishop Metzger. The Bishop received us most cordially, listened to what I, as the spokesman for the Central Council, had to say, but he gave not an inch. When Bennis and I left the Bishop's office, I told him I felt we had accomplished nothing. Nothing happened for a while. I accepted a second term of one year as president of the Central Council in the hope of solving the problem. On one occasion, in an appearance before the Budget Committee of the Community Chest asking for an appropriation for the Central Council, the birth control issue was raised. Rabbi Wendell Phillips became incensed and suggested to me that we start a boycott of the Community Chest; I felt confident he did not actually mean it. Rabbi Phillips went to war and District Judge David E. Mulcahy succeeded me as president. In April of 1944, the Catholic agencies withdrew from the Central Council and Judge Mulcahy resigned as president. Judge Mulcahy also was a highly respected Catholic layman. That was a severe blow, but El Paso lived over it, of course, and all groups later joined together in the United Fund.

Vote on Electric Company Sale

The first real clash I had with Editor E. M. Pooley of the *Herald-Post* occurred in September and October, 1943, over the issue of the City's purchase of the El Paso Electric Company. The *Times* of September 23, 1943, announced on its front page that the city would buy the utility if the voters approved. The $16 million asking price was acceptable, and the election would be called within 30 days. The City Council was informed by Donald Barnes, board chairman of the Engineering Public Service Company, parent company of El Paso Electric, that the Securities and Exchange Commission had ordered it to sell the subsidiary here. A buyer was available for the public transportation system and the two international bridges owned by the El Paso Electric Company.

Mayor J. E. Anderson was quoted by the *Times* as saying:

> The El Paso Electric Co. doesn't have to sell to us. We have been told that one alternative is as desirable as the other. We believe the purchase of the properties will be a good business deal for El Paso.

The *Times* said on September 24 that El Paso qualified voters would go to the polls October 9 to decide whether the city should issue revenue bonds for purchase of the properties of the El Paso Electric Company. The Company had come down $100,000 on the proposed purchasing price. It looked as though the Mayor, the City Council, and most of the business element of El Paso were for the purchase.

As editor of the *Times,* I thought things were being rushed for a proposition of such gigantic proportions. On the front page of the *Times* of September 25 I had an editorial which started the fight with the *Herald-Post* and with what could be called El Paso's power structure.

Here is that editorial in part:

What's The Hurry?

Price agreed upon by El Paso's Mayor and City Council for the purchase of El Paso Electric Co., the speed with which the negotiations were concluded and the early date set for the election cause this newspaper to wonder whether or not the figure of $17,850,000 is a fair price, and why all the hurry.

It is the intention of the City Council to retain the power and light system of the company and to dispose of the international bridges, the traction system and certain properties in New Mexico for which a price of $2 million has been guaranteed. That leaves a total of $15,850,000 which the city would pay for the power and light system.

It is not the purpose of this newspaper at this time to attempt to block the purchase of the utility by the city. Neither does it question the good faith of anyone concerned. But it seems to be rash and unbusinesslike to rush into a $16 million transaction, the largest in the history of this community.

That is exactly what we will be doing unless the City Council talks further about the price and unless it gives to qualified voters of this community more time to learn what it is all about and to make up their minds as to whether they are for or against the proposal.

The election has been called for two weeks from today. That does not allow sufficient time for a thorough study of all the facts connected with a deal of this magnitude.

Attitude of some supporters of the proposal that the price is secondary — that the city soon would make it back — is not sound business. . . .

If the people of El Paso really want to buy the power and light utility it would be a pity to have the proposal defeated at the polls because they considered the price was too high and they thought their representatives in the City Hall had been too hasty.

That is a distinct possibility. Steps should be taken to eliminate those impressions.

The *Times* said on its front page of September 26:

Mayor J. E. Anderson said Saturday that he would convoke the City Council Monday to consider the matter of delaying the election on the proposed purchase of El Paso Electric Company properties for "a reasonable time" from October 9, the date set by the council in the ordinance enabling the purchase.

This action followed an editorial on the front page of the *Times* Saturday entitled "What's The Hurry?"

And in an editorial in that same issue:

El Paso's Mayor and City Council and a number of our leading citizens have become so entranced at a picture of future earnings of the power and light utility under municipal ownership that they believe El Paso Electric Company's purchase would be cheap at any price.

Some supporters of the proposed purchase are so convinced that they are right that they refer to others who may differ for one reason or another as "non-thinkers."

That is going pretty far.

Some of the best business brains in El Paso are oposed to municipal ownership. So are the utilities unless they have to dispose of their properties and are able to sell them at a nice profit. . . .

So far we have been told nothing except that we were offered a "wonderful buy" and given figures running into the millions of how much we can make.

On September 28, the *Times* said on its front page:

The list of qualified voters was expanded Monday on the proposed purchase by the city of the light and power system and the date of the election was postponed from October 9 to October 23.

From a most reliable source, it was learned that every poll tax payer who has property listed on the unrendered list as well as on the rendered list is qualified to vote on the $17,850,000 transaction that would place El Paso Electric Company properties under city ownership and operation. Furthermore any person who owns property which does not appear on either list, rendered or unrendered, may go to the City Hall and render his property any time before the election.

And by editorial the same day:

Let's Talk Price

El Paso City Council did right in postponing the election on the purchase of the El Paso Electric Company's properties to October 23, two weeks later than the date originally set.

Now no one can say that the City Council is in too big a hurry. Time will be allowed for all the facts to be presented and for the people to make up their minds as to whether or not they want the city to make the purchase.

The price of $17,850,000 is the main thing to be discussed.

A *Times* editorial on September 29 said:

Let Them Vote

Decision of the city's legal department that every El Pasoan holding a poll tax receipt or exemption certificate and whose name appears on the city's tax rolls may vote in the election October 23 on whether or not this municipality will purchase properties of the El Paso Electric Company was a reversal of the department's previous stand, but it should please the people of this community. . . .

This newspaper is endeavoring to obtain all the information possible on the proposed purchase of the El Paso Electric Company's light and power system.

When a true picture is presented the *Times* will be entirely willing to leave the decision in the hands of the people. If it would be good for this community to make the purchase we should do so. If it would not be good for the community, we should turn it down.

That is the only fair course to pursue. An honest effort should be made to keep prejudices at a minimum.

A *Times* editorial on October 1 said:

Price Too High

This newspaper again earnestly urges El Paso's Mayor and City Council to reopen negotiations with Engineering Public Service in an effort to obtain a price lower than $15,850,000 for the power and light system of El Paso Electric Company. . . .

It is the opinion of the *Times* that the proposal to buy El Paso Electric Company's properties will be defeated the way matters stand now.

The *Times* announced October 2 the selection of a power plant trustee board, publishing pictures of the board members: Sam D. Young, R. E. McKee, Milton C. Tracy, and George G. Matkin.

A *Times* editorial of October 3 said:

El Paso's Mayor and City Council seem to be convinced that the price of $15,850,000 is the lowest they can get from Engineering Public Service for the light and power system of El Paso Electric Company. So far our city officials have shown no inclinatiion to attempt to reopen negotiations.

Thus as matters stand now the proposal of whether or not our municipality will purchase the utility will be submitted to the voters on October 23 on the original price.

A surprise appeared on the front page of the *Times* October 7. R. E. McKee came out in favor of the proposed purchase by the city of the light and power system "provided the purchase price is materially lowered below that proposed and tentatively agreed to by the Mayor and City Council."

On its front page October 9, the *Times* had this:

Calling the proposed utility purchase a "momentous undertaking" and charging that the city would be paying a tremendous premium, R. E.

McKee Friday called on the Chamber of Commerce to take an active part in the $17,850,000 transaction that is going before the electorate October 23.

The discussion developed into a debate between McKee and E. M. Pooley, editor of the *Herald-Post.*

The Chamber Board of Directors took no action.

Pooley indicated that "this price talk is all hooey."

The *Times* revealed October 12:

Engineering Public Service Company of New York flatly refused Monday to reduce the price for El Paso Electric Company should the voters authorize the city to buy the property October 23.

This information was transmitted to Mayor J. E. Anderson by Erwin H. Will, president of El Paso Electric. The telegram, signed by D. C. Barnes, chairman of Engineering Public Service, parent company of the local utility, was received by Will at 1:10 p.m. Monday.

Meetings were held over the city with speakers for and against the proposed purchase. I recall going to the auditorium of the El Paso Electric Company during the heat of the battle and being warmly applauded by that company's employees.

On October 14, the *Times* announced that the Tax and Legislative Committee of the Chamber of Commerce voted against the proposed purchase. The following voted against the purchase:

C. G. Whyburn, committee chairman, J. C. Peyton, Warren D. Small, W. W. Scott, Paul Harris, G. J. Casselberry, M. E. DeBord, H. A. Markham, Harry J. Ponsford, C. C. Cragin, C. R. Morrill, A. B. Poe and J. P. Sheehan, Leo F. Yetman, treasurer of El Paso Electric, did not vote.

The *Times* said editorially October 17:

The *Times* dislikes to burden its readers with statistics or other masses of figures.

But when a table so misleading as the one that appeared in the public print on the ofternoon of October 12 is given to the people in an effort to prove that this municipality would have made a profit if it had operated the power and light division of El Paso Electric Company for the last 10 years, it is time for someone to try to present a true picture.

The *Times* urges every person qualified to vote next Saturday on the proposed purchase to look into the matter from every angle. It is a cold blooded business deal, and we should be cold blooded and calm in thinking about it. Let us try to keep our political beliefs and affiliations in the background. This is El Paso and we want to do what is best for our community.

Editorially, the *Times* said October 18:

The time has come for the citizen of El Paso to ask himself a few questions in connection with the proposed purchase by the city of the light and power division of El Paso Electric Company for $15,850,000.

First question to be asked is this:

"How will I benefit if the deal goes through?"

Other questions follow:

"Will I receive a lower rate on electricity in my home? If so, when?"

"Will the service be improved? Will taxes be lowered thus meaning a saving to me if I am a home owner or my rent be lowered if I live in an apartment or home owned by someone else? If so, when?"

That editorial also asked who was the prospective buyer of the bridges, traction company, and certain properties in New Mexico. The *Times* continued editorially to insist that the price was too high. On October 20, the El Paso Teachers Association indicated opposition to the purchase, and the *Times* said editorially:

The whole proposition involving the proposed utility purchase is surrounded with mystery and confusion.

To tell the truth, neither the mayor nor any member of the City Council knows exactly what this municipality would pay for the power and light system if the people authorized the revenue bonds.

Finally, on October 21, the *Times* got down to the real point in a front page editorial:

Reject Utility Purchase

The *Times* to the best of its ability has pointed out objectionable features in the proposed purchase by the city of the power and light division of El Paso Electric Company for $15,850,000.

Let's vote the proposed purchase down at the polls this Saturday and wait for a more favorable opportunity if we really want to own and operate our power and light utility.

The *Times* added a postscript editorially on October 22: "A Poor Deal for El Paso."

Editor Pooley had thrown the *Herald-Post* in favor of the proposed purchase. He had used front page charts and figures, trying to convince the people it was a good, sound business deal for them.

Then came election day. The *Times* said in big headlines October 24:

Utility Sale Smothered
By Vote of 2,475 to 651.
Voters Reject Bond Issuance For $16 Million.

In a front page editorial the *Times* congratulated the people of El Paso for refusing to purchase the Electric Company by a vote of almost 4 to 1. That was undoubtedly the worst defeat suffered by the *Herald-Post* in the 26 years Pooley was its editor.

I have always felt the *Times* was on solid ground. The El Paso Electric Company is privately owned today, a taxpayer and an excellent citizen, with many El Paso stockholders. It does not have to go to the voters when it needs money to expand. That was a real hot newspaper fight; the *Herald-Post* was to win its share of the battles in the years to come.

Big Time Politics

The year 1944 was politically eventful for me. I was involved in a fight in the Democratic Party that took me to Chicago for the National Convention, then to Dallas for the second State Democratic Convention. It all started at the El Paso County Democratic Convention held May 9, a quiet affair, but something of a curtain raiser for the fight that was to come. The *Times* announced May 9 that,

> El Paso County Democrats will send a delegation to the state convention in Austin instructed to work for the renomination for a fourth term of President Franklin D. Roosevelt, on the basis of tabulation of precinct conventions.

May 10 the *Times* announced that El Paso County was sending an FDR delegation to the state convention in Austin.

In Austin the fireworks began. I had attended neither my precinct convention nor my county convention, and I was not a delegate to the state convention. I did not go as a newspaperman. The *Times* of May 24 in an Austin Associated Press dispatch reported that Texas Democrats were split with pro-Roosevelt and "uninstructed" delegates holding separate conventions, and they were going to send rival delegations to Chicago.

A couple of days later, Arthur Horn of El Paso told me that El Paso Attorney Robert L. Holliday and I had been named by the pro-Roosevelt convention to represent the Sixteenth Congressional District as delegates to the Chicago convention. Holliday and I were uncertain as to what to do. Texas had 48 delegates to the national convention, and each group would send that number of delegates. President Roosevelt already had announced that he would accept a fourth term, but he had not asked that Vice President Henry Wallace be his running mate.

I went to Chicago as a pro-Roosevelt delegate from Texas and also as a newspaperman, with double credentials. Holliday did not go. I went to Chicago with Charles A. Guy, editor of the Lubbock *Avalanche and Journal.* He went strictly as a newsman, but he was not for Roosevelt for a fourth term.

Our pro-Roosevelt group caucused in Chicago. Mayor Tom Miller of Austin seemed to have charge of things. The "uninstructed" delegation also was on hand. They later became known as the "Texas Regulars." When the contest was taken before the Credentials Committee, that group decided to seat both delegations, giving each of us half a vote .Many of the Regulars walked out, but former Governor Dan Moody did not. I sat beside him in the Texas section of the convention hall.

On July 20, the *Times* carried a Chicago dispatch under this head: "Democratic Party Leaders Urge Wallace To Quit; Aim Ballots At Truman." Guy and I were writing daily dispatches and sending them back to our papers by telegraph. On July 21 the *Times* had a byline story by me from Chicago on the front page telling of the bitterness, even hatred, that was much in evidence among the delegates. They were sharply divided from all over the nation, but the Roosevelt group had control of the convention. FDR was renominated on the first ballot and talked to the convention by radio.

I had heard Senator Harry Truman of Missouri say near the speaker's platform, while eating a hot dog and drinking a Coca Cola, that he did not care about being vice president, but he accepted the nominatiion nevertheless. There was a tremendous ovation for Henry Wallace on the night Roosevelt made his speech. The galleries were packed with Wallace fans and they stormed out of the galleries and started a parade for Wallace. Before anyone could stop her, a woman pro-Roosevelt delegate from Texas grabbed our banner and joined the parade. The convention was adjourned until the next morning. On July 22, the *Times* had a headline saying, "Truman Nominated on Second Ballot." The New Mexico delegation, headed by Governor John J. (Jack) Dempsey, was united and had absolutely no trouble. All of them seemed to be enjoying themselves. Texas Democrats are still split into so-called liberals and conservatives.

Following the Chicago convention, Guy and I took the Twilight Limited for Detroit where we were going to write a series of articles for our papers back home about the tremendous war effort being made by industry in that automobile capital. On the train, we met a man who said he was a brain surgeon. He said he traveled to various cities to perform delicate brain operations. He told us something that has remained with me to this day. He said the Democrats had made a grievous error in nominating Roosevelt for a fourth term. He said they should have nominated Senator Harry Byrd of Virginia. Our surgeon friend told us that Roosevelt had brain damage and that he would not live long. He said that was a well known fact among the better informed medical men in the country. All I know is that Roosevelt took the oath of office for the fourth time. He went to Warm Springs, Georgia, and died of what was called a cerebral hemorrhage in April, 1945. Whether that man we met on the Twilight Limited knew what he was talking about or not is open to conjecture. But we do know that FDR died soon after taking office. I have always wondered whether or not he knew he could not live long and did not want Henry Wallace to be President.

In Detroit, Guy and I went to the various plants, including Willow Run. There we saw B-24 bombers being turned out on an assembly line. I had never seen anything like the job Ford was doing. At a change of shift, men and women workers came marching in, presenting an eerie effect; I thought they resembled zombies as they went to their places. I renewed acquaintance in Detroit with Gerald Dailey, former city editor of the El Paso *Herald-Post,* then on the staff of the Detroit *News.* Dailey helped Guy and me make our appointments with plant officials.

I returned home and began a campaign to support Roosevelt for reelection. That move was not popular with some other *Times* executives. The publisher, Dorrance Roderick, had gone to war and set up a committee to operate his holdings, including the *Times* and KROD. The other members of that committee were not for Roosevelt. They were critical of the editorials I wrote. Publisher Roderick had given me instructions to support Roosevelt. I think I am right in saying the El Paso *Times* was the largest paper in the nation to support Roosevelt four times. Finally, I asked Charles A. Guy of Lubbock, a vice president of the *Times* and who had been assigned by Roderick to act in an advisory capacity to me, to come to El Paso and meet with the committee. He did so and told the other members that he knew I was carrying out instructions. Life was easier for me from then on.

The El Paso County Democratic Convention was held in July shortly after the National Convention in Chicago. I was still in Detroit and did not attend. The expected hassle between those for and against Roosevelt led to the sending of two sets of delegates to the State Demrocratic Convention held in Dallas September 12. At the El Paso County Convention there was an altercation between County Attorney Ernest Guinn and Attorney Jim Hulse, and it was reported that one of them was pushed off a table. I flew to Dallas to cover the state convention; it turned out to be an education in political maneuvering.

The *Times* of September 12 carried this story on its front page under my byline from Dallas:

> All anti-Roosevelt delegations, including Dallas, El Paso, Tarrant and Harrison Counties, were seated Monday night in the State Democratic Convention by the subcommittee on credentials.

When El Paso County's two delegations appeared before the credentials subcommittee presided over by District Judge Otis Dunagan of Gilmer on Monday, the wrangling reached such a point several times that Judge Dunagan had to rap for order.

Highlight of the hearing was when anti-Roosevelt Chairman R. E. Cunningham closed his argument by saying his group wanted no compromise.

"Don't do us like they did in Chicago," he said. "Don't divide us in half. We don't want to sit with them and I'm equally sure they don't want to sit with us. I don't want to sit with CIOers and hoodlums in training."

At this moment a subdued roar started in the back of the room.

"Listen and you can hear them now," said Cunningham.

Then S. A. Sharpe, 3209 Morehead Avenue, El Paso, a pro-Roosevelt delegate, said:

"I resent Mr. Cunningham's assertion. I am a veteran who served as an officer in the U.S. Army. Before that I served in the Navy. I am here because I think the men fighting and laying down their lives today want me here. My record is as good as that of Mr. Cunningham."

"That," said Cunningham, "is Exhibit A." He pointed to Sharpe.

Another highlight was the verbal attack which Attorney W. H. Fryer made on County Attorney Ernest Guinn in questioning his credibility as a witness because of the fracas which took place in the El Paso County Convention last July. In that fracas, Guinn and Attorney Jim Hulse engaged in a personal encounter.

In presenting the case of the pro-Roosevelt group, Guinn contended that the anti-Roosevelt faction did not hold a county convention. With reference to the pledge which was sent to the various precinct conventions, Guinn said:

"It is being charged that it was I who drew up that pledge. I am proud to say I did." . . .

Cunningham charged that Guinn had two muscle men in the person of "Horseshoe" MacIver and this man (he pointed to J. G. Black of the International Association of Machinists AFL) on hand to see that the anti-Roosevelt faction did not get control of the convention.

On September 13, the *Times* had another byline story from me from Dallas:

A battle to the end, with no quarter asked or given by either side.

That would seem to describe the Democratic State Convention being held in Dallas.

In comparison to this gathering, the Democratic National Convention in Chicago was exceedingly tame.

This is a battle for the domination of Texas politics. If the pro-Roosevelt group wins out finally, which it should according to the first show of strength Tuesday afternoon, it means a new state Democratic organization with the Butlers and the Moodys being pushed aside.

State Chairman George A. Butler showed he realized that too because he was not yielding an inch without fighting to the last.

The *Times* again carried my story from Dallas September 14:

With the pro-Roosevelt faction in complete charge of the State Democratic Convention the El Paso delegation headed by R. L. Holliday and County Attorney Ernest Guinn took seats on the convention floor when the session was reconvened at 9 p.m., Tuesday, amid the cheers of other delegates. Pro-Roosevelt delegations from Dallas, El Paso, and Harris Counties were seated after the antis lost control.

The whole question was submitted to a vote of the seated delegates. Robert Calvert of Hillsboro was the floor leader of the pro-Roosevelt group. They voted to seat the pro-Roosevelt delegations.

In the argument put up before the subcommittee of the credentials committee, W. H. Fryer had used some very strong language in referring to County Attorney Guinn. Later in my room in the Baker Hotel, Guinn told me that what Fryer had said was libelous. I did not write what Fryer had said; later I was glad I did not, for time has a way of healing wounds. Ernest Guinn became a highly respected U.S. District Judge in El Paso. W. H. Fryer died some years ago. Guinn died June 9, 1974.

I also wrote this byline story from Dallas:

Texas members of the Senate and House of Representatives were conspicuous by their absence at the convention.

Rep. Wright Patman was the only member of the House who was in Dallas to fight for the pro-Roosevelt faction. Rep. Martin Dies, who was booed when he tried to speak Tuesday afternoon, was looked upon as being a member of the anti-Roosevelt group. No other Texas members of Congress were present.

Perhaps they were wise politically. Time will tell.

The *Times* observed editorially September 15:

Who are the Democrats in Texas?

That does not mean democratic in thought, but members of the Democratic political party as it now is set up. . . .

It seems to be obvious that the Democrats in Texas are those who will support the Democratic Party at the polls in November.

I wrote several editorials expressing the hope that the Republican Party would poll more votes in Texas than the Texas Regulars, who had set up their own group of electors and had them on the ballot. The El Paso *Herald-Post* was supporting the Texas Regulars. On the morning of November 7 I had an editorial on the front page urging the people to vote:

Voters in Texas have still a third choice although it is a negative one. The Texas Regulars are trying to get votes AGAINST President Roosevelt, but not FOR anyone.

As history shows, Franklin D. Roosevelt defeated Thomas E. Dewey and was elected for a fourth term. On page one November 8, 1944, the *Times* reported these figures from Texas: Democrats 505,617; Republicans 107,240; Texas Regulars 77,971. My wish had come true; Republicans polled more votes than the Texas Regulars. Those were rough political times in Texas. Seeds were sown for the birth of a strong Republican Party; many Texas Regulars later joined the Republican Party. Texas needs a strong two-party system.

On January 16, 1958, I was in Juarez to meet the United States Ambassador to Mexico Robert C. Hill (center) and former Congressman Ken Regan (right).

I attended a party for the El Paso Symphony in the Fall of 1954 and visited with conductor Orlando Barera (left) and mayor Fred Hervey (center).

CHAPTER ·VII·

Postwar El Paso

After The War

DURING WORLD WAR II, newsprint was so scarce the *Times* had to curtail circulation by some 9,000. There was not enough newsprint to serve the military personnel in our circulation area. We wound up the war with 39,000 daily and 50,000 on Sunday. There is no way of telling how much we could have grown if newsprint had been plentiful. Roderick had become a major in the Military Government and was assigned to Occupied Germany. Dorrance Roderick, Jr., participated as a combat captain in the Battle of the Bulge. Roderick returned early in 1946 and again took command of our operation. Things began to run smoothly again.

Bill Latham, a combat lieutenant, also returned. During his absence, H. W. Bierhorst had been performing the duties of managing editor. I made Latham managing editor, because that was the position he would have held if he had remained at home instead of going to war. Bicknell Eubanks had left the paper and had joined the *Christian Science Monitor.* Other veteran members of the *Times* staff returned and soon we had a fine organization again. Some of the girls stayed with us, while others journeyed to other jobs. Things returned to normal.

Fort Bliss continued as a major military installation, which it is to this day. Practically all of the air bases in the area were closed. El Paso began a steady growth; the census in 1950 gave us well over 130,000. We felt El Paso's future was well assured, and we were right.

The *Times* continued to grow. Editorial competition between the *Times* and the *Herald-Post* never slackened. I always thought that was a healthy situation. When the two papers took opposite viewpoints, the people were given full details of both sides and were given an opportunity to make a choice. I will write about politics of that period in other chapters. .We had plenty of excitement; there is never a dull moment in El Paso.

Popular Ike Visits El Paso

General Dwight D. Eisenhower returned from the war in Europe a conquering hero, the idol of the American people.. He was made chief of staff and as such began an inspection tour of the various Army installations across the country. Word came to El Paso and Fort Bliss that he soon would be in our community. At the time I was first vice president of the El Paso Chamber of Commerce. The Chamber sent word up through channels asking what our community could do for Ike while he was here. The word came back that he preferred that no festivities be arranged.

On February 24, 1946, General Eisenhower arrived in El Paso. His party, including Major General Alexander Day Surles, the same officer who had accompanied General George Van Horn Moseley to Juarez on that eventful day in February, 1929, and now chief of Army public relations in the Pentagon, went to the Downtown Hilton Hotel, where they were assigned one end of a floor. Then General Eisenhower began inviting those El Pasoans whom he wished to see to come to the Hilton. As first vice president of the Chamber of Commerce and also as editor of the *Times,* I was included. Word came to the *Times* office that General Eisenhower wished to see me in the Hilton. I was doing my work at the time and was late in getting to the hotel. When I arrived, everyone had gone. I gave my name to a military policeman in the lobby; my name was sent up to the floor where General Eisenhower was holding forth and word came back for me to go on up.

When I arrived in the suite occupied by General Eisenhower, only he and General Surles were there. General Eisenhower was just ordering his dinner. He asked me to sit down and chat with him. He was a chain smoker at that time, and he smoked almost a package of my cigarettes before his dinner arrived. He began to talk. He told me all about his war experiences. Then he got off on the subject of the Russians. He said they were in much the same position that we were following our Revolutionary War. I was not taking notes, but my mind was working rapidly. I was making plans for a column that I was going to write. Soon, General Eisenhower's dinner arrived, and I thanked him for his hospitality and left. General Surles, walking with me to the door, put an arm around my shoulder and said, "Bill, of course all the General said was off the record." There went my planned column.

According to a report in the El Paso *Times* of February 25, 1946, General Eisenhower proved that he liked Mexican food. For his meal at the Hilton that Sunday night, the chief of staff disposed of a full plate of enchiladas, tacos, refried beans, and tamales. Then he attacked a large plate of avocado salad and tortillas in earnest. He said it was his first experience with avocado salad, but quickly pronounced it as his favorite dish. The *Times* the following day reported that General Eisenhower said one of his principal concerns during his inspection tour was quick release of unneeded Army housing facilities for civilians. He said Fort Bliss was, and would continue to be, a major Army post: the terrain was suitable for year-round training, there was plenty of room, and there were many permanent buildings.

It was my pleasure to see General Eisenhower on a number of occasions after that. He was always a favorite with the American Society of Newspaper Editors, whose conventions he addressed in Washington. I wonder how history will treat him as President of the United States. At least, we did not get into a war during his eight years in the White House.

Sarah McClendon

An important part of this narrative would be left out if I were not to pay tribute to Sarah McClendon, Washington correspondent for the *Times*. Sarah McClendon is the daughter of a Tyler, Texas, postmaster who had been appointed by President Woodrow Wilson. She received her Washington training under Bascom Timmons, undoubtedly the best known of Washington newsmen from Texas. Sarah served in the WAC during World War II. In 1946 I wrote Congressman R. E. Thomason in Washington and asked him to recommend a capital correspondent for the *Times;* without hesitation, he recommended Sarah McClendon. She was employed at a modest monthly stipend.

Sarah soon made a reputation for herself in Washington. She acted as correspondent for other newspapers, of course, and had her own radio program. Today, I would place Sarah McClendon in the top ten of American newspaperwomen. She is fearless and honest, and completely trustworthy. During the Eisenhower administration, the President would begin to turn red in the face when Sarah McClendon stood up to ask him a question at White House press conferences. Her questions were always pointed, if somewhat embarrassing at times. When President John F. Kennedy and Vice President Lyndon B. Johnson were in El Paso in June of 1963, Lyndon Johnson telephoned and asked that we request Sarah to be nicer to him and the President. Sarah always did a magnificent job of covering the national Democratic and Republican conventions. To sum it up, I would say that Sarah McClendon is a newspaperwoman after a newspaperman's heart. She knows the ropes and her work is superb.

Les and Liz Carpenter, husband and wife, also received their early training under Bascom Timmons. As it will be remembered, Liz Carpenter became Mrs. Lady Bird Johnson's press representative during Lyndon Johnson's years in the White House. She wrote a book which received nationwide circulation. There was a certain amount of jealousy between Liz Carpenter and Sarah McClendon in years gone by. I recall one rainy Sunday morning in Washington that Liz Carpenter called on me in the Statler Hotel and said she could do a better job for the *Times* in Washington than Sarah was doing. I did not tell that to Sarah for a long time. By then, the two of them were so well established and admired each other so much that such a small episode did not count.

Sarah McClendon has a number of El Paso friends. She has visited them often. An interview which she did with Reies Tijerina when he was so much in the news did not please us on the *Times*. So what? I am certain I did a number of things while editor of the *Times* that did not please the publisher. As the old saying goes, "You can't win 'em all."

Earl Warren

Earl Warren always intrigued me. He was a great politician, a man who was elected governor of California on both the Republican and Democratic tickets. A part of his political success was due to his amazing memory for names and faces.

As I wrote before, I first met Warren at the El Paso International Airport in December, 1946, when we were getting ready to embark on a plane for Mexico City to attend the inauguration of President Miguel Aleman. At the El Paso airport, on that early morning, Governor Warren asked me what I thought of New York Governor Thomas E. Dewey. I told him I thought Dewey's moustache was a handicap. Warren laughed and said he was going to tell Dewey what I had said. I suppose we all remember that Dewey was called "The Little Man on the Wedding Cake." Each time I saw Governor Warren in Mexico City, he called me by name.

Later when he became Chief Justice of the United States, I saw him several times in Washington. He continued to remember me by name, and we reminisced about our Mexico City trip. Warren has his place in the history of our country. I have not forgotten that it was the Warren court that gave us all those decisions which changed our way of life. President Eisenhower must take all the responsibility for putting Earl Warren on the Supreme Court, obviously in payment of a political debt.

Some years ago, it was an annual custom of the Hall Syndicate to give a big party beginning at about 11 p.m. following the closing banquet of the American Society of Newspaper Editors' convention. That custom has since been discontinued at the request of the ASNE officers. The Hall Syndicate usually brought part of a New York show to Washington to entertain its guests. Such celebrities as Eddie Fisher and Jimmy Durante were among those appearing. I remember striking up a conversation at one of those affairs with a man of about my age. The talk turned to the relative merits of scotch and bourbon. The man with whom I was talking turned out to be Associate Justice William O. Douglas of the United States Supreme Court. He was a brilliant conversationalist, but I never liked his policies on the Supreme Court.

One comment on the Supreme Court: I think every member should retire at 70, instead of continuing on indefinitely as they presently do. Oliver Wendell Holmes, Jr., may have been the exception, but perhaps he also should have retired earlier. Younger men have a fresher slant on conditions, and we need their perspective in interpreting the law of our land. I also think members of Congress should retire at 70; some of the elderly chairmen of congressional committees are blocking the nation's progress.

A Scotch Mistake

During my nearly 30 years as editor of the *Times,* it was my privilege to know many New Mexico candidates and officeholders. The *Times* enjoyed the largest circulation in New Mexico outside of Bernalillo County (Albuquerque).. I would never have the *Times* endorse a New Mexico candidate. I felt that the people of that state would resent having an out-of-state newspaper sticking its nose into their politics. I would write, however, "If the *Times* were in New Mexico we would vote for so and so." One of the New Mexico men who was highly successful in politics and whom I liked very much was John J. (Jack) Dempsey, who served in Congress for five terms and was governor two terms. This story is about him.

During the war a gambling spot called the Sunland Country Club operated in the Upper Valley just across the Texas border in New Mexico, doing a land office business. In the spring of 1946, during Governor Dempsey's second term, a situation arose that caused tempers to flare. New Mexico officers came down from Las Cruces and arrested El Paso taxi drivers at the Sunland Country Club, took them to Las Cruces by the back road, charged them with operating in New Mexico without a license, and fined them heavily. The next day El Paso officers went to the scene, determined by measuring distances that the El Paso taxi drivers had been arrested in Texas, and issued a warrant for Sheriff Happy Apodaca of Dona Ana County, charging him with false arrest.

That was when Governor Dempsey entered the picture. He telephoned me in the *Times* office. "What's going on down there?" he asked. "What's this I hear about Texas officers having a warrant for the arrest of a New

Mexico sheriff? We can't have that. I'll be in Hotel Paso del Norte tomorrow afternoon.. Please have your chief of police, sheriff and the attorney for the taxi drivers there. We're going to settle this thing."

Right on the dot the next afternoon, I had the sheriff, chief of police, and Victor B. Gilbert, the attorney for the taxi drivers, in Governor Dempsey's suite in the Del Norte.

The matter was settled in this way: Governor Dempsey gave his assurance that El Paso taxi drivers could go to the Sunland Country Club without New Mexico licenses. Gilbert wanted the return of the fines that had been assessed the taxi drivers in Las Cruces. Dempsey said that could not be done, because the money already had found its way into official coffers.

The following Sunday, Joe Black, chief of New Mexico State Police, telephoned me at home, saying he had something in his car for me from Governor Dempsey and would I be so kind as to drive to the Del Norte and get it? I wasted no time. Black transferred a case of scotch from the trunk of his car to mine. I wrote Governor Dempsey, thanking him. I said he owed me nothing, but, at the most, one bottle of scotch would have sufficed since scotch was hard to come by in those days. Governor Dempsey wrote me back he was sorry he did not have two cases of scotch to send me.

If the story ended there, everything would be great. A few days later, I learned that the case of scotch had been intended for Edward M. Pooley, editor of the *Herald-Post*. He had given Dempsey the money and asked him to buy the case for him. It was too late then: I already had given away most of my scotch to friends. Governor Dempsey had to produce another case for Pooley.

The Sunland Country Club seemed to have a monopoly on gambling on the New Mexico side in the Upper Valley. Tom Burchell, who operated a very popular saloon in that general area, also opened gambling games. He did that with the cooperation of Toughy Johnson, well-known El Paso saloonkeeper. I remember telling Tom Burchell I thought he was making a mistake, because his bar was popular with many young El Pasoans. At any rate, the New Mexico State Police arrived soon and destroyed the gambling equipment at Tom Burchell's with sledge hammers, while the Sunland Club was still operating.

For some years gambling had been permitted in New Mexico in such resorts as Hot Springs and Ruidoso. When Edwin L. "Big Ed" Mechem, a former FBI agent, took office as governor in 1951, gambling in the state stopped, and still is stopped. There may be some isolated gambling going on; there probably is, but there are no more gambling casinos like the Sunland Club. Horse racetracks are popular in New Mexico today; the

Sunland Track near El Paso and Ruidoso Downs are extremely well patronized, but there are no gambling halls.

Pigs and Politics

There is an old saying that anything is fair in love and war; I think it should be extended to include politics. I will always think, however, that County Judge Moliere Scarborough was given extremely unfair treatment in his campaign for reelection in the Democratic primary of July, 1946. He was being opposed by Attorney Victor B. Gilbert, but I do not think that Gilbert had anything to do with that unfair treatment.

I had written an editorial in the *Times* of July 16, 1946, endorsing Scarborough for reelection:

> County Judge Moliere Scarborough does not know how to stir up ballyhoo. He flatly refuses to make promises he cannot keep. He has the unhappy faculty of making some folks angry when he says "No." And he doesn't care how big they are—he still says "No."
>
> All that is working against him in some quarters during the present campaign.
>
> This newspaper thinks those qualities in Judge Scarborough, which some citizens of the county do not seem to like, are in his favor. . . .
>
> It is to the best interest of El Paso County to return him to office.

Everything went along smoothly for a few days, and then the *Times* of July 24 had this on its front page:

> Echoes of the three-year-old Ascarate pork barrel and sweet potato episode blared out of a loudspeaker to shatter the aplomb of a routine political rally in Anthony Monday night in what was an apparent "smear" attempt leveled at County Judge M. Scarborough and John L. Andreas. Andreas is a candidate for county commissioner from Precinct 4.
>
> Victor B. Gilbert is challenging Scarborough's bid for reelection while Andreas is seeking to unseat Commissioner Ord Gary.
>
> The four candidates Tuesday vigorously denied knowledge of, or complicity in, the overt loudspeaker presentation which coupled the names of the county judge and challenging commissioner candidate with a hogpen medley of grunts and squeals.

The pigs and sweet potato episode at Ascarate Park had been the object of a grand jury investigation in 1943. Scarborough and Andreas had been members of the Commissioners Court during that investigation.

The *Times* reported July 25, "Pig Squeals But Briefly At Ascarate." On July 27, the *Times* reported:

> County Judge Scarborough wound up his campaign for reelection Friday night in Cleveland Square marked by the absence of "pig squealing," "The Shadow," or other recorded heckling used at earlier political rallies.

The *Times* reported July 29: "Gilbert Wins By 316 Votes," receiving

6,840 votes to Scarborough's 6,524; Gary defeated Andreas by a somewhat wider margin.

There is no way of knowing whether the pig grunts and squealing over the loudspeaker had any effect on the outcome of the election. I think it did, and I also think it was a dirty trick. Judge Scarborough and Johnny Andreas, in my opinion, were public-spirited, honest men. Assistant District Attorney Gill Newsom told me later that he had been at odds with County Judge Scarborough and that he had something to do with the loudspeaker. Judge Scarborough later moved from El Paso to San Antonio, where he still lives.

Dan L. P. Duke

This is the story of Dan L. P. Duke, who was elected an alderman in the administration of Mayor J. E. Anderson in February, 1939, a member of the ticket that defeated Mayor Marvin A. Harlan for reelection. Duke served on the Anderson City Council until Anderson's death February 4, 1947; he had for eight months in 1946 been acting mayor during the illness of Mayor Anderson. Duke and Anderson both said they would run for mayor in the February, 1947, primaries, but Anderson died before the election. .

I had always been friendly with Duke; to this day I admire his courage and determination. When Duke announced for the 1947 primary, he talked to me about serving on his advisory committee, for his ticket composed of Tom E. Rogers, Truett Evans, Ray S. Watt, and R. B. Wicker. Opposed to the Duke ticket was a formidable array headed by Dan Ponder, whose father had been editor of the *Times,* with Karl O.. Wyler, Marty Baumann, Jules Carlin, and E. W. Kayser, Jr., for Council. The *Times* took no part in that campaign. Ponder and his entire "team" were elected. On election night, Duke made such a splendid speech over radio congratulating the victor that some observers said he assured his own election two years hence.

Dan Ponder made an excellent mayor, but he made a few political errors. For one thing, his City Council declined to grant the summer discount for water, thus alienating the city's gardeners, many of whom were women. Then the *Herald-Post* reported that the Ponder police department had shot a number of dogs, and a large number of dog lovers were outraged.

Came 1949 and Dan Duke was back in the field with a brand new ticket. The *Times* had this editorial February 5:

> Two years ago the people of El Paso wanted progress.
> They decided that Dan Ponder and his four candidates for the City

Council who were on his "team" were the best bet to help go ahead and do things.

By a convincing majority, the people of El Paso elected Dan Ponder mayor and placed his "team" in the City Hall.

Since then, El Paso has shown progress. Improvements have been made and are being made. Those things cost money. . . .

The *Times* is not unfriendly to any candidate in the present municipal political campaign. This newspaper does not intend to publish an unkind word about any candidate. This newspaper merely believes that the Ponder administration has given the people what they asked for and that the Ponder administration should have a second term.

The *Times* held to that position. We were supporting the Ponder ticket, but we said not one unkind word about either Duke or his aldermanic candidates. On February 27, the *Times* headline read: "Duke Wins Mayor's Race by 4-3 Margin," Duke receiving 8,748 votes to Ponder's 6,325. The aldermanic candidates who took office with Duke were Archie Gill, Carroll W. Smith, Jr., E. W. Kayser, Jr., and Jules Carlin. A feature of that election was the one-vote victory of Kayser over Lee Riggins. Kayser and Carlin were holdovers from the Ponder administration.

The Duke administration was heading down a rocky road. On the evening of October 1, 1949, Alderman Kayser telephoned me and asked me to come by his home. When I arrived there, all four aldermen were on hand: Kayser, Smith, Gill, and Carlin. Assistant City Attorney Reuben Momsen was also present. The council had split with Mayor Duke and had given him an ultimatum. I listened to what they had to say and urged them to take whatever action they thought advisable.

I went to the office and wrote a byline page one story under this eight-column headline:

Entire Council Breaks With Mayor Duke.

Aldermen Ask Probe Of Police Activities In Gambling; Payoff.

For the first time in the history of El Paso, all four members of the City Council Saturday had broken with the mayor. El Paso's four aldermen, E. W. Kayser, Jr., and Jules Carlin, holdovers from the Dan Ponder ticket, and Carroll W. Smith, Jr., and Archie Gill demanded that Mayor Duke take drastic action in the police department to stop gambling and to quell rumors of payoff.

The four aldermen met with the mayor at noon Friday and gave him an ultimatum. He was either to discharge or retire Chief of Police W. C. Woolverton, Assistant Chief of Police H. S. Bernhardt, and Chief of Detectives Joe Stowe or the aldermen were going to take the matter to the grand jury. Mayor Duke flatly rejected the ultimatum.

I had this editorial in the *Times* of October 3:

Find The Truth.

El Pasoans awoke Sunday morning to find themselves in a very serious situation. Their city government was split wide open. All four aldermen were at outs with Mayor Dan Duke. The aldermen had demanded that the mayor dismiss or retire the three top men in the police department. There was talk of gambling and the ugly rumor of "payoff." The four aldermen have asked the Civil Service Commission to conduct a thorough investigation.

The entire matter is regrettable. But the situation is so grave that it must be cleared up, one way or another. A determined effort must be made to arrive at the truth. It has gone beyond a feud between four aldermen on one side and the mayor on the other. The community as a whole is deeply concerned. The *Times* has all the respect in the world for members of the Civil Service Commission. This newspaper is certain those men will do all they can to encourage and promote honest government. But the grand jury should take hold also and conduct a thorough, far-reaching investigation. . . . A courageous, determined effort must be made to clear the atmosphere. Let the chips fall where they may.

Times Reporter Art Leibson had a front page article October 3 which said:

Mayor Dan Duke struck back Sunday as the rift between himself and the aldermen widened over a demand for a wholesale shakeout of the police department. Less than 48 hours after the council called for the removal of three top police officials for sanctioning gambling in El Paso, Duke issued an order that the aldermen devote the time to their city jobs that is required by law.

The story pointed out that a city ordinance required that aldermen work six hours a day.

The mayor and the City Council joined together in requesting a grand jury investigation. On October 5, the *Times* said that District Attorney Roy D. Jackson and E. G. Magruder, foreman of the grand jury, received the requests from the mayor and City Council. *Herald-Post* Editor E. M. Pooley was a member of that grand jury. On October 19, the *Times* reported that petitions seeking a recall election for the four aldermen were being circulated. The *Times* reported October 25 that charges against the police department officials filed with the Civil Service Commission Monday by three aldermen would be aired at a hearing scheduled before the commission on November 11. The charges were brought by Aldermen A. A. Gill, Jules Carlin, and E. W. Kayser, Jr., with Alderman C. W. Smith, Jr., refusing to join in their action.

The *Times* reported November 11 that El Paso's

. . . three embattled aldermen Thursday overrode a protest by Mayor Dan Duke and employed Attorney W. H. Fryer to represent them at the Civil Service Commission hearing of anti-gaming charges Friday night.

On November 12, the *Times* reported:

Hearing on sensational charges brought against top officials of El Paso's police department collapsed Friday night when the Civil Service Commission refused to hear evidence against the officers. The hearing ended suddenly with a short announcement from Walter T. Ponsford, commission chairman, that no action would be taken until the present El Paso grand jury makes its report.

The grand jury investigation came to naught insofar as the three police officials were concerned.

On November 22, the *Times* reported:

The City Civil Service Commission in its regular meeting Monday night agreed to hear charges of laxity in enforcing anti-gaming laws lodged against three top police officials and set the hearing for Tuesday, November 29.

That hearing lasted until December 20, with numerous witnesses being called. The Civil Service Commission, in a lengthy report, found those accused not guilty. The report talked of personality clashes and urged closer supervision of the police department.

That was the end of the investigation, but dissension in City Hall continued. Aldermen Gill, who had been elected on the Duke ticket, and Kayser and Carlin held a close grip on city affairs. They would not yield in dealing with Mayor Duke. On September 18, 1950, it was reported that Mayor Dan Duke charged Chief of Police W. C. Woolverton with playing politics with Aldermen Archie Gill, Jules Carlin, and E. W. Kayser, Jr., instead of running the police department. Duke and Woolverton had recommended that Lieutenant Harry S. Bernhardt be promoted to captain in his job as head of the traffic division. The three aldermen instead passed up Bernhardt, who was third on the eligible list, and chose Lieutenant I. E. Baggerly.

The mayor was reported as still firm in his decision to push an election for the recall of the three aldermen. It should go in the record that during the height of the trouble in the City Hall, a very warm friend, the late Graves Malone, brought me a pistol, thinking I might need it. I put the gun in a drawer and forgot about it; there was no such danger in El Paso.

The trouble in the City Hall continued for the rest of the Duke term of office. In 1951 he announced for reelection with a new slate of aldermen, accusing the three dissenting aldermen of not having the nerve to run again. At one point, on September 23, 1950, the *Times* reported that Mayor Duke admitted he had been approached by people he respected to settle the dispute without a recall election. Alderman Gill said,

I have not been contacted and I most certainly would be if there is anything afoot. I don't know what the mayor might want, but I am not willing to concede anything on principle. I am not afraid of a recall election.

Dan Duke was somewhat bitter toward the *Times* and me personally during the 1951 election.

On February 24, 1951, the *Times* reprinted a story from the *Herald-Post,* in which Duke had attacked the *Times* and me. I wrote on the *Times* front page:

> When it comes to a matter of veracity between the *Times* and Dan Duke, the *Times* is perfectly willing to leave the decision in the hands of the people. Here is an exact reproduction of Duke's story on the front page of the *Herald-Post* Friday afternoon. Mayor Duke did not furnish the *Times* with a copy of his statement.

Such terms as "bare-faced lie" were used, and I was attacked verbally.

Fred Hervey, El Paso merchant, was running for mayor with a strong aldermanic team. The *Times* on February 25, 1951, announced that Hervey defeated Duke 7,660 to 5,312. Hervey's aldermen were former Sheriff Allen Falby, H. T. Etheridge, Jr., Ernie Ponce, and C. W. Harper. The City Hall was united, and El Paso moved ahead. I will write about Hervey's two terms in another chapter.

In the 1955 election, former Mayor Dan Duke tried again. His opponent was Mike Misenhimer, an El Paso merchant, handpicked by a committee including Hervey, L. Roy Hoard, and me. The count, as published in the *Times* after the February primary, was Misenhimer 11,047, Duke 5,646. Elected with Misenhimer were Aldermen Ernie Ponce, Hal Dean, Richard E. Fletcher, and Tom Burnham. Misenhimer decided he did not want to be mayor and did not serve a day. A committee of business and professional men recommended that El Paso businessman Tom E. Rogers be named mayor to serve out Misenhimer's term, and that was done.

Duke tried again for public office in 1960, attempting to defeat Colonel John E. (Ned) Blaine, a veteran member of the Legislature, with the support of *Herald-Post* Editor E. M. Pooley.

I wrote in "Everyday Events" April 27, 1960:

> During my absence in Washington attending the convention of the American Society of Newspaper Editors, El Paso's afternoon newspaper attempted to make hay building up former Mayor Dan Duke as a senior statesman and as the man who ought to beat State Representative John E. (Ned) Blaine. Since my return I have been amazed at some of the statements made in the afternoon newspaper on behalf of former Mayor Duke. Now let's get the record straight. Personally I have nothing against Dan Duke, but he was a sorry mayor as the people proved by their vote: Duke 5,646; Misenhimer 11,047.

Blaine defeated Duke in the July Democratic primary.

All that is in the dim past. Today Dan Duke and I are friends. We meet each year at the El Paso Electric Company's Christmas party, where we reminisce a little and wish each other a "Merry Christmas."

Ken Regan

Ken Regan and I were warm personal friends. I not only approved of his politics, I liked him as a man and enjoyed being in his company. Regan's first political office was as mayor of Pecos; later he was state senator from the Twenty-Ninth Senatorial District. He moved to Houston, where he was active in the oil business and then he moved back to Midland. And from there he announced his candidacy for Congress from the Sixteenth Congressional District to succeed Representative R. E. Thomason, who had been named United States District Judge.

County Judge Victor B. Gilbert, the *Times* said on June 7, 1947, was the first candidate to file for the congressional seat. That same day, County Commissioner Ord Gary said he planned to resign his present position when he opened his campaign for Thomason's post, but he later decided to stay where he was. The *Times* of June 8 noted that Louis A. Fail of El Paso and James W. Metcalfe of Odessa announced their candidacies to succeed Thomason. S. J. Isaacks, state representative, was quoted in the *Times* of June 27 as saying that "lots of good people" had talked to him about running for Congress. The *Times* revealed July 11 on its front page that candidates who had announced for Congress were Gilbert, Gary, State Representative Woodrow Bean, Pat Hargrove, and L. A. Fail, all of El Paso, and Kenneth Regan of Midland, and J. W. Metcalfe of Odessa.

In "Everyday Events" of August 14, I wrote:

> In my opinion, young Woodrow Bean ignored some of the best advice that was given to him in all of his life. A number of his sincere friends, older, mature men, advised him not to run for Congress at this time, but to run for the State Senate to succeed H. L. Winfield.

The election had been set for August 23 by Governor Beauford Jester. The *Times* said editorially August 15:

> When we look at the whole picture we see that Ken Regan of Midland has made fewer rash promises than any of the more prominent candidates.
>
> Regan has conducted a dignified campaign. He has a convincing record in business and in public life. In contrast, what is Woodrow Bean's principal personal interest? He is a politician and he freely concedes that he is.
>
> Whom do you want to represent us in Congress?

The *Herald-Post* was supporting either Ord Gary or Woodrow Bean, and it published a picture of the two on its front page. Editor Pooley had been sharply attacking Regan, particularly for his oil business activities. The *Times* said August 25 that Regan had a 396-vote lead with 300 votes still uncounted; I had an editorial congratulating Regan, observing, "Now let's forget politics for a while and get down to work."

When the 1948 Democratic primary rolled around. Woodrow Bean again was a candidate for Congress and made a determined effort to unseat Regan, again with Pooley's support. The attack by the *Herald-Post* on Regan became so aggressive and determined that a group of El Pasoans bought a newspaper ad to make a reply. The *Herald-Post* did not publish that ad, but the *Times* did in its Sunday edition of July 18, 1948.

That ad, which occupied practically an entire page, said in part:

> An Open Letter
> To The Editor Of Our Afternoon Paper.
> We the undersigned residents of El Paso County take this means of expressing our disapproval of the attacks through the paper you edit against Congressman Ken Regan.
> A year ago you opposed Mr. Regan only because he was in the oil business and did not live in El Paso. This was a narrow view and was calculated to tear down the good will El Paso had been building in the oil country of West Texas.
> The merchants, wholesalers and manufacturers of El Paso are dependent upon business from West Texas. A great many of our people are making a living out of this business. We want the people of West Texas to know you did not express our sentiments. . . .
> We are trying to build a united, harmonious community spirit in El Paso and in our trade territory. Your attacks on Congressman Regan, who resides in the heart of the oil country, where he is highly respected, makes it very difficult.
> We want you to know that we and the people of West Texas do not approve the type of campaign that you have been waging against our congressman.

More than 400 names were signed to that ad, including many of the top men in El Paso.

On July 20, the *Times* had a page one editorial headed:

> Not Fiction, But Facts.
> The "Gold Dust Twins" have been separated.
> Ord Gary, 65 years old, for county judge.
> Woodrow Bean, 30 years old, for Congress.
> Those are the two principal candidates being supported by the El Paso *Herald-Post* at this time. Last August when we held a special election to name our new member of Congress, the *Herald-Post* supported Ord Gary, 64 years old, and/or Woodrow Bean, 29 years old. Both were defeated, but it was anything to defeat Ken Regan.

Now what do we see? Ord Gary, 65, is being supported for county judge because the *Herald-Post* says we need a sound businessman, a man of mature judgment, to superintend the spending of our $1,400,000 a year. Woodrow Bean, 30 years old, a man with practically no business experience, should be elected to Congress because of his youth, says the *Herald-Post*, where he would have a say in our $275 billion national debt and have a vote in the expenditure of billions of dollars annually. Inconsistency, thy name is the El Paso *Herald-Post*!

Something then happened in that campaign which I must confess cut me to the quick. The *Times* on its front page of July 23 had this:

Yellow Journalism Charge Is Hurled Against the *Times*
Twelve members of the Dean Hawkins Detachment, Marine Corps League, including H. L. McCune, Jr., commandant, signed a resolution attacking W. J. Hooten, editor of the *Times*, for his alleged effort to "discredit and detract" from Woodrow Bean's war record. The *Times* urges that the resolution be read carefully together with the comments of the *Times* editor beside it. Woodrow Bean declined to comment other than to say he knew nothing about it.

The resolution, which followed, contained this paragraph:

Whereas we hereby go on record as saying that if Editor Hooten has seen fit to criticize the war record of a man who served honorably overseas during war time with the Marine Corps, it is only equitable that Mr. Hooten make public his own war record.

The resolution was signed by H. L. McCune, Jr., Ralph H. Weir, Maury Cohen, James F. Collins, James H. Muhn, Jr., Fred G. Davidson, Jack L. Pickle, Julian Stroud, Jr., James E. North, Jose L. Delgado, Floyd Thompson, and Manuel M. Silva.

In the statement from me, accompanying the resolution, I wrote:

Neither as editor of the *Times* nor as a citizen who has lived among you for 30 years have I ever attempted to discredit and detract from anyone's war record. No political race could become heated enough for me to do that.

Then I cited the only editorial I had ever written on the subject. I had written that Bean served in the Marine Corps in World War II and that Regan had served in the Air Corps in World War I. I concluded my statement with this: "As for my war record, through no fault of my own, I have none." That statement was signed by me.

The *Times* announced in headlines July 25 that the voters had reelected Ken Reagan and Gary had lost to Gilbert. On July 26, the *Times* reported that Bean had carried El Paso County 11,371 to 7,072, but the entire district had gone for Regan 25,372 to 17,605.

Regan continued to represent us in Congress with distinction, or so we on the *Times* thought, but the *Herald-Post* continued to harass him. In 1950 Fred Hervey of El Paso and Judge Paul Moss of Odessa announced against Regan. The *Times* supported Regan, as usual. Hervey conducted a spirited campaign, referring to the congressman as "Playboy Ken Regan." Moss campaigned extensively and expensively, with page ads in the newspapers. He apparently did not consider Regan a real Democrat.

The *Times* on July 27 reported Regan and Moss in the runoff. The returns from the Sixteenth Congressional District showed Moss 11,216, Hervey 5,148, and Regan 14,601. In El Paso County, the vote was Regan 3,974, Moss 3,594, and Hervey 2,841. Hervey took no part in the runoff campaign. The *Times* headline August 27 said, "Regan Re-Elected By 4,500 Votes." The count in the district was Regan 23,086, and Moss 18,565, and in El Paso County Regan polled 9,639 votes to Moss's 8,597.

Regan went back to Congress and we thought he continued to represent us well and ably, but the *Herald-Post* did not think so. In 1952, Regan escaped opposition, but in 1954, a potent young state senator named J. T. (Slick) Rutherford from Odessa came on the scene. He had defeated Hill Hudson of Pecos for reelection to the State Senate by an impressive majority. Rutherford told me in my office that if he ran against Regan he would beat him worse than he defeated Hudson. The campaign was a hot one, with both candidates extremely active. The *Times* and the *Herald-Post,* as could have been expected, went at it hammer and tongs. The outcome of that election was a heartbreaker for me. The *Times* headline of July 26 was, "State Senator Apparent Winner by 188 Votes;" the vote was 25,236 to 25,048. Ector County, Rutherford's home, had spelled the difference, giving Rutherford 5,528 votes and Regan 2,060.

Friends tried to get Regan to contest the election, but he would not. He accepted defeat and returned to his Midland oil business. I was a pallbearer at his funeral in Midland on August 15, 1959. I always looked upon Ken Reagan as a fine gentleman.

Unsolved Double Murder

El Paso had a double murder in February, 1948, which has never been solved. On February 9, Rod MacNeil, advertising director of the Newspaper Printing Corporation, while entertaining Maurice Heaton, a visiting advertising man from Los Angeles, took him up on Scenic Drive. At high noon, the two men parked MacNeil's automobile at the summit, overlooking El Paso. While they were viewing the beautiful sight that lay before them, a dark man, described by MacNeil as wearing a red bandanna handkerchief on his head, forced them at gunpoint into MacNeil's automobile. The gunman sat in the back seat with his gun on them, and MacNeil was forced to drive out the Mesa Road and out onto the mesa.

The *Times* of February 10 described what MacNeil later said in Hotel Dieu Hospital. MacNeil said the man told them he was a three-time loser, took their billfolds and watches, and ordered them to walk a distance away. MacNeil said he told Heaton in a low voice that the bandit was going to kill them, and they tried to "jump" him, but the bandit shot both of them, and fled on foot. Heaton was hurt so badly he could not walk. MacNeil placed his coat under his head in an effort to make him more comfortable, and then walked to Mesa Road, to the home of H. Arthur Brown, conductor of the El Paso Symphony Orchestra. He sat down in the living room, where he was found by a maid, who called the police. Heaton was dead when sheriff's deputies reached him. MacNeil was taken to Hotel Dieu, where he died on February 15.

Allen Falby was sheriff of El Paso County at the time. An Indian tracker made the mistake of saying he could find only two sets of tracks. Events showed plainly that the killer was there; he must have been wearing moccasins or soft shoes that left no footprints. The billfolds and watches belonging to MacNeil and Heaton were never found. MacNeil's automobile was not placed under guard to preserve fingerprints; the crowd that gathered was all over it. An El Paso woman, whose name was withheld for fear of reprisal, said she saw a man answering the description given by MacNeil. The killer must have walked to either the Mesa Road or the Upper Valley Highway, where he hitchhiked away. No trace was ever found of him, and the MacNeil-Heaton double murder remains a mystery.

Harry S. Truman

I had a number of occasions to see and talk with Harry S. Truman, once while he was a senator. He was a member of a congressional group which visited El Paso and Fort Bliss at the invitation of Congressman R. E. Thomason. Later I saw him when he said at the Chicago Democratic convention of 1944 that he did not care about being vice president. He visited El Paso as a candidate for vice president, and I was in a group that welcomed him at Union Depot. The *Times* supported Truman when he came here in 1948 during his campaign for reelection and his surprising victory over Republican Thomas E. Dewey. I wrote an editorial headed, "Welcome to El Paso, Fighting Man Truman."

Harry Truman is a 33rd Degree Mason; he was Grand Master of Missouri Masons at one time; he also is a Shriner. I heard him speak at Chicago in 1949 to the Imperial Council of the Shrine. Before starting his speech, he took off his fez, saying he was President of all the people.

I also saw President Truman in the White House on several occasions. The first time was in April, 1946, when he received the members of the American Society of Newspaper Editors in the East Room. The President told us in off the record remarks that the time had come for the United States to get tough with Soviet Russia. He was somewhat humble.

With Truman's election in 1948 he became a changed man. He was President of the United States in his own right, and he stood on his own two feet. He became belligerent toward newspapermen. I can't say I blame him because most of the nation's press opposed him.

In 1951, the convention of the American Society of Newspaper Editors came just after President Truman had fired General Douglas MacArthur as supreme commander in Korea. It was no secret that there had been a tug of war between Truman and MacArthur, and the latter was fired because he apparently refused to take presidential orders in the conduct of the Korean war. MacArthur arrived in Washington by plane shortly after I did; I saw him enter the Statler Hotel. It was expected that he would appear before the nation's editors, but he went straight to his room. Later that evening he sent word that he would like to see the ASNE members in the auditorium of the Statler. I had another engagement, so I did not go.

President Truman was scheduled to address the ASNE convention the next day, but he cancelled his date so that undivided attention could be given General MacArthur's appearance before a joint session of Congress. We had a huge television screen installed at our meeting place in the Statler and heard MacArthur's address to Congress. The day that MacArthur appeared before the joint session of Congress, General Omar Bradley, chief of staff, had an off the record meeting with the nation's editors. He talked from a stage in the auditorium in the Statler. He had large maps on the stage showing the position of United Nations and enemy divisions. General Bradley said if Congress should see fit to declare war the Armed Forces would fight it. But he warned that Soviet Russia had said it would enter the conflict under such conditions.

I always thought Truman was right in firing MacArthur. In our country, the civil government must be supreme; military commanders cannot be permitted to run things to suit themselves. However, I did not approve of the no-win policy in Korea any more than I supported the no-win policy in Vietnam.

When the American Society of Newspaper Editors met in Washington in April, 1952, President Truman had seized the steel industry to prevent a nationwide strike. The visiting editors took part in a presidential press conference. One editor asked, "Mr. President, do you think you would have the same right to seize the nation's press and radio that you had to seize the steel industry?" "The answer is 'Yes,'" Truman replied. "Next question." A blanket of cold air settled over the room. As I wrote before, Truman was already unpopular with the nation's press, and his reply to that question did not really help the situation.

The *Times,* long a stalwart in the Democratic Party, had been gradually turning against Truman. At that time, the *Times* added this paragraph to the paper's masthead which appeared daily and Sunday at the top of the editorial column:

> The El Paso *Times* is an independent Democratic newspaper. Traditionally, it is Democratic, but it will support that which it believes to be right and oppose that which it believes to be wrong regardless of political party.

Truman's seizure of the steel mills was staunchly resisted; the issue of his power to do so was taken to the Supreme Court. Justice Hugo Black, who wrote the majority opinion, said neither the law nor the Constitution gave the President the right to take over the steel mills. The 1952 steel strike was then called; it lasted for 55 days, the longest and costliest in the history of the steel industry.

I wonder what history will have to say about President Truman. It was he who ordered the atomic bomb dropped on Japan. He took over when FDR died and led the country to a successful conclusion of World War II. It was he who ordered American forces into action in Korea. Despite the occasions the *Times* disagreed with Truman and despite our editorial policy in the national elections of 1952, I think he was a strong President. He was not afraid to make world-shaking decisions. I still like the editorial I wrote in 1948 in which I called Truman a "Fighting Man."

Note: Harry S. Truman died December 26, 1972.

At an April, 1961 editor's convention in Washington, I visited in the old Supreme Court Chamber with Lyndon B. Johnson (then Vice-President), Charles Guy of Lubbock, William Stevens of Houston, and Jake Mehaffey of Texarkana.

CHAPTER ·VIII·

The Nineteen-Fifties

The Bataan Memorial Trainway

THE BATAAN MEMORIAL TRAINWAY, a project dreamed about for many years, the depression of the railroad tracks through Downtown El Paso, was one of El Paso's greatest achievements. Its total cost was $5.5 million, $2 million of which the people of El Paso voted by 3,707 to 345 as a bond issue on January 4, 1947. Dan L. P. Duke was acting mayor when the bond issue was approved and he was mayor at the dedication on August 21, 1950. I remember riding through the entire depression in an automobile with Mayor Duke before the tracks were laid.

The *Times* on August 22, 1950, had this big headline:

$5.5 Million Trainway Dedicated
Sunset Limited, Flat Car Train Run In Channel.

A byline story by Dale Cockerill said in part:

Thousands of El Pasoans Monday afternoon proudly witnessed the dedication of the $5.5 million Bataan Memorial Trainway and cheered when the first train, Southern Pacific's gleaming Sunset Limited, rolled into the city's long awaited train depression.

The solemn dedication ceremony at the Union Depot took on a circus air later when civic officials, rail leaders and Trainway boosters climbed aboard six gaily decorated flat cars pulled by a locomotive engineered by Mayor Dan Duke and followed the streamliner through the depression.

A bit of levity was added to the occasion when E. H. Will, who acted as Mayor Duke's "fireman," appeared in a pair of overalls that had been outgrown by Mayor Duke, a railroad engineer in private life.

Times Reporter Joe Parrish wrote in another byline story:

Credit for the Downtown Trainway belongs first to the people of El Paso, Mayor Dan Duke said in an address at a cocktail dinner held in the Country Club Monday night celebrating completion of the project.

Times Reporter Bob Chapman reported that 456 men attended a luncheon in Hotel Cortez that same day celebrating completion of the Trainway. It was a big occasion in El Paso.

This community had dreamed for many years of doing something about the railroad tracks that traversed the business district, with trains at times holding up traffic for long periods. *Times* Reporter Raymond J. Stover had an article in the *Times* of August 27, 1937, interviewing former Mayor Tom Lea, who said an effort was made in 1916 during his administration to correct the situation. The plan then was for a subway from Campbell Street past Santa Fe Street, with the railroads agreeing to bear the entire $1 million cost of the project. Stover quoted Lea,

> I went into office with a promise to remove the downtown railroad crossings. It was a campaign pledge of every administration since then.
>
> After the railroad officials had the matter thoroughly presented to them they agreed to do their part to relieve the traffic situation caused by long trains passing over the important crossings.
>
> After the contract was signed the City Council unanimously passed an ordinance providing that the railroads should construct the subway, eliminating railroad tracks on Main Street and paving the thoroughfare. They agreed to start the work within 30 days.
>
> It became necessary, however, for us to call an election upon the proposed closing of the intersection of Durango and Main Streets, which was desired by the railroads to prevent having to depress the tracks at the Union Depot.
>
> Certain opposition developed. Some folks talked of how the smoke from trains would be concentrated in the subway and would create a nuisance. Others opposed the project because they believed the railroads should be forced to build around the city, buying right-of-way along the river and building new tracks and yard facilities completely away from the city's downtown area.
>
> Immediately after I left office, Mayor Charles Davis called the election. It was held in July of 1917 and badly defeated.

Mayor Marvin Harlan and other mayors talked of track depression, but something always prevented it. Today, pedestrians and motorists passing over the Trainway do not even realize it is there. It was indeed a tremendous improvement for El Paso.

Lyndon B. Johnson

Lyndon Johnson and I were good friends in the old days, when he was a young congressman trying to unseat United States Senator W. Lee (Pappy) O'Daniel, when he defeated Coke Stevenson in 1948 by 88 votes, when he was a senator in Washington, when he was Senate majority leader, and when he was vice president. After President John F. Kennedy's assassination in Dallas November 22, 1963, Johnson took on a new proportion for me: he no longer was "Lyndon," he was "Mr. President." I have a number of pictures taken of me with Lyndon Johnson and I have a file of letters from him. The *Times* supported him when he ran for the Senate against O'Daniel, and he carried El Paso County. He asked me to call him "Lyndon" years ago; just about every newsman in Texas called him by his first name.

In my opinion, Johnson will go down in history as one of the most effective majority leaders the Senate ever had. Under Republican President Dwight D. Eisenhower, he and Sam Rayburn, as Speaker of the House, did a tremendous job for the American nation.

During the convention of the American Society of Newspaper Editors held in Washington in April, 1953, Senator Johnson and Secretary of the Navy Robert Anderson, another Texan, invited the Texas editors in attendance to go on a cruise down the Potomac on the secretary's yacht, the *Sequoia*, and I am confident they all accepted the invitation. Just as we were preparing to leave the dock, Secretary Anderson and another man whom I did not know were piped aboard. We all wondered who the other man was. He turned out to be a newspaper editor from Bay City, Michigan. Anderson's secretary had run the list of editors in attendance at the convention, picking out those from Texas. She concluded there could be only one "Bay City," and that was in Texas; thus the Michigan editor was invited to the Texas party. He had accompanied Secretary Anderson aboard by coincidence. We made him an honorary Texan. Lyndon Johnson and Bob Anderson were wonderful hosts.

During the April, 1961, convention of the ASNE in Washington, Vice President Johnson gave a cocktail party for the visiting Texas editors in the old Supreme Court quarters in the Capitol. I have a picture taken at that party. In it with Johnson and me were Charles A. Guy of Lubbock, Jake Mehaffey of Texarkana, and Bill Stevens of Houston. It was during that evening that I unintentionally angered Speaker Sam Rayburn; he and I had been friends for years. In conversation he asked me, "Bill, what do you think of my boy?" referring to Vice President Johnson. I asked him in turn, "While you were at it, Mr. Sam, why didn't you make him President of the United States?" Rayburn began to shake in anger. I was sorry immediately. I knew that Sam Rayburn had done his utmost at the Los Angeles 1960 Democratic Convention to get the nomination for Johnson, and that, after Kennedy was nominated, Rayburn felt it was somewhat a personal victory when Johnson was given the Vice Presidential nomination. The nation lost a man, in the death of Sam Rayburn, who always reminded me of a solid, sturdy oak tree.

When I was in Washington in April, 1964, for another ASNE convention, Lyndon Johnson was in the White House. Early that evening, as I was getting into a tuxedo to attend the annual banquet of the National Women's Press Club as the guest of *Times* Washington Correspondent Sarah McClendon, a White House call came that President Johnson expected me, along with other Texas editors, to come to the White House immediately. We were received in the President's living quarters in the White House, where Lady Bird, the lovely first lady, made us feel at home. The President talked and joked with us; he obviously was pleased to see some Texas friends. Those of us who were going to the women's banquet were late, but it was worth it.

On another occasion, in April, 1966, after Johnson was elected President, he invited the Texas editors to the White House. I have a picture of our group taken with him on the White House lawn. We all sat around a long oval table and the President had us take turns in asking him any questions we wanted to. It was then that the President told us he intended to appoint a Negro to the Supreme Court. I heard him say in the White House that he expected Russian bombs to drop on the White House right after he ordered the first bombing of Haiphong harbor.

In April, 1968, President and Mrs. Johnson invited all the ASNE editors and their wives to a White House reception. I was one of those Texans who were extremely proud to have a Texan as President of the United States. I was sorry to see Lyndon Johnson become so involved in Vietnam, but I am convinced he did exactly what he thought was right. I recall that when Johnson talked of being a candidate for the Democratic nomination in 1960, the *Times* spoke very favorably of him. When he became John F. Kennedy's running mate, the *Times* supported Richard Nixon, the Republican nominee. The *Times* strongly supported President Johnson in 1964.

It was my privilege to greet President Johnson when he was in El Paso to meet Presidents Adolfo Lopez Mateos and Gustavo Diaz Ordaz of Mexico. I received an invitation to attend the dedication of the great Lyndon Johnson Library at The University of Texas at Austin, but I had been ill and did not attend. I wonder what place history will give Lyndon Johnson. I think he was a man who strove to be loved; perhaps he tried too hard. I shall always have a warm place in my heart for him.

Note: Lyndon Johnson died January 22, 1973.

Fred Hervey

Fred Hervey had a turbulent but highly successful four years in the City Hall, one of the best mayors El Paso ever had. He had courage, and he did what he thought was the right thing for El Paso as a whole. The *Times* supported him from the beginning. During Hervey's administration, the city limits were extended in all directions, except across the Mexican boundary to the south. Today El Paso is a home rule city with its city limits north, east and west solidly established, taking in a large part of El Paso County.

The principal problem was annexing the Lower Valley, since most of the citizens there did not want to come into the City of El Paso. Hervey made speeches in Ysleta, telling the people they would be better off as a part of El Paso. On December 11, 1954, the *Times* reported that County Judge Hugh McGovern ruled that the City of El Paso could legally proceed with the annexation of additional Lower Valley area.

The *Times* quoted Mayor Hervey December 18 as saying,

> There are many urgent reasons for immediate annexation, including making it possible for Valley residents to vote on the administration under which it would be governed for the next two years.

On December 22, 1954, there was talk at an Ysleta High School meeting of legal action against the city. The *Times* said December 24:

> The Lower Valley will be annexed before the February city election, Mayor Fred Hervey announced Thursday after the City Council had acted unanimously in approving on first reading an annexation ordinance. The council approved the ordinance and immediately authorized publication of a new ordinance excluding from the annexation about 5,000 acres below Ysleta. Mayor Hervey said the new ordinance will move through the council "on schedule," allowing first reading Jan. 27 and adoption the following Thursday.

The *Times* on March 13, 1955, said the Lower Valley voted to incorporate the City of Ysleta, the measure carrying by 2,754 to 637. The *Times* said June 25, 1955:

> The city's annexation of the Lower Valley was legally sanctioned Friday in an Eighth Court of Civil Appeals ruling which voided the City of Ysleta incorporation election held earlier this year.

Some of the sting for Lower Valley residents was removed when the Ysleta Independent School District retained its identity. The annexation was probably Mayor Hervey's principal achievement. The *Times* had supported annexation of the Lower Valley right along.

Hervey had a number of other problems. In 1951 the city decided to submit an $11 million revenue bond issue for the Water and Sewer Department. The *Herald-Post* immediately opened up its big guns against the bond issue. Mayor Hervey, supported by the *Times,* contended that we must have additional water supplies. *Herald-Post* Editor E. M. Pooley said, editorially, time and again: "There's plenty of water; go find it." The *Times* reported on October 14, 1951, that the referendum for water revenue bonds was defeated 2,937 to 2,071, and for sewer revenue bonds 2,821 to 2,146.

Hervey had defeated Dan Duke in the February, 1951, Democratic primary. He was unopposed in the City Democratic primary February 28, 1953. Aldermen Tom Burnham, Hal Dean, Ernie Ponce, and Clarence Harper were elected for the second Hervey term.

Another fight developed in the city in the spring of 1954. A charter commission, chosen to write a new City Charter, had after long and hard labor come up with a proposed new Charter providing for a city manager form of government. Mayor Hervey and the *Times* supported the new charter, and the *Herald-Post* opposed it. Mayor Hervey did not interfere when city policemen and firemen canvassed the city in pairs opposing the charter, claiming it would adversely affect their pensions. The *Herald-Post* reported on May 31, 1954, that the charter was soundly defeated, 6,369 votes against, 2,997 for.

Mayor Hervey and County Judge Hugh McGovern deserve the credit for the City-County Building, a $3 million remodeling job on the old Court House. City and county governments are now concentrated in that one huge building. Hervey and McGovern had visions of this being the first step in the merger of the city and county governments.

I would like to digress from the Hervey story for a moment and pay a tribute to Judge McGovern. It was his work while county judge in obtaining right-of-way for the Freeway through El Paso County that put this community far ahead of the rest of Texas in that field. Interstate 10 runs from county line to county line, right by downtown El Paso, a modern improvement we have had for a long time.

Work on the City-County Building was exceedingly slow. The completed building was dedicated May 30, 1959, with United States Senator Ralph Yarborough as the speaker. Among the honored guests were former Mayor Hervey and former County Judge McGovern.

Mayor Hervey had continuing difficulties with *Herald-Post* Editor Pooley. Pooley regularly dubbed Hervey "The Hamburger King." The *Herald-Post,* in reporting a meeting of the trustees of the City Employes Pension Fund, quoted Hervey as saying, "After all, we only passed the 65-year-old rule to get rid of one employe." Hervey filed a libel suit against the *Herald-Post* and Editor Pooley on September 23, 1953, for $125,000, alleging that statement was untrue and damaging to him. On March 16,

1954, a jury in district court brought in a verdict in favor of Hervey, giving him $20,000 actual and $5,000 exemplary damages, but the Eighth Court of Civil Appeals reversed the lower court, holding that Hervey was a public figure. Hervey told me after Pooley had retired that he and the former editor had decided to bury the hatchet.

Hervey is an eminently successful businessman with widespread interests. In 1973, after this account was written, Hervey ran for Mayor against five other candidates, and, after a runoff against Hector Bencomo, became mayor. His entire ticket went into office with him.

Visit to Babicora

William Randolph Hearst's Babicora Ranch in Chihuahua was one of the largest to be found anywhere. Ed Ardoin, an El Paso cattleman, was manager of Hearst's ranching interests in Mexico. Hearst built a magnificent home on Babicora and he and Marian Davies spent some time there during the war. It was reported that he feared a Japanese submarine would appear and shell his castle-like California home at San Simeon. I had always wanted to visit Babicora, but invitations to outsiders were few and far between.

In 1952, negotiations were under way for the Mexican Government to take over Babicora and Ardoin no longer was manager. In June the El Paso Chamber of Commerce sent a good will delegation to Chihuahua City to pay a courtesy call on Governor Oscar Soto Maynez. I was chairman of that trip, and some of El Paso's top men went along; Congressman Ken Regan came from Washington to go with us. In Chihuahua City, an old friend, Jose Navarro Elizondo, who was acting as manager of Babicora, invited *Times* Publisher Dorrance Roderick and me to leave the good will party and fly to Babicora with him, and we accepted.

A young Mexican flier in a small plane with no radio flew us over the mountains from Chihuahua City to Babicora. We had an enjoyable couple of days in that magnificent home. The young Mexican flier came back for us two days later and, radio or not, he flew us to Juarez like a homing pigeon. I have often wondered what happened to that beautiful home on Babicora. It was wonderful to live like a king for a couple of days.

The Times Goes Republican

The year 1952 was an extremely important one in the history of the El Paso *Times*. As far back as anyone could remember, the *Times* had been a Democratic stalwart, supporting party nominees, right or wrong. In

1952, the *Times* supported General Dwight D. Eisenhower, the Republican nominee for President of the United States. Personally, I felt that way, too, and I wrote the pro-Eisenhower editorials with strong convictions.

Looking back over the copies of the *Times* of 1952, I found this editorial on May 20:

> Override Veto
>
> It is a foregone conclusion that President Truman will veto the tidelands bill which gives title to oil rich areas to the various states where it belongs.
>
> That seizure by the federal government, which was upheld by the Supreme Court of the United States, is undoubtedly one of the most flagrant steals in all history.
>
> Unless President Truman's veto is overridden by Congress, it will be another disgrace to be added to the long list of disgraces that have occurred during the Truman Administration.

That editorial seemed to sound the sentiments of the people of Texas, as they rallied to the Eisenhower banner in November, 1952.

I started out in earnest and early to take part in politics that year. I attended my precinct convention and was chosen a delegate to the county convention. At the county convention I was chosen a delegate to the state convention in San Antonio, helping to lay the groundwork for a split with the Truman Administration. On May 23, Sarah McClendon in a dispatch from Washington said:

> A delegation of Loyal Democrats of Texas in an effort to save Texas from going Republican will call at the White House at 2:30 p.m. Friday. . . . to try to get President Truman to change his stand of opposition to state control of the tidelands. . . .
>
> Both the Shivers faction and the Loyal Democrats fear that if Truman vetoes the tideland bill that Texas will go Republican in the presidential election.

In the El Paso County Democratic Convention, the unquestioned leader was Attorney Thornton Hardie, a strong advocate of state ownership of the tidelands. The El Paso delegation went to San Antonio under the banner of Governor Allan Shivers, but some did not agree. The *Times* of May 27 printed a dispatch from San Antonio which said:

> Texas anti-administration Democratic leadership once more attacked the national party Monday and set the stage for a certain bolt by the "liberal" faction at Tuesday's state convention.
>
> Protesting delegations from rump conventions in a bloc of nearly 30 counties, opposing Gov. Shivers and the conservatives, were denied seats by an overwhelming majority of the Executive Committee.

In "Everyday Events" of May 27, I wrote:

As this arrives in the hands of readers of this column, I will be in San Antonio to attend the State Democratic Convention as a delegate from El Paso County.

W. R. Blair, Col. Jack Ballantyne and I, forming a "Little Entente" or the "Three Musketeers," were to take a plane for San Antonio at 6:35 p.m. Monday, arriving there two hours later. Other El Pasoans attending the convention already had departed.

If events occur as expected, with a bitter fight on the floor in San Antonio and a walkout of so-called "Loyal Democrats," I should have considerable to write about.

As a little background, readers of this column might be interested in having a few of my thoughts on the subject.

In 1944, I was a pro-Roosevelt delegate to the Democratic National Convention in Chicago, I thought I was right then.

At this time, I am definitely against the "Loyal Democrats" because I don't believe they know what they are doing.

In my opinion, the conduct of President Truman in the last few years, particularly his outlandish attitude toward the tidelands, has changed the opinion of a majority of Texans toward the Democratic national leadership.

If the National Convention, also to be in Chicago this year, persists in backing up President Truman in his policy toward the tidelands, Texans attending the convention should walk out.

I do not want to see Texas in the Republican column in 1952, but I believe it will be there if President Truman stands by his guns on the tidelands and the National Convention backs him up.

I'm expecting to go to Chicago also to give readers of this column a firsthand account of what goes on there.

Governor Shivers had wired me expressing pleasure at the prospect of my being chosen to be among the Texas delegation to the National Convention. The *Times* reported in a San Antonio dispatch May 28:

Texas Democrats exploded Tuesday into two fighting factions, one electing national convention delegates promising to support its presidential nominees and the other refusing. The regular convention was dominated by Gov. Shivers and his conservative friends. . . .

Delegates to the National Convention from the 16th Congressional District were Attorney Eugene Smith of El Paso and Attorney Tom Sealey of Midland. Alternates at large included L. F. Miles and W. J. Hooten of El Paso and Mrs. Howard Hodge of Midland. . . .

The walkout came after Loyalists tried to win recognition for their delegates pledged to all out party allegiance. They lost on a point of order and Maury Maverick cried, "Let's go." They went.

It was revealed that Governor Shivers' personal choice for the Democratic nomination was Senator Richard Russell of Georgia. I wrote in "Everyday Events" of May 29:

El Pasoans starred in all four of the political conventions held Thursday.

In San Antonio, two women residents of Fabens, Ruby M. Wortham and Jewel Risinger, were among the Loyal Democrats who walked out of the State Democratic Convention following a call by Maury Maverick. . . .

At the regular convention, Attorney Eugene Smith of El Paso and Tom Sealy of Midland were named delegates to the National Convention with Maurice Bullock of Fort Stockton and Mrs. Henry M. Bailey of Alpine, as alternates.

Two El Pasoans, Leo Miles and I, were named alternates at large by the regular convention.

At the Republican convention held in Mineral Wells, Tad Smith, son of Eugene Smith, was named a delegate to the GOP National Convention by the Eisenhower group who walked out of the regular convention and held their own. . . .

R. E. (Bob) Cunningham, who was elected permanent chairman of the El Paso County Convention earlier this month, was named chairman of the 16th Congressional District delegation to the state convention. He handled that very efficiently.

Two other El Pasoans, Alderman Allen Falby and Alderman Clarence Harper, were named to the Committee on Delegates to the National Convention. Perhaps that is why two El Pasoans, Leo Miles and I, were named as alternates at large.

At the Republican National Convention held in Chicago, the Texas Eisenhower group was seated. A *Times* dispatch from Chicago July 8 said:

Texas' Eisenhower supporters voted jubilantly with the winning side Monday in the Republican convention's first test of strength between Gen. Eisenhower and Sen. Taft.

A *Times* headline July 12 said:

Ike Pledges Total Victory; Nixon Chosen Running Mate.

An Austin dispatch in the *Times* of July 14 said:

There had been hints that some Southern delegations would walk out of the National Convention in Chicago if the Shivers Conservative slate from Texas is not seated.

In a Chicago Associated Press dispatch by Dave Cheavens on July 19, the *Times* reported:

Two tough talking Texas delegations yelled "Victory or Nothing" Thursday in their demands to be seated at the Democratic National Convention.

The *Times* reported July 19 that Senator Estes Kefauver and Averell Harriman joined forces in an effort to seat disputed Texas and Mississippi delegations pledged to support any presidential candidate nominated by the Thirty-First Democratic convention. On July 21, I wrote from Chicago:

Maury Maverick, heading a pro-administration delegation of 52 members charged that Shivers is guilty of making nothing but foggy statements.

Maverick Saturday night attended a press conference in the Conrad Hilton Hotel with the delegation from Minnesota headed by Sen. Hubert Humphrey.

With the Minnesota delegation were four Negroes wearing badges bearing this slogan: "Seat Texas Maverick."

I wrote from Chicago July 22:

At the very first session of the Democratic National Convention it looked as though Governor Adlai Stevenson of Illinois could have the nomination for the presidency if he wanted it.

On that same day the *Times* published a dispatch from Chicago by Inez Robb of the International News Service quoting Governor Shivers as saying he could not promise support for a platform pledging federal ownership of disputed tidelands.

In the *Times* on that same date, a Chicago dispatch said:

W. J. Hooten of El Paso made the motion at the Texas caucus Tuesday morning that precipitated favorable action on the new rules change by the majority of the Texas delegates led by Gov. Allan Shivers.

Hooten took one look at the resolution and said: "I can go along with this."

As Shivers explained later, it is just what the Texas law now says, that officials shall put the nominees of the party on the Democratic ticket under the Democratic column.

Later Tom Sealy of Midland modified Hooten's motion by adding that the rules change is adopted as is but with the explanation that this does not mean the delegates are taking a pledge to support the nominees or the party platform unseen.

Under a Chicago dateline July 25, I wrote:

Texas' 52 votes remain pledged to Sen. Richard B. Russell until the senator releases them, Gov. Allan Shivers said Thursday.

I also wrote that Texas' delegates took a pledge to assure the convention nominees a place on the Texas ballot and that Texas would stay with Senator Russell until he left the race.

The *Times* carried a headline July 26: "Demos Nominate Stevenson." On July 27 the *Times* headline said: "Stevenson And Sparkman Team Leads Democrats Against GOP; Sen. John J. Sparkman of Alabama Vice President."

I wrote from Chicago:

With the Democratic Convention over, many Texans probably are asking themselves just what their delegation, headed by Gov. Allan Shivers, did at the national conclave.

A simple answer to that question is:

They cast their 52 votes for Sen. Russell of Georgia on all three ballots and did not waver and vote for Adlai Stevenson even though the Illinois governor was nominated "by acclamation."

Sen. Sparkman was nominated vice president without aid from Texas. When the word came down to the state delegations that Sparkman was Stevenson's choice for a running mate, Gov. Shivers declared that Texas could not support him.

Shivers contended that Sparkman was against Texas in the fight to regain control of the tidelands.

The *Times* published an Associated Press article August 15 saying:

Gov. Allan Shivers' rampant forces were in firm control of Texas Democratic Party machinery Saturday as the party held its county conventions.

Most of the meetings were mild, sugar and honey affairs, with Shivers forces in firm control.

The Democrats of Texas began preparing for the State Convention to be held in Amarillo.

On September 5, the *Times* said:

Delegates from El Paso County will go to the State Democratic Convention in Amarillo prepared to work for a ballot arrangement permitting Texas Democrats to vote for Republican nominees without voting Republican. R. E. Cunningham was named chairman. . . .

Delegates of the 29th State Senatorial District will caucus at 8 p.m. Monday in the lobby of the Herring Hotel in Amarillo. Present at the pre-trip meeting were Mr. and Mrs. R. E. Cunningham, W. C. Burgie, Ben Turner, Thornton Hardie, K. B. Ivey, Homer Hirsch, Mrs. William Flournoy, Leo F. Miles, State Rep. S. J. Isaacks, W. J. Hooten, Col. Lucius Patterson, Mayor Fred Hervey, Volney Brown, and Eugene Smith.

The battle at the Amarillo convention was hot. A September 8 dispatch from Amarillo said:

Shocked and furious anti-administration Texas Democrats growled "Bolt" and "Third Party" Sunday as delegates girded for Tuesday's state convention.

Gov. Allan Shivers' sudden surprise announcement Saturday that he had given up his search for a "legal and honorable way" to let Texans vote for Dwight D. Eisenhower as a Democrat bomb-shelled the pre-convention crowd.

A stiff fight was put up in an effort to keep Stevenson and Sparkman off the ballot in Texas. R. E. Cunningham of El Paso was among those who wanted their names kept off. That group was reminded time and again that the Texas delegation to the Chicago National Convention had pledged to put their names on the ballot. The *Times* headline of September 10 said: "Texas Democrats Put Stevenson on Ballot; Ask Shivers To Work For Ike."

I returned home from the Amarillo convention and the *Times* prepared to do battle in support of Eisenhower. The *Times* had been the leading voice in the Democratic Party in the Southwest for a long time, but in the Sunday *Times* of September 14 we had an editorial written by me in collaboration with *Times* Publisher Dorrance Roderick favoring the election of Eisenhower. Under the heading "Elect Eisenhower President of U.S.," the editorial said in part:

> After much thought and observation, the *Times* recommends that its readers vote for Dwight D. Eisenhower for President of the United States. In coming to that decision, this newspaper was not unmindful of this statement of policy which it has published under its masthead for some time:
>
> "The El Paso *Times* is an independent Democratic newspaper. Traditionally it is Democratic, but it will support that which it believes to be right and oppose that which it believes to be wrong, regardless of political party."
>
> The *Times* is convinced that the election of General Eisenhower as President would be right and to the best interests of the nation as a whole for these reasons:
>
> Conditions in our Government in Washington have become so unsatisfactory under the leadership of Harry S. Truman that a new broom is needed to sweep out the mess.
>
> Gov. Adlai Stevenson, the Democratic nominee for President, is so burdened with obligations that he could not correct those unsavory conditions as well as General Eisenhower, even though we assume Stevenson personally would like to do so.
>
> If the *Times* thought Governor Stevenson could do a better job of straightening out our Federal Government than General Eisenhower could, we would endorse him for election without a moment's hesitation.
>
> JUST TOO MUCH
>
> In arriving at its decision to support General Eisenhower, the *Times* believes it is entirely consistent with its frequent protests in recent years against the trends in Washington.
>
> The *Times* has had enough of creeping socialism, influence peddling, mink coats, tax frauds, Communist infiltration in high places, etc., which have hit a new high since 1948.
>
> But, equally important, the *Times* has become increasingly alarmed over the effort to centralize too much power in the Federal Government, to the detriment of state government, such as the seizure of the tidelands.
>
> The *Times* lays much of the present unsavory condition in Washington at the door of President Truman mainly because he is not a strong leader.

He is impetuous. He jumps before looking and then does not have the courage to admit his errors and try to correct them. . . .

WE WANT ACTION

Regardless of those facts, however, the *Times* did not rush in to endorse or support anyone. It made no pre-convention commitments.

This newspaper has carefully observed the campaign methods of General Eisenhower and Governor Stevenson.

Eisenhower unquestionably has advice from some sources objectionable to the *Times,* but, when he is elected, we believe he will do his own thinking and have the courage of his convictions.

Stevenson is a polished politician who in political debate probably could tie Eisenhower in knots. But we are not interested in Stevenson's debating ability. What we want is the unsavory condition in Washington straightened out. The *Times* believes Eisenhower, with his direct approach, could do better than Stevenson could.

REALIGNMENT NEEDED

The *Times* further believes that present wide political differences throughout the land portend a realignment of political affiliations.

The *Times* has wanted such a realignment since 1944 when it became apparent that many Democrats, mainly those in the South, had reached a point where they felt they had no political home and that many Republicans, mainly in the North, felt the same way.

The *Times* sincerely hopes that the next four years will bring about such a realignment. The *Times* wants to feel at home in any political party with which it becomes affiliated even temporarily.

After a vigorous campaign by both the Republicans and the Democrats, election day, November 4, 1952, rolled around. The *Times* in a big headline November 5 announced: "Ike Wins in GOP Landslide; El Paso Follows Trend to Ike." Eisenhower, the second Republican in 100 years to carry Texas, received 677,390 Texas votes to Stevenson's 581,397. In El Paso County, the count was Eisenhower 14,108 to 10,341 for Stevenson. Dwight D. Eisenhower became President, Texas got its tidelands back and holds them to this day, and the El Paso *Times* continues to be an independent newspaper.

That was the last time I ever played a personal part in politics; after that election, I sat on the sidelines. A personal highlight of the 1952 campaign involved my daughter Grace and me. As editor of the *Times* I came out for Eisenhower. As editor of the *Prospector,* publication of the then Texas Western College, she came out for Adlai Stevenson. *Time Magazine* took note of that situation and had a story about us.

Richard M. Nixon

Richard M. Nixon always seemed to be a favorite of the American Society of Newspaper Editors. I believe he appeared before that group more times than any other man. I was at the ASNE luncheon in April, 1954, when Vice President Nixon, answering a question off the record, said he favored sending American armed forces into Indo-China to help the French. The American press respected Nixon's wishes to be off the record, but an English journalist published what Nixon had said, and it then was published world-wide.

Secretary of State John Foster Dulles tried to soft-pedal what Nixon had said, claiming the United States had no intention of sending troops into Indo-China, After his 1960 defeat for the presidency and after his defeat for the California governorship, Nixon continued to appear before the ASNE. It was obvious that the editors liked him; he always handled himself well. The *Times* supported Nixon in 1960 and again in 1968.

Nixon as President seems to be having some difficulty with the press. He has been criticized for not holding more press conferences. By the way, I never did think presidential press conferences were fair, with him having to stand there and answer questions, many of them loaded. In the old days, Presidents, when they held press conferences at all, demanded written questions submitted in advance.

Nixon also has Watergate and tax problems. He seems to be in deep trouble.

Working Trip to Europe

Publisher Roderick assigned me to accompany a group from the United States Society of Editors and Commentators to Europe and the Middle East in March, 1956. It was not a sightseeing trip, but one on which I was to interview kings, presidents, foreign ministers, and prime ministers and write a series of articles for the *Times*. I made that trip and wrote articles from Madrid, Casa Blanca, Tunis, Rome, Athens, Cairo, Tel Aviv, Paris, Bonn, and London.

The Middle East was then in turmoil, just as it is today. The interview we had with Colonel Gamal Abdel Nasser impressed me a great deal. We were all seated at a large oval table, when suddenly the curtains were drawn and there was Nasser. He talked to us an hour, then submitted to questions for another half hour. He said the Americans of the days of our Revolution would understand the problems of Egypt today better than we did. He kept referring to the British as "the enemy still at the canal."

I was also deeply impressed by an interview we had with Prime Minister David Ben-Gurion in Tel Aviv. He reminded us of a character right out of the Old Testament. In one breath he hurled defiance at the enemies of Israel and in the next he held out the olive branch to his Arab neighbors.

Ben-Gurion said he knew Israel could not have a high standard of living if its neighbors were living in poverty. At one point a member of our group told Ben-Gurion the Arabs feared that the Israelis were ambitious to extend their boundaries from the Euphrates to the Nile. "Those people are ignorant," he thundered. "When we were led out of Egypt we were told never to return."

In Rome we were honored by an audience with Pope Pius. I held a number of medallions in my hand when we were blessed by the Pope. I brought them home and gave them to my Catholic friends, who appreciated them greatly.

An interview we had in London with Lennox Boyd, secretary of state for colonial affairs, left a bad taste in my mouth. At the time, there was trouble on Cyprus because of the activities of Archbishop Makarios, and Boyd was highly critical of the conduct of the United States in that situation.

My contact and experience on that journey were of much value to me.

The Battle of 1957

Tom E. Rogers was sworn in as mayor of El Paso in April, 1955, after Mike Misenhimer, elected by a tremendous vote in the Democratic primary, said he did not want to serve. I was a member of the committee which met on a Sunday afternoon and recommended to the City Council that Rogers be named to serve out Misenhimer's term. I thought Rogers made an excellent mayor. He was conservative, thought well before he acted, and was a credit to the city.

When Rogers announced for election in the 1957 City Democratic Primary, he was opposed by County Clerk Raymond Telles. Telles and his ticket, calling themselves the "People's Ticket," had the support of the *Herald-Post*. The *Times* was for Rogers and immediately dubbed the Telles ticket "The P-for-Pooley Ticket." There followed one of the roughest and toughest campaigns in the history of El Paso. The candidates, Rogers and Telles, never said particularly unkind things about each other, but the *Times* and the *Herald-Post* fought each other tooth and toenail.

We had front page editorials. The following appeared in the *Times* February 17, 1957:

A Serious Matter

It seems impossible that any man who offers himself for mayor of a city the size of El Paso could be so careless in talking about city affairs.

Speaking before the Sertoma Club, the head of the "P-for-Pooley" ticket said the city should have sold $3,829,000 in bonds by now and be working on improvements for which they were voted last November.

The candidate spent some time in the City Clerk's office last week looking for campaign ammunition .If he had taken five minutes to ask City Clerk Joe Herrera about these bonds he would have learned the facts. He would have learned that the city was obligated not to market the bonds until 90 days after the Public Service Board sold its own bonds in November.

The *Times* said editorially February 18:

Two Weeks To Go

Clear The Atmosphere

As we enter the last two weeks of the campaign preceding the March 2 City Democratic Primary, let's endeavor to get down to brass tacks.

Judson Williams, manager of the ticket headed by Mayor Tom Rogers, is asking that the opponent, County Clerk Raymond Telles, discuss the campaign issues with Rogers on a joint television program. Mayor Rogers has added his voice to the invitation.

It is assumed, of course, that the sponsor of the "P-for-Pooley" ticket will have to be consulted before a reply will be forthcoming.

The *Times* said on its front page February 21:

City politics hit a torrid pace Wednesday when the candidates faced off before the Del Norte Club in Hotel Paso del Norte.

The candidates set a slow starter pace, but a flood of questions from the floor drew fire and ended with County Clerk Raymond Telles asking: "Any more loaded questions?"

Before the curtain rang down on the noon political rally, Telles answered a question, "Who are the Kingmakers?" with "I can only refer you to Pooley."

The *Times* said February 22:

County Clerk Raymond Telles again dodged a television debate with Mayor Tom Rogers when the candidates for mayor appeared Thursday before the Rotary Club in Hotel Paso del Norte.

The invitation was renewed by Mayor Rogers asking Telles to appear with him on a half hour televised program where the men could give their views and answer questions on city affairs.

Mayor Rogers repeated the invitation Thursday and Telles carefully sidestepped by first saying he had not been asked personally and later by insisting he had nothing to debate.

That Page One article was accompanied by a front page editorial with this head: "TV Offer Still Open." The editorial declared the people were still waiting at their television sets, and asked, "How about giving him the green light, Mr. P."

The *Times* said in a front page editorial February 24:

Exploding a Myth

Let's nail down the phony claim that Raymond Telles has been something special as a county clerk.

Taking credit for turning in money to the county from the operation of the clerk's office makes about as much sense as if the tax collector were to boast of turning millions into the treasurer.

In a front page editorial March 1, the *Times* said:

People's Ticket

El Paso goes to the polls Saturday for a showdown. . . .

Tom Rogers stepped out of his business two years ago to become mayor after Mike Misenhimer, elected by the biggest vote ever given a local candidate, could not serve. Tom Rogers has had two fine years as head of El Paso's city government, giving us an economical, level-headed administration, serving efficiently and courteously in a period of most difficult decisions.

He is opposed by a ticket that is the echo of the *Herald-Post*. There is not one good reason why it should be trusted with the reins of our municipal government. . . .

Instead they have campaigned on holes in the streets, tumbleweeds near the stockyards, audits of city departments covering years before Tom Rogers ever walked into the City Hall.

On May 3, the *Times* had this big headline: "TELLES ENTIRE TICKET WINS."

County Clerk Raymond L. Telles swept to the Democratic nomination for mayor in Saturday's Democratic Primary by more than 2,500 votes out of a record 34,863 in defeating Mayor Tom Rogers. Telles carried with him his entire aldermanic ticket without a runoff.

South Side, East Side and Lower Valley precincts gave Telles a runaway lead that Rogers could not overtake.

Aldermen elected with Telles were Ernie Craigo, Ted Bender, Ralph Seitsinger, and Jack White. The count was Telles 18,688, Rogers 15,934.

The *Times* front page carried statements from both Rogers and Telles.

The *Times* said editorially Monday morning:

County Clerk Raymond Telles has been nominated mayor of El Paso by the largest vote ever cast in a Democratic primary in this community. The *Times* congratulates him and all his ticket. . . .

As a good citizen the *Times* willingly will abide by the decision and will continue to work for a better El Paso.

But the fight was not yet over. A write-in campaign for Mayor in the general election April 9 was started by M. R. Hollenshead. The *Times* said on its front page April 8, "El Paso's first organized city write-in political campaign swings into high gear Monday with volunteer workers urging support for M. R. Hollenshead in Tuesday's general election."

The *Times* reported April 9 that Hollenshead had made a strong race, under the circumstances, but Telles had won easily, 16,895 to 8,787.

Attorney George Rodriguez, a good friend of mine and now a district judge in El Paso, said to me after the election, "That was a revolution, not an election." It certainly was an outpouring of Mexican-American votes, and many Anglos also voted for Telles.

Raymond Telles served two terms as mayor of El Paso. He had what I would call a "warm" administration, constantly endeavoring to make friends with the people. He and I never were unfriendly, and in later years we became very good friends.

To keep the record straight, however, I feel that I should relate an incident that occurred between us in connection with an editorial I wrote July 15, 1958. The issue involved a critical tour of the new city jail in the City-County building taken by Mayor Telles with reporters on the day before he left for two weeks of active duty as an Air Force officer and while County Judge Hugh McGovern was on vacation. The absence of both Telles and McGovern effectively defeated further exploration of an important issue bearing upon the Democratic primary election, less than two weeks away. The editorial wondered whether the Mayor had intentionally precipitated the issue just before his departure in an effort to influence the election.

The editorial prompted an emotional letter from Telles, hand-delivered to me in my office on the afternoon of July 23, 1958, by Mayor Pro Tem Ralph Seitsinger. I have kept that letter in my personal file since that time. It was five pages, single-spaced, and quite vituperative, charging me with "malicious insinuations" and "unjust accusations." He disclaimed any interest in any of the County political contests except as a voting member of the community, and he mentioned two previous occasions in particular in which he thought I had been unfair to him.

I feel no animus whatever in raising this matter. I believe Raymond Telles felt better after getting that off his chest. We are warm friends today. He came to the *Times* office on October 20, 1960, to attend a gathering held in observance of my 20 years as editor. Telles served with distinction as our ambassador to Costa Rica. He came home and was chairman of the United States-Mexican Commission of Development and Friendship (CODAF). He ran unsuccessfully for Congress against Richard White in 1970. Today he has a highly important position with the Office of Economic Opportunity in Washington. I wish him well.

El Paso Couple Disappears

El Paso and the Southwest have had a number of mysterious disappearances and murder mysteries, but one of the most baffling cases in modern history concerns William D. Patterson and his wife, Margaret, who disappeared late March 5 or early March 6, 1957. Former *Times* City Editor Ed Engledow and *Times* Reporter Bill Cook, both of whom are no longer with the paper, had much to do with investigating the disappearance. Bill Cook and his wife rented the Patterson home at 3000 Piedmont and lived in it during much of the investigation into the couple's disappearance. I was in the Patterson home while the Cooks were living there. Engledow and Cook, in 1958, wrote a resume of the Patterson case and left it in the *Times* files.

Engledow and Cook wrote in part:

The latest and most baffling mystery of the U.S.-Mexican border, where mysteries are not uncommon, is the disappearance of William D. and Margaret Patterson, well-to-do operators of an El Paso photo supply house.

The Pattersons came to El Paso penniless in the early 1940s. He began work as a street photographer. As their financial condition improved, they opened a photo supply shop and their business success has been phenomenal. They expanded into the wholesale field and the firm has grossed at least $250,000 annually for the past several years.

The couple enjoyed their financial success. They purchased a luxurious home in one of the better sectors of town. They drove a Cadillac and a Volkswagen. They owned a summer cabin on Elephant Butte Lake in New Mexico. They made frequent vacation trips into Mexico, devoting much time to fishing. They frequently took part in the night life of Juarez.

On the surface, they were living the happy life of a couple who had found a hard-earned financial success and were enjoying it to the utmost.

Before March 5, 1957, there was no indication of the things which were to come.

It was on that night that the Pattersons disappeared. D. G. Kirkland, a business friend, told police that during the early morning hours of March 6, he received a telephone call from Patterson. Patterson told him "Margaret is on one again," and indicated she had found another woman's picture in his billfold. He told Kirkland he was parking his Cadillac in the driveway of Ward's Motor Clinic and asked Kirkland to have minor repairs made on the car. He indicated he was leaving town "for a few weeks," according to Kirkland.

Cecil Ward, operator of the Motor Clinic, where the car appeared the next morning, was a personal friend of Patterson's. On March 4 he had spent some time with them. He planned to help Patterson work on his boat in the Patterson garage on the night of March 5, but became ill and cancelled the date.

On March 16, 1957, Herbert Roth, free lance auditor who kept the Pattersons' books, received a telegram dated the previous day and sent from Dallas.

It instructed Roth to put Kirkland in charge of the business. He was to have Art Moreno (a photo shop employe) cancel reservations in Washington, D.C., for the couple's attendance at a photographers' convention. He was to rent the house for nine months, sell the house trailer and use the money in the business, and license both autos for use of the firm.

Roth was urged to handle things as quietly as possible. The telegram was signed "Pat." Subsequent investigation determined that it was sent from a pay phone near Love Field in Dallas. It has never been substantiated that it was ever sent by Patterson who habitually used the long distance phone in preference to a telegram.

During the summer months of 1957 nothing was heard of the Pattersons. Ward became disturbed, although Roth repeatedly indicated to him that he was not worried. Sometime during the summer, Ward's concern took him to the sheriff's department and an undercover investigation was launched. On Aug. 15 the El Paso *Times* uncovered the disappearance and broke the story.

The investigation has continued and has been expanded since that date. At the editorial insistence of the *Times,* the Department of Public Safety entered the case early in 1958.

False reports and leads have been numerous. The Pattersons have been reported in a Texas sanatorium, on the West Coast, in Mexico, etc. All have proved false.

Since the disappearance the operation of the business by Roth and Moreno has been above question. Early in 1958 the first court action was taken when Roth was appointed receiver and the firm is now operating under court direction.

So far as can be determined, no one has profited from the disappearance. No one except the Pattersons' families could profit in the future and the couple would have to be declared legally dead before they could share in the estate.

A letter purportedly was received from Laredo in which Patterson was supposed to have written that he was all right. That letter was introduced in a court of inquiry into the Pattersons' disappearance. District Attorney William E. Clayton was quoted by the *Times* on August 16, 1958, as saying the Laredo "mystery letter" which had been used in the June court of inquiry was not signed by the missing man.

The *Times* of June 27, 1964, said:

Mr. and Mrs. W. D. Patterson, who disappeared March 6, 1957, were declared legally dead late Friday by Judge Richard Crawford in the County Court-at-Law.

Judge Crawford appointed Herbert Roth of El Paso, a certified public accountant, as the administrator of both estates and authorized that their wills be probated.

The Patterson case appears in the news every so often, but no trace has ever been found of either of them. My personal belief is that both of them were murdered the night of their disappearance and are buried somewhere on the mesa near El Paso. What was the murderer's motive?

Your guess is as good as mine, but I have never been able to believe that anyone, of his own volition, would walk off and leave a lucrative business such as the Pattersons had in El Paso.

End of The City Democratic Primary

The *Times* is entitled to a great deal of credit for spearheading the drive to eliminate the City Democratic Primary, but its efforts would have failed if City Democratic Chairman Robert Haynsworth had not supported the charter amendment which meant putting himself out of office. Haynsworth was quoted in the *Times* of January 10, 1959, as branding the City Democratic Primary "entirely unnecessary."

That article in the *Times* added:

> In a landslide of opinion started by a *Times* editorial Friday morning which pointed out it cost the mayor $2,400 to file for reelection, other prominent El Pasoans fell solidly in line with the stand that the primary is wasteful and unnecessary. Former mayors joining in the plea to eliminate the City Democratic Primary were Tom E. Rogers, Dan L. P. Duke, Dan Ponder, Fred Hervey, and U.S. District Judge R. E. Thomason.
>
> The mayor of El Paso receives $9,600 a year. Of this he must pay back $2,400 each two years as a filing fee for his office to help finance the Democratic primary. It amounts to a $100 a month pay cut which is not deductible from income taxes.
>
> Judge Thomason said: "Primaries staged by any political party in a city election of the type El Paso traditionally has had are a waste of time, money and effort."

The *Times* said April 10, 1959, that Mayor Raymond L. Telles joined the five former mayors in backing the charter amendment eliminating the primary.

The *Times* reported on April 15 that the charter amendment dropping the City Democratic Primary carried 7,089 to 4,577. The city general election today is nonpartisan. Anyone who wishes to be a Republican on the state and national levels still can offer himself for mayor or alderman of El Paso without partisan disadvantage. In that way, the city does not deprive itself of the services of good men because of their party affiliation. The School Board also operates in that manner. The 1959 charter change was a great step forward for El Paso.

In that same election, as reported in the *Times* of April 15, El Paso County voters gave a resounding approval to a $3.7 million bond issue for a new City-County Hospital. The magnificent City-County Hospital was built with Hill-Burton assistance; it was named for Judge R. E. Thomason. I am convinced that if the voters had known what the new hospital district would mean in additional taxes, they might not have approved the bond issue; the hospital district taxes are almost equal to the levy by El Paso County. I think the R. E. Thomason Hospital is a decided asset to El Paso.

Prominent Attorney Slain

Dr. Harold Eidinoff on January 28, 1959, shot and killed Attorney Ted Andress at the International Airport. Andress was a prominent lawyer and president of the El Paso School Board.

The *Times* of January 29 published a full account of the slaying. The trouble apparently began when Mrs. Eidinoff sued for divorce. She went to El Paso Attorney Leo Jaffe who set a fee of $5,000. Eidinoff insisted that was too high and retained another lawyer. The divorce was obtained. Jaffe sued Eidinoff for the $5,000 fee, contending that he had been retained, and Andress represented Jaffe in that action. Jaffe obtained a judgment against Eidinoff; a nude picture of Eidinoff appeared in the case. Trouble developed between Eidinoff and Andress. Andress won a suit against Eidinoff for slander, and started action to seize some of Eidinoff's property to satisfy the judgment.

The city was shocked on that January evening in 1959 when Andress, returning from a school meeting in San Francisco, was shot down by Eidinoff at the airport. Eidinoff had concealed a pistol in a hollowed-out book and had so disguised himself that acquaintances at the police station had difficulty in recognizing him.

After much legal argument, Eidinoff obtained a change of venue to Lubbock. Following a lengthy trial there, Eidinoff was adjudged insane and was committed to the State Hospital for the Insane at Rusk. For several years, Eidinoff instituted legal actions seeking release and contending he was sane. Each year, the El Paso district attorney journeyed to Rusk to oppose Eidinoff's petitions, and each time Eidinoff was sent back to the hospital.

Finally, on November 4, 1968, following a hearing on an Eidinoff application, he just disappeared. It was reliably reported later that he had gone to New York and that he was practicing medicine there, but apparently no effort was made to return him to Rusk. Several El Pasoans who had been victims of Eidinoff's wrath were reported fearful that he might return to El Paso, but, as of this writing, nothing further has occurred.

On June 5, 1963, President John F. Kennedy came to El Paso. I joined him on the platform at El Paso International Airport as he addressed the crowd.

CHAPTER ·IX·

The Nineteen-Sixties

John F. Kennedy

JOHN F. KENNEDY'S assassination in Dallas November 22, 1963, was a great tragedy, but I never saw any reason to blame the people of Dallas for that event, any more than the people of Los Angeles should have been blamed when the late President's brother, Robert F. Kennedy, was killed there. Dallas just happened to be the city where Lee Harvey Oswald killed the President.

Frankly, I was disappointed in the conduct of President Kennedy during the unsuccessful invasion of Cuba in 1961. I don't pretend to know what he should have done, but I heard him say, at a luncheon of the American Society of Newspaper Editors in the Statler Hotel in Washington on April 21, 1961, that the United States would not abandon the Freedom Fighters at the Bay of Pigs. But we did.

President Kennedy's "eyeball to eyeball" confrontation with Soviet Premier Nikita Khrushchev later during the Cuban missile crisis was hailed as a victory for the United States, but I don't know whether it was or not. The Russians are supposed to have withdrawn their missiles from Cuba, but the United States in return had to give its word not to invade Cuba. Since then Cuba apparently has been turned into an armed Communist camp only 90 miles from our shores. It has never made sense to me that we are fighting communism in Southeast Asia, half way around the world, but tolerating it at our back door.

I heard John F. Kennedy make a great speech in Washington in April, 1960, telling the nation's editors why his Catholic religion should make no difference in his candidacy for the Democratic nomination for President. He was applauded warmly and made many friends that day; it was a wonderful speech. As history shows, he went on to receive the nomination and win the Presidency.

I saw President Kennedy and Vice President Johnson when they were in El Paso in June, 1963. *Herald-Post* Editor R. W. (Pete) Lee and I drove to the International Airport together to meet them. We were invited to sit on the platform of dignitaries to hear President Kennedy's address. I was presented to President Kennedy by Texas Governor John Connally. I was impressed by the way Kennedy looked persons presented to him straight in the eyes, as if he were trying to determine what they were thinking about.

Perhaps I am somewhat prejudiced, but I never liked the way President Kennedy appeared to place Vice President Johnson on a shelf. On his side of the bargain, Johnson never overlooked an opportunity to praise Kennedy. Neither did I like the way the Kennedy clan turned on Johnson after he became President. President Johnson put over the Kennedy program in Congress after Kennedy's death, and it looked to me as though much of the abuse that Johnson received later derived from parts of that Kennedy program.

John F. Kennedy has his place in history, and it is terrible that he was shot down, but there is absolutely no way of telling how history will be shaped by unexpected, unscheduled, and sometimes violent events.

Woodrow Bean

When young Woodrow Bean first offered himself for Congress in the special election in 1947 to fill the vacancy created by the resignation of Representative R. E. Thomason, who had been named a federal judge, Thomason said that Bean had "political *it*." That must have been true, as this account will show. Bean began serving in the Texas Legislature as an extremely young man; he was only 29 when he first ran for Congress. He lost to Ken Regan in 1947 and again in 1948.

Then Bean became a candidate for the State Senate in the special election of November 2, 1954, called to replace State Senator J. T. (Slick) Rutherford, who had been elected to Congress. Other candidates for the State Senate were Attorney Frank Owen III of El Paso, a member of the House, and Fred Wemple of Midland. The *Times* supported Bean and the *Herald-Post* supported Wemple.

In going through Bean's file in the *Times,* I ran across this excerpt from an editorial which appeared in the *Herald-Post* October 7, 1954:

> In the campaign now being waged there are two candidates from El Paso — Frank Owen and Woodrow Bean.
>
> Mr. Bean, we have learned to our sorrow, is not politically reliable. He doesn't seem to understand loyalty. He is an opportunist. He seeks office only for the benefit of Woodrow Bean. Today you may think he is on your side; tomorrow you will find he isn't and never was.

That was the same *Herald-Post* which had supported Bean for Congress against Ken Regan.

Results of the special election November 2, 1954, as reported in the *Times,* were Frank Owen 8,282, Fred Wemple 6,798, and Woodrow Bean 6,026. Thus Owen won a seat in the State Senate without the support of either El Paso newspaper.

Bean was elected El Paso County Judge in July, 1958, defeating Ken Braxton by some 200 votes. He was an energetic county judge; he was in that office when the new City-County Building was dedicated and when the Sun Bowl was built.

By 1962 he had acquired quite a state-wide reputation, and he offered himself for congressman-at-large from Texas in the Democratic primary May 5, 1962. The *Times* supported Bean for Congress, with several complimentary editorials, until he was charged with failing to file his income tax return. The *Times* in a page one editorial May 1, 1962, withdrew its support from Bean, saying in part:

We Cannot Support Bean

The *Times*, in good faith, endorsed the candidacy of County Judge Woodrow Bean for the Democratic nomination for congressman-at-large.

We did so in the belief that he would be of good service in Congress to the entire State of Texas, and more particularly to his native West Texas.

It is now, with regret, that we withdraw that endorsement.

We cannot support any man for public office who admits that he has flaunted the law of the land, particularly through open defiance, as is in the case of Woodrow Bean. He has admitted that he has not filed a federal income tax return since the year of 1952.

In what we think was a ridiculous press conference in Houston after declining to make any statement in his home city of El Paso, Judge Bean made assertions that we cannot permit to go unchallenged.

For example, Judge Bean was quoted by the Associated Press as saying in Houston:

"At least 50,000 people in my home county and throughout Texas knew it (that he had not filed an income tax return since 1952.) It was an issue in my campaign for county judge and I have been elected six times by the people who know me in El Paso County in spite of it."

We condemn those statements as being untrue. If Judge Bean's income tax was an issue in the 1958 campaign, when he was elected county judge here, we did not know about it. And if Bean has been elected six times by the people who know him in El Paso County, in spite of it, we do not know about that either. And we think we have been on top of the news for many, many years.

Judge Bean also was quoted as saying he believes the federal income tax is "economically unnecessary, illegal and immoral."

For a man holding the office of county judge and running for Congress to make such a statement is amazing. We did not think Judge Bean was capable of such open defiance of the law. . . .

In plain words, Woodrow Bean has defeated himself, at least it would seem he has destroyed the chance he had of being elected to Congress.

We are astounded that he even offered himself knowing that he had violated the law and that he would be caught up with, sooner or later.

Came the election May 5 and Woodrow Bean astounded the State of Texas by leading the field for congressman-at-large, despite his income tax troubles; he led Joe Pool of Dallas by 226,782 to 201,278, carrying El Paso County impressively, 4,126 to 1,463. Pool defeated him in the runoff June 2, 1962, 570,743 to 448,449, and in El Paso County 9,826 to 6,363.

On June 18, 1967, Bean pleaded guilty to charges of having filed no income tax returns for the years 1956-61; the *Times* of September 27, 1967, stated he was fined $5,000 and placed under five one-year suspended sentences. He was released on three years' probation. Federal tax liens totaling $41,341.90 were filed against former County Judge Woodrow Bean and his wife Maxine, encumbering property owned by the couple until the tax claims were paid.

I agree with Judge Thomason's 1947 comment that Woodrow Bean had "political *it*." He probably would have been elected congressman-at-large in 1962 if it not been for his income tax troubles. Today, he is a power in state Democratic politics; press dispatches from meetings of the State Democratic Executive Committee quote what Bean has to say. He was chairman of the El Paso Housing Authority. Later he was named chairman of the State Advisory Council on Housing.

For my part, I always liked Woodrow Bean; he was an outgoing person. He was mostly a little too liberal for me, but he has an uncanny knack for winning political friends. The day after an election, Bean would walk into my office in the *Times* and shake hands with me, even though we had opposed him, and say, "There's always another time." He is that sort of fellow. It was a hard chore for me to write that page one editorial withdrawing support from him when the scandal broke during his race for congressman-at-large.

The Civic Center

I wish I had a nickel for every word I have written down through the years in support of a civic center for El Paso. That project always was high on my list of community "musts," because I have seen other cities forge ahead with civic centers or convention halls while El Paso lagged behind.

Dr. Maurice Spearman in 1960 headed the first move to get a civic center in El Paso. I wrote many columns and editorials in support of that project. The election was held November 8, 1960, on that and several other issues. The bond issue for construction of the Sun Bowl was approved but the proposed civic center and other issues went down to defeat. The vote for the Sun Bowl was 13,896 for and 12,310 against, and the civic center lost 11,977 for and 12,890 against. The late Marshall Willis, who had led the Stadium drive, and all athletic buffs in the city were elated over the Sun Bowl victory.

In 1962, a power-packed organization headed by Banker Sam D. Young was started in El Paso, with a civic center as its principal project. The *Times* and the *Herald-Post* strongly supported the proposed civic center; the *Times* had a series of front page articles. A site was selected in Downtown El Paso, and an issue of $7.75 million general obligation bonds was proposed, along with a tax of 3 per cent on room occupancy in hotels and motels. The community's young business and professional men went on television and talked convincingly for the civic center. But we were doomed to disappointment again; the *Times* headline of December 12 said, "Center Issue Defeated; Tax Approved." The bond issue lost 11,394 to 9,020, but oddly enough the voters approved the room occupancy levy on hotels and motels, 11,123 to 9,717.

The civic center idea lay somewhat dormant for a while and then the *Times* revived the proposal, with a straw vote conducted in the home edition of our Sunday *Times*. The result showed conclusively that the people of El Paso wanted a civic center but were divided over its location. I wrote many columns and editorials again stressing the necessity of a civic center. There had been some talk that Mayor Ralph Seitsinger had not given full support to the proposal during the 1962 election. I was convinced that Dr. Judson Williams, who in 1968 was in his third term as mayor, was for a civic center, but he was waiting for the right time to submit it to a vote, since he did not want to see the issue defeated a third time.

Finally, Mayor Williams called an election for June 22, proposing a $15 million bond issue for the civic center, with no increase in property taxes, and gave the project his wholehearted support. The *Times* again conducted a vigorous campaign. Mayor Williams' leadership was superb. The issue carried 12,829 to 10,431.

The civic center is being erected in much the same location as that proposed before the 1962 election. There have been a number of delays in the construction. No date was set for completion of the job when the City

Council entered into the construction contract, and no penalty was provided. I am not being critical, but it seems to be obvious that is the main reason in the delay of completion. I hope the people of El Paso will be satisfied with the civic center, but I fear some will say it is not large enough.

The main problem was caused by the delay in finishing the theater area.

Almost A Woman Mayor

If circumstances had developed just a little differently, El Paso could have elected a woman mayor in 1961. Mrs. Julia Breck, wife of Dr. Louis Breck, a prominent El Paso physician, conducted a vigorous campaign and went into the runoff with Alderman Ralph Seitsinger, who had been on the City Council of Mayor Raymond Telles. Mrs. Breck was very well known in El Paso; she had strong opinions on numerous controversial subjects, and she was a strong candidate.

The *Times* reported on March 25, 1961, that, in a field of six candidates, Mrs. Breck had run second to Ralph Seitsinger. The runoff campaign was vigorous and spirited. The *Times* reported April 5, 1961, "Ralph Seitsinger won Tuesday's runoff election for mayor in heavy voting that cut across ticket lines and narrowly defeated two aldermanic candidates running with Seitsinger on the 'Peoples Ticket.'" Seitsinger defeated Mrs. Breck 17,253 to 15,755, and for aldermen Bert Williams defeated Ernie Craigo, Ray S. Watt won over John D. (Dan) Patton, and R. R. (Buck) Rogers beat Albert Armendariz; Ted Bender had won an aldermanic seat in the first election.

Mayor Seitsinger had a turbulent two years in office. On several occasions, irate citizens practically took charge of City Council meetings. It was during Seitsinger's term that the second unsuccessful bond issue election on the civic center took place. I heard comment that Seitsinger did not provide sufficiently strong municipal leadership for that important project. Seitsinger is a likeable person, but city politics got somewhat out of control during his administration. He offered himself for reelection in 1963 against potent competition and did not survive the primary.

Dr. Judson F. Williams

Dr. Judson F. Williams, in my opinion, must rank among the strong mayors El Paso has had in modern times. He had knowledge, confidence, resourcefulness, and unflinching courage. Williams had the support of El Paso's business community, but he stood on his own feet. It was during Williams' administration that the gigantic project got under way of giving the Chamizal Zone to Mexico, with the construction of new bridges across the Rio Grande, relocation of displaced families, and the fixing of the new river bed as the permanent boundary line between the United States and Mexico. Williams in 1963, with a strong aldermanic ticket, ran against an impressive array of candidates.

The campaign was on a high level, but no punches were pulled. The *Times* took no part in the campaign preceding the first election, beyond reporting what the various candidates had to say. In the election on March 30, 1963, the *Times* reported Williams polled 9,198, Charles B. Moore 7,233, Ralph E. Seitsinger 5,678, and Mrs. Julia Breck 4,865, followed by four also-rans, with Dr. Williams and businessman Charles B. Moore entering the runoff.

Both men, with their aldermanic candidates, asked for *Times* support, but since either was entirely acceptable, we withheld endorsement. The *Times*, in a front page story by George Kinsinger on April 10, 1963, said:

> Dr. Judson F. Williams led three members of his "All El Paso Team" to victory in Tuesday's runoff election for mayor and alderman in one of the most closely contested races in the city's history.
>
> Dr. Williams, executive vice president of the White House Department Store, defeated businessman Charles B. Moore by a scant 831 votes out of a total of 34,039 cast, carrying 39 of the city's 60 voting precincts.
>
> In an even closer race, Fred McKinstry, member of the Moore "Sound Business Government" ticket, edged out retired Sears, Roebuck manager Joe E. Walters by 83 votes.

The *Times* reported Williams received 17,342 votes to Moore's 16,511; winning aldermanic seats were Hector Bencomo, Ashley Classen, Fred McKinstry, and Oliver Nordmarken.

The City ran smoothly during Mayor Williams' very successful first two years in office. In 1965 Williams was opposed by two "Ed Langs," but one of them belatedly added the name "Earl" to his name to signify the difference. The *Times* of March 26, 1965, reported that Judson F. Williams won handily, polling 16,429 votes to 8,946 for Ed (Earl) Lang and 2,613 for Ed Lang. Ed (Earl) Lang continued in the limelight, and in 1967 he again was a candidate for mayor against Williams.

On March 26, 1967, George Kinsinger had this on the front page of the *Times*.

> Mayor Judson Williams gained a near two to one margin over Ed (Earl) Lang to win a third two-year term as El Paso's mayor Saturday, sweeping three of his four "All El Paso" team running mates into office with him.
>
> Oliver G. Nordmarken, an original member of Williams' 1963 ticket,

failed to gain a majority and went into the runoff with J. Warren (Pappy) Hoyt.

The vote was Williams 15,589 and Lang 8,661. The *Times* refrained from endorsing either Nordmarken or Hoyt in the runoff. We had only praise for Nordmarken, but we could not recommend voting against Hoyt, who had for years directed all Sun Carnival Parades and had rendered many other services to the community. Hoyt won in the runoff and served on the third Williams Council.

It was during Mayor Williams' third term that a charter commission, headed by Jack Vowell, Jr., proposed a new city charter. The *Times* had reported faithfully on developments on the charter commission. When the charter was completed and submitted to the people, the *Times* opposed it. Our principal objection was that the proposed new charter had to be either accepted or rejected in its entirety. El Paso voters rejected the proposed charter, said the El Paso *Times* of July 30, 1967, by a decisive 8 to 1 margin, 9,733 to 1,233. Later Mayor Williams submitted a list of amendments which were approved. Mayor Williams had to his credit that he submitted the civic center to a vote again and it was approved. The *Times* supported Williams every time he ran except the first. Mayor Williams resigned March 1, 1969, to enter private business, and Alderman Ashley Classen finished out his term.

I should like to tell where I first met Judson Williams, of whom I have always been personally fond. Frank Junell was public relations man at the College of Mines and organizer of the Southwest High School Journalism Association. He and I traveled to various West Texas high schools and attended meetings of that association. In 1938, Junell asked me to go with him and be the speaker at the annual banquet of the Grandfalls, Texas, High School Journalism Department. Grandfalls is a small community southwest of Odessa. There we met a young journalism teacher, Judson Williams, whose father had been assistant pastor of the First Baptist Church in El Paso. Williams impressed me then as a go-getter. Later he joined the faculty of the College of Mines and obtained a doctor's degree. Thereafter he became an executive of the White House Department Store. In addition to his success in politics, he also was seriously mentioned for president of The University of Texas at El Paso. Today Judson Williams has a prominent place in the El Paso business community.

In and Out of Congress

Representative J. T. Rutherford of Odessa, who defeated Ken Regan for Congress in 1954, lasted eight years on Capitol Hill. He was defeated in the 1962 general election by Republican Ed Foreman, also of Odessa.

Republican United States Senator John Tower, said the *Times* of November 2, addressed a capacity crowd at a dinner in Hotel Paso del Norte in support of Foreman, phrasing the crucial need for forceful voices to express the conservative will of the American people.

In an editorial November 4, the *Times* said in part:

> Foreman's opponent, J. T. Rutherford, has had almost eight years in Congress to prove of value to the nation and his district. We think he has fallen down.
>
> We need a conservative and a man with get up and go. We have that man in Ed Foreman.

The *Times* on November 5 said 30 prominent El Pasoans who had termed themselves "Democrats and Independents for Ed Foreman for Congress" had issued the following statement:

> We the undersigned Democrats desiring to express our confidence in the honesty, integrity and conservatism of Ed Foreman and believing these qualities to be of utmost importance in a candidate for Congress, warmly endorse the candidacy of Ed Foreman.

In the Democratic primary that summer, Congressman Rutherford had experienced a rough and tumble campaign against El Paso Attorney Tom Diamond, in which he was charged with dealings with Billie Sol Estes. This statement appeared in the *Times* of May 24 in a dispatch from Austin:

> United States Representative J. T. Rutherford reported to the Texas secretary of state that he received a $1,500 check last January 17 from Billie Sol Estes.

A dispatch from Dallas appearing in the *Times* of August 8, 1962, said:

> An El Paso bank official was subpoenaed Tuesday to bring records of the bank accounts of Rep. J. T. Rutherford and his wife for examination by the special grand jury checking promoter Billie Sol Estes.
>
> Rutherford, in whose 16th District Estes built much of his financial complex, has been repeatedly linked to the bankrupt financier. . . .
>
> Rutherford acknowledged last May that he received a $1,500 check from Estes as a campaign donation when Estes visited his office Jan. 17.
>
> Rutherford was quoted as saying, "I could have dropped my teeth" when he found a record of the Estes donation.

District-wide returns from the general election of November 6 showed Foreman the winner over Rutherford, 41,627 to 35,044. Foreman carried El Paso County 16,618 to 16,087.

Republican Ed Foreman lasted only two years in Congress, and then El Paso Attorney Democrat Richard C. White rode into office with President Lyndon B. Johnson's 1964 landslide, 64,871 to 50,808. The *Times* did not endorse either Foreman or White. White was an effective vote getter. The vote in El Paso County was White 34,608 and Foreman 21,337.

White had won the Democratic nomination for Congress by defeating El Paso Attorney Malcolm McGregor. Congressman Foreman had predicted to me in Washington before the Democratic primary that McGregor would face him in November. White proved to be a resourceful and energetic campaigner; he was too much for McGregor and for Foreman.

Richard White is making an effective, hard-working, conscientious congressman. He proved his strength by handily defeating former El Paso Mayor Raymond Telles in the 1970 Democratic primary. I predict that Richard White will remain in Congress about as long as he wants to.

A feature of the 1962 election was the campaign by Mrs. Lydia Stark for county school superintendent; she advocated abolishing the office, since the last county school had become an independent district. Mrs. Stark piled up the biggest Republican vote in El Paso County, said the *Times* November 7, defeating the Democratic incumbent, John T. Bean, by more than 3,500 votes, 17,706 to 14,124. Mrs. Stark's wish came true; the County Commissioner Court, all Democrats, abolished the office.

The Mayor of 1969

The campaign for mayor of El Paso in 1969 produced a spirited race. Former Alderman Bert Williams was back in the running. So was Ed (Earl) Lang. The top runner was former Chamber of Commerce president Peter de Wetter, who barely squeaked by without a runoff. The vote was De Wetter 16,418, Lang 4,021, and Williams 12,031, said the *Times* of March 30.

I heard De Wetter say in an address before the Rotary Club of El Paso that South El Paso housing was the most important problem facing the community. South El Paso has its objectionable features, but the low rent there is attractive to the residents and makes it difficult for the owners of that property to offer all modern conveniences. Residents of South El Paso move to other parts of the city when their circumstances permit it. New people coming from Mexico keep up the pressure on South El Paso accommodations. It is a tremendous problem, but, compared to some cities, El Paso's "slums" are minor indeed.

Mayor de Wetter undertook turnkey construction to help correct the housing situation. The new turnkey housing was to be constructed in various parts of the city. The Lower Valley received the most attention, but some residents there protested the increased load on the public schools. Those turnkey projects are rapidly being completed; I hope they bring the necessary housing relief.

I think Peter de Wetter was a good, sound mayor, and I mean absolutely no criticism of him, but I thought he should have made an agreement with the contractors who are building the civic center for a completion date, with a penalty clause. The longer the civic center completion is delayed, the more convention business El Paso will lose.

Although I had retired, I watched the election of Bert Williams in 1971 over Alderman Clinton Wolf. Hector Bencomo, alderman under Mayor Judson Williams, and Sal Berroteran, a member of the Judson Williams and the De Wetter councils, were two of Bert Williams' aldermanic candidates. The *Herald-Post* supported the Wolf candidates in the runoff. The *Times* supported the Williams slate. All of the Bert Williams ticket won, with the exception of Glenn Woodard, who lost to independent candidate Tony Petry.

Mayor Bert Williams also tried to do something about South El Paso. The people of El Paso voted on urban renewal. I am glad I did not have to make the decision whether or not the *Times* should support the urban renewal proposal. Basically, I am opposed to urban renewal, but it is clear that conditions have changed. El Pasoans soundly defeated urban renewal in November, 1972. Cities and school districts all over the nation have men whose sole duty is to figure out ways and means of taking full advantage of available federal funds, but that does not make it right. I still think states, counties, cities, and school districts should stand on their own feet and retain their sovereignty, not be controlled by Washington. With the national debt what it is, I wonder where all that federal money is coming from.

Editors and politicians meet frequently, and in the picture above I visited with Richard C. White in Washington in April, 1967.

CHAPTER ·X·

Of Many Things

Men in Politics

A TEXAS POLITICIAN whom I always liked, but whom I never supported, was Ralph Yarborough. I am certain that I wrote the first newspaper story about him that ever appeared. Yarborough had come to El Paso early in 1927 right out of law school. He joined the prestigious law firm of Turney, Burges, Culwell and Pollard. His main job seemed to be filing papers in the court house. I was covering that beat for the *Herald*. In those days, *Herald* reporters had to turn in so many feature stories a week; I wrote one about Yarborough and his filing of papers for that big law firm. Yarborough has mentioned that to me several times down through the years.

Yarborough wanted to be governor of Texas, but he was defeated every time he ran. He became a district judge in Austin and I was told by my friend, the late Charles Green, editor of the Austin *American-Statesman*, that Yarborough was an excellent judge. He ran for the United States Senate and was elected. The *Times* never supported him because he was too liberal; I have sometimes wondered whether he was liberal because he wanted to be or because that was where his political strength lay. I am not questioning his sincerity, but I do not believe that Yarborough was a liberal at first.

I saw the senator almost every year in Washington, and we always reminisced about old times in El Paso. When Yarborough was running for reelection he always called on me, even though we were not supporting him. I received a very friendly telegram from him upon my retirement. I did not think the people of Texas would defeat Ralph Yarborough, but they chose Lloyd Bentsen over him. Then later Barefoot Sanders defeated him for the Democratic Senatorial nomination, only to lose to John Tower in the Nixon landslide of 1972.

The two governors of Texas whom I admired the most were Allan Shivers and John Connally. When Shivers first ran for lieutenant governor in 1946, State Senator H. L. (Heinie) Winfield of Fort Stockton brought him to the *Times* office and introduced him to me. Winfield, whom we supported, recommended Shivers, who then also was a state senator. The *Times* supported him for lieutenant governor, and he won. A year later, I was master of ceremonies and Shivers was the speaker at the annual banquet of the El Paso Chamber of Commerce in Hotel Paso del Norte. Shivers was a strong leader and a very forceful man.

In 1952, while Shivers was governor of Texas, he led the Texas delegation to the Democratic National Convention held in Chicago and battled for the tidelands. As an alternate delegate-at-large from Texas at the convention, I saw the masterful way he handled things. He wanted a commitment from Adlai Stevenson that the tidelands would be returned to the states, but he never got it, and he later led Texas in support of the Republican nominee, Dwight D. Eisenhower. Texas got its tidelands back. Shivers supported the Republican nominee for President, Richard M. Nixon, in 1960. He later became president of the United States Chamber of Commerce. He is now a member of the Board of Regents at The University of Texas. Shivers was, and still is, truly a great Texan.

John Connally had a bitter foe in Senator Ralph Yarborough, and practically all of the liberal element in Texas was against him. The only criticism that I could ever make of Connally was that he did not appoint enough West Texans to state boards and commissions, but he was a strong governor and led the state along the path of progress. Connally barely beat Houston Attorney Don Yarborough for the Democratic nomination for governor in 1962. The *Times* had strongly supported Connally. On election day, before the votes were counted, Connally told me by telephone from Austin, "Bill, regardless of how the vote goes, I want to thank you for the strong support the *Times* gave me."

I have always regretted that Connally and Ralph Yarborough did not oppose each other for office so the voters of Texas would have been given a clearcut choice. In one sense they did, for Connally was a leader in Lloyd Bentsen's successful Senatorial race against Yarborough in the 1970 Democratic primary. Connally did an outstanding job as secretary of the Treasury in President Nixon's Cabinet, and managed the "Democrats for Nixon" in 1972, helping to carry Texas and other traditionally Democratic states for the Republican candidate. Connally turned Republican early in 1973. That should strengthen the Republican Party in Texas, and I think we need two strong parties in this state.

About Speeches

During my years as managing editor and editor of the *Times,* I made many speeches in various communities in the Southwest. At one time or another, I have been on the program at just about every wide place in the road. I was the speaker at three annual banquets of the Pecos Chamber of Commerce. I have talked to luncheon clubs, lodges, conventions, and practically all other types of gatherings. I never was much of a speaker, but my job called for me to try.

In a January, 1951, meeting of the New Mexico Press Association in Truth or Consequences, I was the banquet speaker. In that talk I chided the legislative branch of our government for surrendering its constitutional authority to the executive branch. I said the same thing in a talk at a night meeting of the Kiwanis Club in Roswell later in 1951. J. J. (Jim) Kaster, then district governor of Kiwanis and later El Paso's postmaster, was at that meeting. It was particularly interesting to me to see United States Senator Lloyd Bentsen make much the same assertions at the annual banquet of the El Paso Chamber of Commerce on September 13, 1971. The closest tie we have with our government in Washington is our congressman. The President is far removed from us and a United States senator has so many constituents that he cannot pay much attention to the average citizen.

During the summer of 1955 I addressed a meeting of the New Mexico Press Association held in Ruidoso, in which I said the nation's labor unions had accomplished their goals since federal law had given them all they had striven for down through the years, and I saw no need for the labor unions to continue. They should retire and rest on their laurels. Remember, I was talking to newspaper publishers. The *Times* quoted me on the front page the next morning and the *Labor Advocate* of El Paso sharply criticized me, the labor unions on the newspaper demanding equal space in the paper to reply. I finally weathered that storm without too much difficulty. I recall, however, that in the lobby of the Navajo Lodge that evening I came across Lincoln O'Brien, a progressive New Mexico newspaper publisher, who patted me on the back and said I had more courage than brains.

Maybe so, but I think today the nation's labor unions have entirely too much power. They can practically shut down the country, and the citizen is forgotten in the struggle between capital and labor. The Taft-Hartley Act helped some, but Congress is afraid of organized labor, as indeed also are most candidates for President. Some day, the American people will wake up and become the bosses in this country, and the laws then will protect the public against capital and labor alike.

One of the most aggressive unions in the United States is the American Newspaper Guild, which started with newspaper reporters but has expanded to include other newspaper employes. It appeared in El Paso during the depression when I was managing editor of the *Times.* I thought I should belong to any organization of reporters, and I attended the organizational meeting held in the room of *Herald-Post* Reporter Marshall Hail on Montana Street. I resigned when it became a member of the CIO; I had considered it a purely professional organization. There is no doubt that the Guild has raised the pay of working newspapermen, but it is difficult for a union reporter to be objective in covering the news. The Newspaper Guild remained in El Paso for about 15 years, negotiating contracts with the *Times* and the *Herald-Post,* and then it disappeared from the scene. In its day, the Newspaper Guild has put good newspapers out of business; it is a potent union.

Back to my speech-making career. I think the highlight of my speaking career came in January, 1959, when President Roger Corbett of New Mexico State University had me deliver the address at their commencement after the institution became a university.

Following my return from Europe and the Middle East in 1956, I made some 35 speeches before luncheon clubs and other organizations. In retirement I am relieved of that responsibility; my present status has decided advantages.

Unusual Friends

It has been my good fortune down through the years to have many friends, and I value each one. Among my unusual friends I would place Roark Bradford and his wife Mary Rose; Owen (Slim) Matthews, sheriff of Grant County, New Mexico; and Thomas E. Kennedy, president of the United Mine Workers of America.

Roark and Mary Rose Bradford started coming to El Paso for the winter in 1933, living in a suite in Hotel Paso del Norte. Bradford, America's foremost writer of Negro stories, had a market for all the stories he could turn out. He was author of OL' MAN ADAM AND HIS CHILLUN' from which Marc Connelly took his immortal play GREEN PASTURES. The Bradfords and I became very good friends. They were "night people;" I would go to their suite for a chat after I finished work on the *Times.*

Bradford once asked me to bring him some copy paper, and I took him a supply of the green paper we used to publish extras. Being from New Orleans, and somewhat superstitious, Bradford thought that green paper brought him luck and wanted more; even after he returned to New Orleans I sent him a supply by mail. The Bradfords continued coming to El Paso for the winter for about 15 years and made many friends in El Paso. He died in New Orleans around 1951, and Mary Rose died in Los Angeles in 1969. They easily were among the most colorful people I ever met.

Sheriff Slim Matthews of Silver City was a most interesting Southwesterner. I am proud that he and I were good friends, even though he may have been somewhat on the rough side.

One day Slim made me a regular deputy sheriff of Grant County. He said now I would have to have a "wee-pun," and he gave me a blackjack covered with the soft hide off a testicle of an unborn calf and autographed it "Slim." I still have it and would not take anything for it. Slim Matthews ran a wide open town in Silver City. One time he ran for reelection and won on a campaign that Grant County did not need a sheriff.

In those days I traveled to most of the conventions of the New Mexico Sheriffs and Police Association with Ray C. Suran, special agent in charge of the FBI office in El Paso, whose jurisdiction then included all of New Mexico. I was a dues-paying member of the association, and even had insurance with it which applied in the event I was killed while on duty. I was present at the meeting in Las Cruces in 1946 when Slim Matthews was defeated for president of the sheriffs association by Roy Kerr, sheriff of Hidalgo County (Lordsburg). Slim was offered the vice presidency, but he refused it.

I met Thomas E. Kennedy through his wife, the former Evelyn Fay, to whom I was introduced in Washington by Congressman Ken Regan in 1954. Mrs. Fay had accompanied me to several banquets of the American Society of Newspaper Editors and after she married Kennedy in 1959 they had me to dinner every time I was in Washington. Kennedy succeeded John L. Lewis as president of the United Mine Workers of America; earlier he had been lieutenant governor of Pennsylvania. He and I hit it off great talking politics. He was continuously inquisitive concerning what the people of Texas were thinking and talking about. In 1960, he favored a Democratic ticket of Senator Stuart Symington and Senator John F. Kennedy. Tom Kennedy was quite a man; he died in 1966. I valued his friendship highly.

The Wrong House

In August, 1945, Allen Bruce and I flew to Albuquerque to represent El Paso at the annual meeting of the Albuquerque Chamber of Commerce. We visited Secretary of Agriculture, later Senator, Clinton P. Anderson in his home while we were there. Bruce and I, in a borrowed car, drove to the University of New Mexico where he was graduated, and went to a dwelling which at one time was his fraternity house. We boldly entered and began to walk around, not knowing the house had been taken over as a dormitory by a women's organization. We soon learned when a young woman appeared obviously fresh out of a shower. We beat a hasty retreat. Dan Burrows, editor of the Albuquerque *Tribune,* poked big fun at us in his column.

It was during that trip to Albuquerque that Bruce and I called on an old friend of his, Lester Cooper, the son of a Presbyterian minister. We arrived at his home before Cooper did and we planned a charade with Mrs. Cooper. When Cooper arrived, Bruce introduced me as a Presbyterian minister. We carried on that masquerade for a half hour, knowing that Cooper was craving a drink but deferring to the visiting "Reverend." Finally I blurted out, "How long does a fellow have to wait around here for a drink?"

El Paso on The March

One of El Paso's main attractions that I have seen grow from its inception in 1935 is the Southwestern Sun Carnival with its Sun Bowl football game. The first football classic was played in the El Paso High School Stadium January 1, 1935. The El Paso Kiwanis Club brought in a powerful team from Ranger to play a composite team of El Paso high school players coached by College of Mines Coaches Mack Saxon and Harry Phillips. The El Paso team won.

Dr. C. M. Hendricks conceived the idea of an organization patterned after that of the Tournament of Roses in Pasadena, California, with its Rose Bowl. Dr. Hendricks had practically no financial backing at first and he proceeded carefully. He asked Chester Chope, managing editor of the *Herald-Post,* Jack Castel, managing editor of the *World News,* and me to handle publicity. We wrote and helped circulate the publicity for the fledgling Southwestern Sun Carnival.

The first pageant, or parade, on January 1, 1936, which wended its way through El Paso's business district, on Texas Street, Mesa Avenue and Montana Street, was tremendous. The floats were practically all homemade. One particular float that I remember portrayed the meeting in El Paso and Juarez in 1909 of Presidents William Howard Taft and Porfirio Diaz. Roy D. Jackson was perfect as President Taft.

The football game that afternoon between the New Mexico State College and Hardin-Simmons ended in a 14-14 tie. The *Times* was not prepared for the magnitude of the first parade and football game, and we were two or three days getting the pictures published. In future years, we organized for the occasion and took the Sun Carnival in our stride.

Dr. Hendricks has been dead for some time. But the Southwestern Sun Carnival has grown and prospered. We have the 30,000-seat Sun Bowl, which was voted by the people of El Paso County and deeded to The University of Texas at El Paso. The Sun Bowl football classic is televised and millions of Americans see it. We also have a great invitational basketball tournament. And the coronation of the Sun Queen is a colorful affair every year. The Southwestern Sun Carnival has really arrived and now receives the national publicity it so richly deserves. It is a source of great satisfaction, if somewhat amazing, that year after year, the organization goes forward with new men and women handling the various functions.

Another El Paso County attraction which has grown with the years is the Fabens Cotton Festival. That began in a small way in 1947, when Robert H. Vickers, general manager of the Fabens Cotton Compress, had a few people in for cocktails and dinner in the backyard of his home in Fabens. Newly elected Congressman Ken Regan and I were among those present. The Fabens Cotton Festival, held in the Compress, has grown year after year, with various organizations sponsoring young women who compete for the honor of being named queen of the festival. The winner goes on to Memphis and competes for the title of Maid of Cotton.

I was a judge of the young women participating in the Fabens Cotton Festival in 1953. Miss Beverly Pack, now Mrs. James A. Dick, Jr., was the winner; she went on to Memphis and was chosen Maid of Cotton on January 6. 1954.

Robert H. Vickers is dead, but his son, Bob, carried on, serving as master of ceremonies at the annual Cotton Festival and as host at a large cocktail party held in the Vickers back yard at Fabens. Young Bob died March 1, 1973. I have missed only one of the Cotton Festivals, the one in 1970 when I was ill.

A Well-Kept Secret

Dave Lawson, operator of the Knickerbocker Club, was a political power in El Paso and was recognized as the top man in the gambling fraternity. I knew him to speak to, but we never were close friends. This is a story of a well-kept secret.

About 12:30 a.m., one night in the spring of 1936, I was in the composing room of the *Times* making up the home edition, when Lawson entered and approached me. He inquired if he had ever asked a favor of me, and when I replied no, nor I of him, he said, "Now I'm going to ask you to do something for me."

Lucy Stevenson, top woman in the red light district, had suspected her husband, Buddy Stevenson, of consorting with another woman. On this occasion, Lucy supposedly saw Buddy up the street and decided to take a pistol shot at him. Lawson said he had left the Knickerbocker Club and was walking to his car; the bullet hit Lawson in the back of his trousers, and he had just come from having his superficial wound treated. "No one would ever believe that Lucy Stevenson was not shooting at me," Lawson said. "I don't want any mention of it in the paper. I would never live it down." There had been no police report on the incident and I agreed not to publish anything about it.

Talk of "Payoff"

I have heard all sorts of rumors down through the years about a "payoff" in El Paso for the protection of gambling and prostitution. There seems to be no doubt that some public officials have taken money at times, but it has been rare. I have also known several newspapermen who took money for favorable publicity or for the suppression of publicity. There was talk at one time that the "payoff" while the Knickerbocker Club was flourishing ran as high as $1,500 a week. Trying to prove such a thing or to convict anyone for it would be well nigh impossible.

In the 1930s, the *Times* carried on a game. We would send reporters to the various clubs and report gambling was in progress. The next day we would report that the gambling was closed. Of course, it opened again. Perhaps some men in public office favored an open town. There never was a man with higher ethical standards than Mayor R. E. Sherman, and yet El Paso had a zone of tolerance while he was mayor. Slot machines were operating, purportedly under a federal injuction, and a person could buy liquor by the drink in El Paso's bars. Then Sherman declared determined war on organized gambling; the gamblers helped finance the campaign of P. D. Lowry who ran unsuccessfuly against Sherman in 1935.

I recall one incident when I sent two new *Times* reporters to the gambling places and they reported gambling in progress. The next day I was called before the Grand Jury. I asked that I not be forced to divulge the names of the two new reporters, because, if they were seen entering the Grand Jury room, the gamblers would identify them and in the future would not admit them to the gambling places. The foreman of the Grand Jury agreed with me. The next morning, however, the assistant district attorney informed me he would have to have the names of those two new *Times* reporters; they were Martin O'Neil and LeRoy Nigra.

One incident occurred in 1930 while I was city editor of the *Herald* which I shall never forget. A prosperous looking man traveling with hunting dogs and a cook stopped in El Paso on his way to Arizona. He had known Mrs. Hooten while she was a student at the University of Arizona in Tucson; he was at that time a mining man. He invited us to have dinner with him at his motel and in turn was invited to my home for dinner. Late in the evening he told me he operated slot machines in San Antonio and wanted to extend his operations to El Paso. He asked me what my salary was and said he would match it if I would arrange for El Paso officials to return any of his seized slot machines to him instead of destroying them. I told him I was not interested.

Outstanding Mayors of El Paso

I have been asked a number of times who I thought was El Paso's outstanding mayor of the last 50 years. The mayors must be placed under different categories. R. E. Thomason brought industry to El Paso. R. E. Sherman saved the city's credit. Dan Ponder was progressive, and under him the city started to build. Fred Hervey extended the city limits to where they should be. Judson Williams was a dynamic leader, and won the election for the civic center. I could not name one best mayor; El Paso has been fortunate in that we have had some wonderful mayors.

I have not forgotten a wonderful thing that Mayor J. E. Anderson did in 1941. He and his City Council enacted an ordinance banning fireworks in the city limits. I can take part of the credit for that. At dusk on the Fourth of July I took my family to Scenic Drive. El Paso resembled a battlefield, with deafening noise and flashes lighting up the night in all directions. The next day I told Mayor Anderson I was going to write an editorial suggesting that El Paso adopt a no-fireworks ordinance, and he said he would go along. Today, El Paso has such an ordinance and the Fourth of July is usually a pleasure.

Matter of Advertising

This part of the United States, the El Paso Southwest, has always needed to present a united front in telling the world what it has to offer. An organization was formed for that purpose in 1940. It was called the Associated Southwestern Chambers of Commerce. Lloyd P. Bloodworth, assistant manager of the El Paso Chamber of Commerce, was the moving force behind that organization. An initial meeting was held in Ruidoso in the summer of 1940, but I attended the big meeting in Silver City in August, 1941, with representatives there from as far away as Midland on the east, Tucson on the west, and Carrizozo on the north. It was a fine program.

It looked as though the ASCC was going to be a success, and it was for a while, with such men as Dudley Yard of Pecos, Bill Collyns of Midland, and Dr. R. E. Blaney of Carrizozo taking an active part. The organization fell apart during World War II; Allen Bruce and Dan White of El Paso and Dudley Yard of Pecos officiated at the demise. I still think it was a great idea that should be revived, because the El Paso Southwest has much to offer, and it pays to advertise.

El Paso County made a serious mistake when it discontinued advertising through the El Paso County Board of Development. That program was successful while it lasted, but it was discontinued under the regime of County Judge Colbert Coldwell. The people of El Paso County in 1948 had voted to authorize a levy of up to five cents per $100 valuation for advertising purposes, but that was never done. Whatever funds the County Board of Development received were doled out by the Commissioners Court. At one time, El Paso County placed advertisements in national magazines and thousands of inquiries were received. Whether it means anything or not, El Paso more than doubled its population between 1950 and 1960 while that advertisement program was in effect. I have never understood why that project was discontinued.

Things Accomplished

One of the things that I am proudest of as editor of the *Times* was the effort of the paper, along with Sheriff Allen Falby, to get juveniles out of the County Jail. Children running afoul of the law had been placed in jail along with hardened criminals. Falby had always tried to have the children placed elsewhere. He and I worked together for establishment of the El Paso County Juvenile Detention Home. That home was dedicated June 25, 1950, definitely a forward step for El Paso.

The operations of the County Juvenile Detention Department have come under serious recent criticism. The chief county probation officer, Morris Raley, was indicted. His first trial resulted in a hung jury, but at his second trial he was convicted and given a probated two-year sentence. The NBC gave a program on the treatment of juveniles in which El Paso County was prominently mentioned. The *Times* was highly critical of that department but that happened under the new editor of the *Times.*

I hope things work out satisfactorily. It is certain that we must be careful in dealing with children, but we also must never forget that good boys and girls are seldom taken to the Juvenile Home, nor that those boys and girls formerly were put in the County Jail. They must be given expert care, with sympathy and firmness, but coddling has no place in that operation.

Talking about juveniles, I served on the El Paso County Grand Jury in the fall of 1952 which decided to investigate gangs of young El Pasoans who apparently were out of control, with talk of the "Counts," the "Dukes" and the like. For one thing, a mob of youngsters was said to have entered and wrecked the home of Mrs. H. L. Birney. The Grand Jury decided to call a number of young El Pasoans along with their fathers to appear before it and voted to request the city's news media to publish the names of those young El Pasoans and their fathers.

Karl O. Wyler of KTSM was also a member of that Grand Jury; the *Times* and KTSM did as requested, but the *Herald-Post* ignored the request. One prominent El Pasoan summoned before the grand jury with one of his sons, told me his mother was ill and that if the *Times* published her grandson's name it would kill her. What were we supposed to do, publish all the names except that one? We published all the names and the good lady did not die. I don't know what good that Grand Jury accomplished.

Another thing of which I am proud is the cooperation of the *Times* with County Judge Victor B. Gilbert in helping to establish the Victor B. Gilbert Annex at the City-County Hospital, as it then was called. In those days, persons charged with insanity were lodged in the County Jail and then given a jury trial before the County Judge, with the County Attorney prosecuting. Upon conviction, the unfortunate person was committed to the State Hospital for the Insane in Big Spring.

Judge Gilbert moved to provide better surroundings for the mentally unbalanced. The Victor B. Gilbert Annex was the result; it was accepted December 5, 1951. The *Times,* under my editorship, supported that move. I have a letter in my retirement book from Dr. J. Edward Stern, a prominent El Paso psychiatrist, commending me for the part I played in obtaining better treatment for the mentally retarded.

The Victor B. Gilbert Annex is no longer in use; its purpose is served at R. E. Thomason General Hospital. And the ruling of psychiatrists is now sufficient to commit persons suspected of being insane.

Libel Suits

Among newspapermen talk about libel suits usually is taboo, but if we are going to have a record, how can libel suits be ignored? During the almost 30 years I was editor of the *Times,* we had a number of close calls but only three libel suits, and only two of those went to trial. The third, brought against *Times* Reporter Art Leibson and the *Times* by County Commissioner Richard Telles, was dismissed before trial.

The first suit, or series of suits, began in 1954 after State Representative Stanley Caufield led in instigating a State legislative investigation of purported connections between local officials and the underworld. State Representative Joe Pool of Dallas brought a subcommittee to El Paso and conducted closed hearings. The *Times,* rightly or wrongly, was critical of the whole procedure. *Times* Reporter Art Leibson found himself in the middle of the controversy, and in the heat of battle some uncomplimentary things were written.

Nothing came of the state investigation, but State Representative Caufield filed suit for damages against a number of El Pasoans as well as the *Times.* He filed several suits before it was over, with the *Times* as the target. One day, while we were in Judge Hans Brockmoller's court on one suit. *Times* Publisher Dorrance Roderick and I were served with papers in another of Caufield's suits filed in Corpus Christi. *Times* Attorney Louis A. Scott finally settled the Caufield suits. I never had anything against Caufield; it was just one of those things that may happen as the result of a fight.

The other suit against us was brought in 1965 by Dr. Richard Trexler, who had been a professor of history at The University of Texas at El Paso. He had organized an anti-Vietnam war protest demonstration in San Jacinto Plaza. The demonstration caused quite a bit of comment, including letters to the editors of El Paso's newspapers. In the middle of that discussion, the *Herald-Post* published some assertions attributed to Trexler which helped prompt a highly critical letter to the editor of the *Times.* The Trexler suit for $250,000 damages involved that letter.

Shortly before the alleged libel occurred, *Times* Managing Editor Bill Latham developed a heart condition and he was taken off the copy desk at night and given a day assignment, which included handling letters to the editor.

Attorneys for Trexler were Jesus Ochoa of El Paso and Warren Burnett of Odessa, one of the most successful trial lawyers in Texas.

Representing the *Times* were Attorneys Schuyler Marshall and George Finger. What helped save the day for the *Times* was the fact we had editorially supported the constitutional right of the Trexler group to demonstrate against the war, upholding their right of dissent. In my column "Everyday Events" we even published the Bill of Rights.

While I was on the witness stand, our attorneys had me read into the record editorial after editorial and column after column I had written defending the rights of the dissenters. We did not agree with them, but we supported their constitutional right. Our side took the position that Trexler was a public figure. Burnett had me on the stand several hours under cross examination, trying to make me admit that I would not have passed the letter which we had published, but I admitted nothing. Burnett also put *Herald-Post* Editor R. W. (Pete) Lee on the stand and tried to make him admit that he would not have published the letter, but he would not. *Herald-Post* Reporter Loretta Overton, my former secretary, who had written the *Herald-Post* article precipating the alleged libel, made an excellent witness for the defense.

The jury returned a verdict in our favor, which was appealed. The Eighth Court of Civil Appeals held that District Judge Edwin F. Berliner had erred in his charge to the jury defining malice, and we appealed that to the Supreme Court of Texas, which ruled in our favor. Of course, Dr. Trexler was a public figure. The trial court and the Supreme Court of Texas followed the law as laid down by the Supreme Court of the United States. Thus ended the Trexler case, which caused us no end of trouble and expense.

During the following Christmas holidays, Justice Robert Hamilton of the Supreme Court of Texas, who had ruled in our favor in the Trexler case, said to me in my office, "Bill, I did not send you a Christmas card. I thought you would rather have that decision." Judge Hamilton had formerly been chief justice of the Eighth Court of Civil Appeals and had lived in El Paso. He has many friends here.

Before his suit came to trial, Dr. Trexler had left U. T. El Paso and had joined the faculty at Occidental in California. Later he received a grant for continued study in Europe.

New Herald-Post Editor

R. W. (Pete) Lee and I got along well together after he succeeded Ed Pooley as editor of the *Herald-Post* in February, 1963. He called on me just before he took over and we chatted for an hour. I told him that Pooley and I had many fights and that I expected he and I would have some in the future. Lee laughed and said he did not expect any fights, and there were none for the seven years we opposed each other. We worked more for the improvement of El Paso, and we often found ourselves together in editorial policy.

Lee and I had one particular newspaper friend we both admired very much. He was Chet Johnson, whom I knew in Arizona more than 50 years ago, Chet's first wife, Julie, borrowed a stick pin from me for "something borrowed" when they were married in 1921. Julie since had died and Chet had remarried; Lee knew him on the San Francisco *News.* Lee told me that Chet Johnson talked about me in his delirium before he died. Perhaps that mutual friendship with Chet Johnson helped Pete Lee and me to get along well together.

Lee became very active in the civic life of El Paso. In 1970, he was president of the El Paso Chamber of Commerce. He has been very active in the Boy Scouts and the National Conference of Christians and Jews, among other community endeavors. He is well liked and highly respected. In their editorial behavior, Pete Lee and Ed Pooley are a study in contrasts. Take your choice: it all depends on what you want in a newspaper. Do you want excitement and fights or operation at a friendly, even keel?

Gets Wide Circulation

Undoubtedly the most widely circulated contribution that ever appeared in my column "Everyday Events" was "Merry Christmas Amigos." Beginning in 1948, I published it every year until I retired. Here is part of the "Everyday Events" column of December 21, 1967:

Since Christmas of 1948 this column every year has published a charming poem, part in Spanish and part in English. It is called "Merry Christmas Amigos."

That poem, since first appearing here on Dec. 21, 1948, has gained wide circulation and publicity. It has appeared on Christmas cards and has been read at Christmas parties and at luncheon clubs.

It was sent to me by Marie de la Torre, who at that time was employed by Harry L. Hussmann, Jr. Inc., on Dec. 20, 1948, with this note:

"One of our salesmen brought this in and passed it around and we all thought it was so original that I was appointed to make copies for everybody.

"As this is Saturday and there will be little time to do it before Christmas, and also because I am sure there are a lot of other people in El Paso who also would like to have a copy, I am sending it to you for publication. It will save me a lot of work and it will give you a 'different' way to say 'Merry Christmas' to your readers."

I understand Mrs. de la Torre is still with Warner Brothers in Los Angeles where she has been for some time.

Here it is again with my compliments and with the hope it brings much more pleasure:

MERRY CHRISTMAS AMIGOS

"Tis the night before Christmas and all through the casa
Not a creature is stirring, Caramba! Que pasa?
The stockings are hanging, con mucho cuidado
In hopes that St. Nicholas will feel obligado
To leave a few cosas aqui and alli
For chico y chica (and something por mi!)
Los niños are snuggled all safe in their camas
(Some in camisas and some in pajamas).
Their little cabezas are full of good things
Todos esperan que Santa will bring!
Santa is down at the corner saloon
(Muy borracho since mid afternoon);
Mama is sitting beside la ventana,
Shining her rolling pin para mañana,
When Santa will come en un manner extraño
Lit up like the Star on the Mountain, cantando,
Y Mama lo manda to bed with a right,
Merry Christmas a todos y a todos good night!"

Isn't that wonderful? I never tire reading it, which I have done every Christmas since 1948. I should have kept track of the number of persons who have asked us for copies of that poem in the intervening years. That poem, I hope, will keep its popularity forever.

Another Era

It looks as though another era is looming for the El Paso *Times,* the newspaper I have loved as I do my own children. I have watched it and been a part of it for many years. On March 6, 1972, an announcement appeared on the front page of the *Times,* made by *Times* President and Publisher Dorrance D. Roderick and Paul Miller, chairman of the board of the Gannett Newspapers, that a stock merger was being arranged by which it would become the fifty-fourth member of the Gannett Newspapers. From my point of view, nothing but good can come of that.

I know that the *Times* for the last 41 years has stood on its own feet. I would call it a personalized newspaper, owned and published by Roderick and reflecting him. As a member of the Gannett Group it will retain its personality; all newspapers in that group are autonomous. As I write of my almost 52 years in the newspaper business, I want my last words in the record to be congratulations to Dorrance Roderick for making that Gannett deal.

On May 12, 1966, I presented Miss Maud Isaacks with a resolution passed by the Texas House of Representatives upon her retirement.

The widely read Ann Landers visited my office on June 12, 1965.

Governors of two states frequently visited my office. Above, Governor Price Daniel of Texas visited March 18, 1960. Below, Governor Jack Campbell of New Mexico came July 1, 1964.

The TIMES *staff gathered to look over the Diamond Jubilee edition, April 28, 1956, including Bill Montgomery, Bill Latham, Jim Halloran, Ruby Burns, Ed Engledow.*

Federal Judge R. E. Thomason came to the office on March 31, 1970 to wish me well on my retirement as editor of the El Paso TIMES.

INDEX